M

Peter Byrne's study of God and realism offers a critical survey of issues surrounding the realist interpretation of theism and theology. Byrne presents a general argument for interpreting the intent of talk about God in a realist fashion and argues that judging the intent of theistic discourse should be the primary object of concern in the philosophy of religion. He considers a number of important ideas and thinkers supporting global anti-realism, and finds them all wanting. After the refutation of global anti-realism, Byrne considers a number of important arguments in favour of the notion that there is something specific to talk about God which invites an anti-realist interpretation of it. Here he looks at verificationism, the writings of Don Cupitt, forms of radical feminist theory and the ideas of D.Z. Phillips. The book concludes with a discussion of whether theology as a discursive, academic discipline can be interpreted realistically.

Offering a comprehensive survey of the topic and of the leading literature in the field, this book presents key arguments for exploring issues brought to bear upon the realism debate. Students and scholars of philosophy of religion, philosophy of language, metaphysics, theory of knowledge and theology, will find this an invaluable new contribution to the field.

ASHGATE PHILOSOPHY OF RELIGION SERIES

Series Editors

Paul Helm, King's College, University of London, UK
Jerome Gellman, Ben-Gurion University of the Negev,
Beer-Sheva, Israel
Linda Zagzebski, University of Oklahoma, USA

Due to the work of Plantinga, Alston, Swinburne and others, the philosophy of religion is now becoming recognised once again as a mainstream philosophical discipline in which metaphysical, epistemological and moral concepts and arguments are applied to issues of religious belief. The *Ashgate Philosophy of Religion Series* fosters this resurgence of interest by presenting a number of high-profile titles spanning many critical debates, and presenting new directions and new perspectives in contemporary research and study. This new series presents books by leading international scholars in the field, providing a platform for their own particular research focus to be presented within a wider contextual framework. Offering accessible, stimulating new contributions to each topic, this series will prove of particular value and interest to academics, graduate, postgraduate and upper-level undergraduate readers world-wide focusing on philosophy, religious studies and theology, sociology or other related fields.

Titles in the series include:

Mystical Experience of God
A Philosophical Inquiry
Jerome Gellman

Religious Diversity
A Philosophical Assessment
David Basinger

Rationality and Religious Theism
Joshua L. Golding

God and Realism

PETER BYRNE
King's College London, UK

ASHGATE

Published by
Ashgate Publishing Limited
Gower House, Croft Road
Aldershot, Hants
GU11 3HR
England

Ashgate Publishing Company
Suite 420
101 Cherry Street
Burlington, VT 05401–4405
USA

Ashgate website: http://www.ashgate.com

British Library Cataloguing in Publication Data
Byrne, Peter, C.Ss.R.
    God and realism. – (Ashgate philosophy of religion series)
    1.Philosophical theology 2.Realism
    I.Title
    210

Library of Congress Cataloging-in-Publication Data
Byrne, Peter, 1950–
    God and realism / Peter Byrne.
        p. cm.—(Ashgate philosophy of religion series)
    Includes bibliographical references and index. (pbk. : alk. paper)
    1. Religion—Philosophy. 2. Realism. 3. God.
    I. Title. II. Series.
    BL51.B89 2003
    211—dc21   2003041779

ISBN 0 7546 1461 1 (Hbk)
ISBN 0 7546 1467 0 (Pbk)

This book is printed on acid-free paper

Typeset in Times Roman by Tradespools, Frome, Somerset

Printed and bound in Great Britain by Antony Rowe Ltd, Chippenham, Wilts

Contents

Preface

The Plot of This Book

This book offers a critical study of issues surrounding the realist interpretation of theism and theology. Three distinctions are central to its argument. The first is between judging the intent and judging the success of talk about God. The second is between anti-realist interpretations of theistic talk which are based on global grounds and anti-realist interpretations which are based on contrastive grounds. The third is between theistic discourse *per se* as an object of interpretation and theology as an object of interpretation. The plot of the book is determined by these distinctions.

Chapter 1 sets out the distinctions. The last of the three creates a case for a separate treatment of the realist pretensions of academic theology as a discipline of intelligence. Such a treatment is postponed to the final chapter of this study. Chapter 1 contains a general argument for interpreting the intent of talk about God in a realist fashion. It is difficult to mount such an argument, for, as Chapter 1 makes plain, there is a great variety of conceptions of deity. There is no single sense to the notion of God. The general argument proceeds by identifying something generic to worthwhile conceptions of deity. Worthwhile conceptions are those with some relevance to the life of religion. This generic element is a theodicy, a type of response to the human perception of evil which draws upon two ideas: there is a moral teleology to human life and the world and there is some final good which consists in living in right relation to the source of this teleology. Chapter 1 establishes what is taken to be a strong *prima facie* case for a realist interpretation of the intent of theistic discourse. Only with a realist interpretation can the generic offer of a theodicy by theism make sense. The presentation of the case shapes the rest of the argument up to the end of Chapter 6: we are now looking for such counter-arguments against this realist interpretation as might overturn the strong presumption thus established.

In Chapter 1 and elsewhere, I make plain that many anti-realist interpretations of theism are based on an adverse judgement on the success of theistic discourse in its many concrete forms. Theistic discourse fails to establish the existence of a *theos*. This book roundly dismisses commentary on these forms of anti-realism as uninteresting to its main purposes. It is not the purpose of this book to establish the plausibility or truth of some generic core to theism. And, in a fashion, anti-realism that is motivated by a judgement on the success of theism is uninteresting and uncontroversial (or it ought to be). It is a fact that in the present and recent past very many philosophical commentators on religion have been wholly unpersuaded of the truth of any concrete form of theism. It is not surprising, nor should it be found objectionable, that many in turn have wanted to reinterpret theistic discourse so that it retains some cognitive or pragmatic value. Particular versions of this endeavour may, of course, raise interesting philosophical issues, but the endeavour should occasion no great disputes, once its context is appreciated.

The shape of the argument which flows from Chapter 1 to the end of Chapter 5 is based on the premise that major anti-realist interpretations of the intent of theistic talk in current philosophical and theological reflection are based on global grounds. That is to say, such interpretations are fashionable because it is fashionable to think that *no* human thought and discourse is capable of referring to realities which are truly independent of human representations. Contemporary academia is awash with variants on the theme that human thought and discourse somehow construct, determine or shape their objects of reference. Theological anti-realisms are in large measure a reflection of these strands of global anti-realism. Chapters 2 to 5 thus endeavour to pin down and criticise global anti-realism. Chapter 2 specifies what is at stake. It outlines a minimal metaphysical view which refutes global anti-realism. Paralleling the argument of Chapter 1, this metaphysical view is presented as *prima facie* strongly warranted. Chapters 3 to 5 aim to show that arguments for global anti-realism currently in circulation are not strong enough to overturn this *prima facie* case for global realism.

There is inevitably much in Chapters 2 to 5 that is not specifically to do with the philosophy of religion or theology. Contemporary theological anti-realists are riding on the back of what they take to be obvious anti-realist truths that come down to them from contemporary philosophy, linguistic theory and so on. It is therefore necessary to track these alleged truths to their source. However, the treatment of global anti-realism does try to keep as close as possible to discussions in philosophy of religion and theology. Thus Chapter 3 discusses relativism as a ground for anti-realism by reference to two books by Joseph Runzo, where it is developed specifically in the context of providing a philosophy of religion. The development of Runzo's general arguments into a philosophy of religion is traced and commented on. Chapter 4 looks at the broad category of epistemological grounds for anti-realism. Attempts are made to link these discussions in general philosophy to the philosophy of religion by examination in the course of the chapter of Ayer's critique of religion and by discussion of the use some contemporary philosophers of religion have made of Carnap's 'Empiricism, Semantics and Ontology'. Chapter 5 discusses an array of arguments from postmodernism and poststructuralism for anti-realism by reference to two sources: the post-1984 writings of Don Cupitt and some feminist theologians. In both those sources postmodernist 'insights' are applied to religion.

There is a recurring theme in Chapters 2 to 5: magic. I take myself to be examining variations on the theme that language creates/shapes the world and therefore variations on the theme that human words have the power to create and alter what is so. Thus I see myself as tracing, in the writings of intellectuals of the late twentieth century/early twenty-first century, the survival of the ancient magical belief that manipulating symbols can, of itself, change things. This survival is one of the unintended consequences of the linguistic turn taken by philosophy and allied disciplines in this period.

Chapter 6 is specifically on the philosophy of religion. It looks at contrastive, theistic anti-realism: that brand of anti-realism which seeks specific reasons why theistic discourse should be denied an anti-realist interpretation. The chapter deals in two kinds of reasons: those related to the alleged obvious incoherence in any attempt to refer to a transcendent *theos* and those related to an ethical/political critique of the generic moral vision behind forms of theism. Neither kind of reason is found to be persuasive.

Chapter 7 brings the weary reader home with a discussion of whether theology as a discursive, academic discipline can be interpreted realistically. It is meant to bear out a point made in Chapter 1: one can interpret theism realistically while interpreting theology non-realistically. One can take the realist intent of theism seriously without taking the realist intent of theology seriously.

What is the point of this book? The reader will gather that it is in part a negative enterprise. Chapters 2 to 5 in particular aim to diagnose the errors in the false claims of anti-realist philosophical perspectives. Negative work of this kind can nonetheless be liberating. Liberated from the confusions of global and contrastive forms of anti-realism, the student of religion or theology can appreciate the positive point that it is of the essence of religion in general and of theism in particular to attempt to refer to realities which exist beyond human representations. This enables a better understanding of the meaning of religion and of its relation to good and evil (matters I have tried to pursue at greater length in Byrne 1998).

The pervasiveness of the error-ridden, magical view of human thought and language I try to diagnose in what follows should strike any student of contemporary religious thought. Such pervasiveness is one offshoot of the largely baneful influence of postmodernism in those parts of the academy devoted to theology and the study of religion. Though the errors might stand out most clearly in the writings of a Don Cupitt, they are there in sober, mainstream academic theology. Too many theologians nowadays are convinced that postmodernism and linguistic constructivism face them with major intellectual problems (for an example see Patterson 1999).

The final chapter of the present work argues that there is an intellectual challenge which contemporary theologians need to face in connection with realism. It is not one which emerges from post-modernity but from an inductive, cultural critique developed by comparing theology with science. It has its roots in a very familiar problem: how to match the extravagance of theological claims about God with the paucity of cogent arguments in favour of them. It is the challenge of good, old-fashioned religious scepticism.

Technical Matters

This book uses the Harvard system of citation. It thus has no footnotes. Emphasis in quotations is always as in the original source unless I specifically state otherwise.

There is no agreement in the literature as to how the opposite of realism is to be named. Some writers use 'non-realism', others 'anti-realism'. For the sake of simplicity, Chapters 1 to 6 oppose realist metaphysical theses with *anti-realist* ones. However, in Chapter 7 I found it more natural to write of *non-realist* accounts of the status of intellectual disciplines such as science or theology as opposed to realist accounts of them.

Acknowledgements

Part of this book was read to audiences at King's College London and the University of Uppsala. I am grateful for the patience of those folk and the feedback they provided.

Charlotte Byrne gave invaluable assistance in matters to do with the style and presentation of the typescript. The editors of the series provided helpful comments on the penultimate draft. I am particularly grateful to Paul Helm for a lengthy list of typos and linguistic infelicities.

Chapter 1

Theistic and Theological Realism:
An Analytic Account

The literature in philosophy of religion and theology is full of discussions of realism. This book is written out of the conviction that there is not much order in these discussions. The debates between theological realists and theological anti-realists generate more heat than light. We need some distinctions to clarify the key terms in the debate. Having made the relevant distinctions, we need an ordered presentation of the arguments for and against the various forms of theological realism we shall distinguish.

An Initial Definition of Realism

The first distinction we need is between types of realism and the various objects of realist/anti-realist analysis. There are disputes about the nature and measure of realism to be applied to religion. There are also disputes about what to apply the measure to. With regard to the latter distinction, we must separate the question of whether theistic belief/ discourse or concepts are to be interpreted realistically from the question of whether theology (here primarily *Christian* theology) is to be so interpreted. We need the distinction because we must allow that some may think it apt to give a realist interpretation of the fundamental claims or concepts of a theistic tradition such as Christianity while denying this interpretation to the adumbration of these claims in theological reflection. For example, it is conceivable that one might regard as vain and spurious the pretensions of academic theology in Western universities to be an enterprise with a realist thrust, even though one accepted that the more minimal claims of non-reflective believers were capable of realist interpretation. More will have to be said on this distinction at the end of this chapter and in Chapter 7. Until that point is reached, my discussion will concentrate on what is involved in giving the claims and concepts of minimal theism a realist interpretation.

What then is it to give a realist interpretation of the claims and concepts of a minimal theism? Debates between realists and anti-realists are rooted in other areas of philosophy, such as philosophy of science

1

and metaphysics. They then get carried over to the philosophy of religion. It is a fact that there is no uniform account of what is at issue between realism and anti-realism in these other areas of philosophy. Susan Haack distinguishes four forms of realism (and their denials) concerning the interpretation of science. To these she adds five metaphysical and epistemological stances (with their opposites) concerning the general nature of truth which also count as forms of realism (Haack 1987: 276 and 287). Her four realist theses about science ('theoretical realism', 'cumulative realism', 'progressive realism' and 'optimistic realism') all pertain to the interpretation of scientific discourse and activity. They are hermeneutical theses. This reflects the fact that realist versus anti-realist debates in the philosophy of science concern how to interpret the scientific enterprise. Michael Devitt by contrast sees realism as fundamentally a metaphysical stance. That is to say, realists are philosophers who affirm something about what exists. They affirm that reality exists independently of the mental. Such an assertion – that there is a reality which exists independently of our thoughts or beliefs – is too thin for Devitt. It says nothing about what kinds of things exist independently of the mental. It is compatible with affirming that independent reality is devoid of structure and form and thus with saying that our conceptual activities are responsible for there being distinct kinds and types of things. We would then be, in large measure, constructors of the world we know (see Chapter 2 below for an exploration of this idea). To have any bite, realism must assert that 'Tokens of most current common-sense and scientific physical types objectively exist independently of the mental' (Devitt 1997: 23). Realism then makes the concrete metaphysical claim that there are things independent of us which instantiate most of the current common-sense and scientific concepts we employ.

Devitt's realism is precisely not a hermeneutical thesis. It is not a thesis about the interpretation of discourses. It is a claim about what exists. As such, it is not, in his view, a thesis that can be confirmed or disconfirmed by *a priori* epistemological or semantic theories in philosophy. One of his 'maxims' for conducting the realism dispute is 'Settle the realism issue before any epistemic or semantic issue' (Devitt 1997: 4).

There is much that is sensible in Devitt's definition of realism and the strictures which flow from it. The fundamental question we shall pose under the heading of 'realism' is one that bears on the question of what might exist, and particularly on whether a structured, formed world exists independently of our representations. It is also true that many philosophers have wanted to settle this question by first establishing some thesis in epistemology or semantics – as if the uncertainties of debates about what there is can be replaced by the certainties of *a priori* reflections on the nature of meaning or on the limits of knowledge. We will see these pretensions illustrated in a number of the chapters which follow. They are indeed in many instances little more than pretensions, being based on the vain and false belief that common-sense and scientific opinions are less sure than philosophers' theorising about the nature of meaning or knowledge. There is every reason to be sceptical about philosophers bearing *a priori* proofs that something cannot be or something else must be. The roots of many of the themes in realist versus anti-realist debates lie in philosophical attempts from Kant onwards to tell us what the limits of knowledge and sense are. Three cheers must be offered for Devitt's scepticism about the relative uncertainty of the claims which flow from these attempts compared with the certainty of common-sense and scientific claims. But Devitt is wrong to imply that the realist issue cannot be, in some guises and contexts, an hermeneutical one in which semantic and epistemological questions are to the fore. It is with good reason that we ask whether scientific discourse is to be interpreted as the outcome of interactions between human beings and a reality independent of them. Our enquiries will be directed at the extent to which the rise and fall of the theories of science can only be explained by making some reference to human discovery of independent realities. This is a question about the sources of scientific belief, about what processes control the acceptance and rejection of theories and about the kind of meaning scientific statements can have. A primary issue in the interpretation of science will be whether the explanation of the evolution of scientific thought can be explained wholly in terms of realities existing in the human, social world. Proponents of the strong programme in the sociology of knowledge maintain that it can. Realists will be those who claim that this is only part of the story. They will say that it is essential that we make reference to the role real-world influences and factors play in the explanation of the development of science (see Harré 1986: 14). The label 'realism' is appropriate for this hermeneutical stance because it concerns how far science does develop in response to the mind-independent real. Haack's four types of scientific realism are very much concerned with this type of issue. We shall see that when, in Chapter 7, we come to the question of how far the discipline of theology can be given a realist interpretation, it will be matters of explanation and hermeneutics which are to the fore.

There is a relation between the hermeneutical (semantic and epistemological) questions about realism and the bare metaphysical issue of realism raised by Devitt. If we had a proof that no mind-independent reality existed, then that would settle the hermeneutical questions raised under the banner of 'realism' in advance. A core realist claim of a metaphysical kind, to be discussed and defended in Chapter 2 below, is a necessary condition for taking the hermeneutical questions raised in realism/anti-realism debates seriously. This claim is to the effect that there is a mind-independent reality and it is a structured,

formed reality. We do not impose form and structure on a reality which
is in itself devoid of these things (more about this in Chapter 2). What
this bare metaphysical claim enables us to do is to take seriously the
intent of language users to refer to things of one kind or another in an
independent world by means of common-sense and scientific concepts.
If the intent behind the use of common-sense and scientific concepts to
refer to independent realities of definite kinds cannot be taken seriously,
we shall either have to dismiss the talk which enshrines those concepts
or we shall have to offer a revisionist interpretation of that talk.

We are here approaching the most fundamental question about
theistic discourse which we can raise under the heading of realism versus
anti-realism. Can the *apparent* intent behind talk of God to refer to an
entity existing in some sense beyond us and the universe be taken
seriously? The realist answers 'yes' and the anti-realist 'no'. Note that
we are once more departing from the model for characterising realism
offered by Devitt. That model would bid us take the core realist
question concerning theism to be: 'Is there a mind-independent reality
corresponding to the concept of "God"?' Devitt's definition of 'realism'
confronts us with the following questions. When we ask of a way of
thinking whether it is to be interpreted realistically, are we judging
character of the intent (the meaning) behind its terms and concepts, or
are we judging whether its governing intent is successful, whether there
is an actual correspondence between its types and appropriate extra-
mental tokens? As Devitt reviews the merits of a realistic interpretation
of common-sense and scientific concepts, he considers himself to be
answering the question of whether there really are tokens for most
common-sense and scientific types. Transferred to the debate about
theism, this way of understanding matters would make opting for a
realist interpretation of theistic discourse to be nothing less than
deciding that a God of the appropriate kind really existed. A proof that
there was no God of the kind the typical believer thinks he or she is
worshipping would constitute a proof of anti-realism for theism. This
may seem odd. It is surely worthwhile to say that while Richard
Swinburne and Quentin Smith disagree over whether God is real, they
agree in a realist interpretation of theistic discourse. Contrariwise, while
Smith and Cupitt both agree that the God of traditional theism does not
exist, the former gives a realist interpretation of theism while the latter
does not. What Smith and Swinburne agree on is that the governing
intent of theistic discourse and belief is a realist one. Realism brings out
the meaning of theism. Cupitt contends that we can reinterpret theism
so that it still makes sense, is still a viable intellectual option, without an
intent to refer to a God of the appropriate sort.

The import of the questions 'Are we judging the character of the
intent (the meaning) behind its terms and concepts of theism, or are we
judging whether the governing intent of theistic discourse is successful,

whether there is an actual correspondence between its types and appropriate extra-mental tokens?' rests on what would follow if we had a proof that there was no God of the appropriate sort. Would theism be impossible as a mode of thinking in that case? Or: would possession of such a proof be irrelevant, since nothing of significance in the presuppositions and meaning of this way of thinking would thereby be lost? If the governing intent of theistic discourse is to refer to a reality existing independently of the mental, then a proof that there was no God beyond human thought would be a refutation of theistic talk. Something of vital significance to the meaning of core theistic claims and concepts would have been lost thereby. This need not entail that nothing could be redeemed from theistic talk. It would be judged a failure as making a successful reference to a God beyond human thought but we might find a reinterpretation which retains some point to it. This is what Julian Huxley does in *Religion Without Revelation*. According to Huxley, concepts defining the Christian concept of God do not refer to any transcendent being. There is no divine Trinity. Christianity as ordinarily understood is false. But the concepts of Christianity can be reinterpreted. In particular, 'Son', 'Spirit' and 'Father' can be taken, with much loss of original meaning, to refer to naturalistic entities – to human life, to human ideals and to non-human nature respectively (Huxley 1957: 31–3).

The question of the governing intent behind theistic discourse is not to be settled by psychological survey. An answer to it will reflect an understanding of the meaning of theistic claims. This understanding will in part be based on a perception of what kind of thing counts for and against them. It will also reflect a sense of the role they play in the lives of believers. Is that role, we can ask, such that they need to be thought of as having referential import to sustain it? We will see that philosophers of religion disagree on how that last question is to be answered. Despite the fact that philosophers offer conflicting readings of the intent of theistic discourse, we must note that making realism a matter of judging its intent leaves the realist/anti-realist debate philosophically more tractable than otherwise. No clear-cut proofs or disproofs of God's existence are on the horizon. The realist question, difficult though it is, is not the impossible question of whether there really is a God.

To this point we have established what appears to be one clear question at issue when the realist status of theistic discourse is discussed: 'Is its governing intent to refer to a mind-independent reality?' However, the question is too easy. Let us make it more complicated. To establish whether theism is to be interpreted realistically or otherwise we need to show that we can take seriously its intent to refer to a mind-independent entity of an *appropriate* kind. The appropriate objects of reference for common sense and scientific realism are things and stuffs existing in spatio-temporal, physical reality. Complications do arise if we ask our realist question about those parts of scientific theorising containing terms purporting to refer to unobservable things, stuffs or structures in nature. An interpretation of science which says that they do not refer (say, because unobservables are 'convenient fictions') is an anti-realist one. But so, presumably, is one which says that theoretical terms are roundabout ways of referring to observables (like talk of the 'average Englishman'). The appropriate tokens of many scientific types for a realism worth its name would be things, stuffs and structures now, or in principle, undetectable by observation (extended by instruments or not). Why is this so? Well, because it appears to be the case that key activities in science, such as explaining and predicting phenomena, depend on our taking concepts such as 'electron' or 'magnetic field' to refer to aspects of nature which are real yet unobservable. Science appears to be an enterprise designed to uncover the inner workings of nature. It aims, *prima facie*, to explain nature's surface goings-on by hypothesising and investigating unobservable things, structures and stuffs.

To make our first realist question about theism at all precise we will have to specify the appropriate object to which theistic concepts appears to refer. We will have to say that the appropriate object is mind-independent and *transcendent*. So now we might define realism for theistic discourse as: 'the governing intent behind the concept of God is to refer to an extra-mental, extra-mundane, transcendent entity'. At this juncture problems abound. They stem from the difficulties in initially defining 'extra-mundane, transcendent' and the problems increase when we come to apply any such definition to possible and actual versions of theism. It will transpire that it is enormously difficult to attain clarity and agreement on what 'transcendent entity' means in these contexts. The nature of transcendence in the definition of theism is something that will be explored in a later section of this chapter.

Global versus Contrastive Realism

So far we have realism toward theism as a stance directed at minimal, core theistic concepts which states that the use of these concepts is governed by an attempt to refer to a transcendent, mind-independent reality. Theistic anti-realists deny this intent. They can do so on at least two kinds of ground. They may be theistic anti-realists because they are global anti-realists. On the other hand, they may be theistic anti-realists while being *global* realists. In the latter case, they will contrast the realist intent of normal talk about the world with the anti-realist intent of theistic talk. They are then *contrastive* anti-realists when it comes to theism, citing reasons pertaining to the specific character of theistic discourse and thought which make it deserving of anti-realist interpretation.

The global anti-realist is someone who denies the fundamental global realist claim that there is a structured, mind-independent world to which human beings can refer and which makes their statements true or false. It is no easy matter to pin down the precise character of the metaphysical assumption which underpins global realism. A preliminary attempt will be made to do so in this section. More will be said about the issues for and against global realism in Chapter 2.

Our preliminary attempt begins with Haack's five variants on realism and anti-realism in metaphysics (1987: 283). 'Minimal realism' affirms that truth is not definable in terms of what is relative to a community, individual or theory. A proposition is true just in case things are as it says they are. The opposing thesis is 'radical relativism'. 'Ambitious absolutism' states that truth-bearers are non-linguistic entities (for example, propositions rather than sentences) which can be individuated without reference to a language. Its opposite is 'modest relativism'. 'Transcendentalism' is the thesis that 'truth may outrun us'; that is, that there can be truths beyond human discovery and recognition – even in principle. It is opposed by various forms of 'verificationism' (such as positivism and pragmatism). 'Nidealism' affirms that the world is not constructed from human mental states or representations and is opposed to forms of 'idealism'. 'Scholastic realism' states that some things really are alike, independent of our categories. By contrast, 'nominalism' affirms that our categories of classification are optional, unconstrained by any pre-existent kinds or properties in the world.

In Chapter 2 we shall argue that what is crucial to global realism is a doctrine (styled 'innocent realism' after another paper by Haack [Haack 1996]) which is a combination of nidealism and something which is allied to scholastic realism. The doctrine of innocent realism tells us that, for the most part, the world exists independently of us and our representations of it. It is ontologically independent of human beings. It would exist even if there were no creatures like us. It is epistemically independent of human beings in so far as our concepts refer to, and beliefs are made true by, things and characteristics in a world whose nature is not established by those beliefs and concepts. This entails that nidealism will go hand-in-hand with some version of scholastic realism. It will do so to the extent that our minimal global realism maintains that the independent world is not an undifferentiated stuff which is moulded by our beliefs and concepts. Minimal global realism need not take sides in the debate about the nature of truth-bearers that is highlighted by the opposition between ambitious absolutism and modest relativism. It will, however, take sides on radical relativism versus minimal realism. Our minimal global realism will recognise that we make many statements about parts of the world which are independent of human beings. Nidealism in combination with some form of scholastic realism states that those parts of reality exist and have the characteristics they do independent of the cognitive activities of human beings. They thus constitute truth-makers which are independent of the concepts and beliefs belonging to human communities and individuals. Transcendentalism is then suggested. There can be truths of which we may remain forever ignorant because there is a body of truth-makers which exists quite independently of our cognitive activities. In the next chapter I shall argue that forms of verificationism imply the denial of a minimal, global realism.

Theistic global anti-realism denies the existence of a world of things and properties existing ontologically and epistemically independent of us. It will therefore deny that there could be a God who exists ontologically and epistemically independent of us. Theistic contrastive anti-realists will point to specific facts about concepts and statements concerning the divine which indicate that this part of our thought and discourse cannot be taken to be about a reality independent of us. Global theistic anti-realists avow general metaphysical, epistemological or semantic theories which indicate that no talk can be taken to be about a mind-independent world. In later chapters we will look at examples of global theistic anti-realism in the work of Joseph Runzo and Don Cupitt, amongst others. Contrastive anti-realists think that such things as characteristic religious attitudes or typical relationships between religious language and action show theistic discourse cannot be interpreted realistically. D.Z. Phillips and Don Cupitt (again) will illustrate this mode of argument for us.

Realism/Anti-realism and Truth

There are connections between notions and theories of truth, on the one hand, and minimal global realism and minimal theistic realism, on the other. But the connections are not simple. It would be a mistake, for example, to say that minimal global realism is logically equivalent to a correspondence theory of truth. This is a mistake because one can espouse a correspondence theory and be an idealist. We shall follow White's definition of a correspondence theory of truth:

> ... the Correspondence Theory remains faithful to the basic and indisput-able principle that p is true if and only if p. A particular statement *says that* this is how things are – that is, says that this is a fact – and what is said is true if and only if this *is* how things are, that is, if this is a fact. [White 1970: 108]

A philosopher could maintain that there is no external world, as commonly understood, while still espousing a correspondence theory of truth. He or she could regard material things as constituted by sense impressions in the fashion of phenomenalism. But the truth of material object statements could still be characterised as a matter of their correlation to facts, facts about the character of our sense impressions.

It follows from the above that we cannot define minimal theistic realism in terms of a doctrine about the truth of theistic statements. Alston defines theistic realism in terms of the application of 'alethic realism' to religion. Alethic realism has three components:

1   The statements in our selected mode of discourse are genuine factual statements (as opposed to being the expression of feelings or attitudes).
2   The statements in our mode of discourse are true or false 'in the realist sense of those terms' (that is, a sense which honours the core elements of a correspondence account of truth as outlined above).
3   The facts that make the statements true hold independent of human cognition. (See Alston 1995: 39.)

There is nothing to stop Alston defining 'realism' any way he chooses, but I think it can be shown on reflection that a helpful account of realism in relation to theism needs a stronger account of the independence of truth-makers for factual statements than Alston provides (Alston's third clause above). He, in effect, wants to make it sufficient for realism that truth-makers are epistemically independent of human beings. I contend that, *for the vast majority* of our statements about reality, truth-makers must be ontologically independent of human beings as well as epistemically independent. (The minority which is a proper exception to this rule is those of our factual statements which are about human beings or the humanly, socially constructed world more generally.) We can support this point by direct consideration of minimal realism for theistic discourse.

Alston's conception of alethic realism ignores the fact that after distinguishing between two ways of arguing for theistic anti-realism – on global or contrastive grounds – we can distinguish between two further types of anti-realism about talk of the divine. A Braithwaite-type view which interprets talk of God as a convenient fiction, as non-referential, is a form of anti-realism. Braithwaite's position makes religious discourse expressive of commitment to a way of life and of the imaginative 'stories' which give psychological stimulus to maintaining that commitment and thus falls foul of Alston's criterion (1) (see Braithwaite 1971). But Feuerbach's account in *The Essence of Christianity* is also anti-realist because it makes talk of the divine a roundabout way of talking of human nature, its possibilities and key characteristics. Feuerbach's God is real. It is no fiction. The word 'God' refers for Feuerbach – and to something extra-mental – but not to something of an appropriate sort. The appropriate sort of thing is a transcendent entity, an occupant of 'sacred space'. Moreover, the Feuerbachian programme gives most theistic claims truth when suitably reinterpreted. They are true if they do correspond to the relevant facts about human nature. The problem is that they are true of the wrong kind of object. Feuerbach's reinterpretation of theism and Christianity allows the statements of religious discourse to be correspondence-true of something which is independent of human cognition, namely human nature, its key characteristics and its future possibilities. But it is not yet realism because it reduces that to which 'God' refers to something that has no ontological independence of human beings at all. Talk about God just is another way of talking about human beings and their species-nature. Feuerbach's account of religious concepts fits the requirements of Alston's alethic realism but it is not a realist interpretation of those concepts.

The key point about Braithwaite's anti-realism is that it gives the core terms of theistic discourse a non-referential gloss. We can style it 'instrumentalism' in consequence. A Feuerbach-type view allows the core terms to be referential but reduces the object of reference to something mundane and indeed human. This is anti-realism as reductionism. (Le Poidevin registers the same distinction as that between theological instrumentalism and positivism: 1996: 109.)

The distinction between instrumentalist and reductionist theistic anti-realism reinforces the original definition of minimal theological realism we offered: core theistic concepts refer to appropriate mind-independent realities. Feuerbach's referent for theistic concepts is a mind-independent reality in one sense (the human essence is not dependent on human beliefs) but it is not an appropriate reality since it lacks any transcendence of the human and the mundane.

Thus far we have two distinctions among types of theistic anti-realism to draw: global versus contrastive (a question of what grounds anti-realism), and instrumentalist versus reductionist (a question of what type of interpretation is given to theistic terms). It is evident this will give us four modes of theistic anti-realism: global instrumentalist, global reductionist, contrastive instrumentalist and contrastive reductionist. Alas for our sanity, we can introduce a further distinction among types of theistic anti-realism: 'descriptive' versus 'revisionary'. This will give us potentially eight forms of theistic anti-realism.

This last distinction relates to what the anti-realist thinks he or she is doing: describing the actual character of the governing intent of theistic discourse or recommending a revision of that intent. This is an important distinction whose merits can be seen once we remind ourselves of reinterpretations of theism of the kind found in Julian Huxley. It is a fact about many nineteenth-century and later philosophers and thinkers that they came to regard theism in general, and Christianity and Judaism in particular, as false. To reach that conclusion they must have initially interpreted theism realistically. Some of them (Huxley is an example) nonetheless wished to find something of value which can be redeemed from the wreckage. Instrumentalist or reductionist reinterpretations of theism follow. The choice between descriptive or revisionary theistic anti-realism is a question of whether any sample anti-realist thinks he or she is reporting on the governing intent theistic symbols have been used with or recommending a governing intent they ought now to be used with. Many revisionary interpretations of theism have been grounded in the perception (whether accurate or not) that something about modernity has made traditional religious claims impossible to maintain. They are false in the light of modern science and/or historiography. They are nonsense (or non-factual) in the light of modern epistemology or semantics. Thus a new governing intent for them must be forged. Hence, we have forms of revisionary anti-realism. Such anti-realism can surround itself with the language of conscious reworking of the faith or of saving it from its dominant, but now outmoded, past interpretations (as we find in the writings of Cupitt).

A further blow to our sanity comes from the fact that this same distinction can operate in realist accounts of theistic and religious discourse. The realist interpreter of key theistic concepts may argue that they can be taken to be about an appropriate (that is, transcendent) mind-independent object only if they are recast. The realist may agree with those anti-realists who say that theistic concepts as ordinarily understood cannot be so taken. Theological reconstruction is needed to rescue a realist intent for theism. In an earlier study I explored attempts to reinterpret religion in moral terms (Byrne 1998). Some of those endeavours are exercises in revisionary realism. A common starting-point for them is that the personal God of traditional Christianity, Judaism and Islam is no longer credible (on metaphysical and historical grounds). They will offer an account of religious symbolism which allows it an intent to refer to a sacred, transcendent reality but whose character is no longer fixed through images of the personal. It is rather given through the role this reality must play as a ground to the moral life (Byrne 1998: 16–17). I think a good case can be made for saying that the account of theological language in Kant's Critical Philosophy embodies revisionary realism. Kant can be interpreted as arguing that traditional theological discourse has been an attempt to break the bounds of sense. Revise it, or the intent behind it, and it can function referentially (Byrne 1998: 63–5). In a way, those many attempts by theologians in the theistic traditions to reinterpret the seeming anthropomorphic language of traditional faith and devotion can be seen as attempts at revisionary realism. A Maimonides could be interpreted as telling us that we cannot honour the realist intent behind the language of the faithful while its anthropomorphic character is left untouched.

An Appropriate Object for Theistic Discourse

Minimal theistic realism states that the key concepts of theism are governed by an attempt to refer to an appropriate extra-mental reality. An appropriate reality is one that is ontologically independent of us and is in addition a sacred, transcendent reality. 'Sacred' invokes an evaluative category and 'transcendent' an ontological one. The sacred is that which is supreme in value and the transcendent is that which exists beyond or apart from the world of spatio-temporal things. 'Transcendence' is the key category in any attempt to fill out the content of minimal theistic realism. It is to that category we will look in endeavouring to discern whether descriptive or revisionary accounts of theistic discourse are reductionist or not. 'Reductionist' only has any precision as a label by reference to a point of comparison provided by 'transcendent'. 'Transcendent' provides the signal that any referent for 'God' must make this entity epistemically and ontologically independent of human beings to a degree which allows it to be an appropriate object of reference for theistic discourse. Transcendence in the object of reference can be considered appropriate by reference to two deeper standards: historical and functional. We can appeal to the meaning that theistic claims have historically borne. Substituting a non-transcendent referent for 'God' may be thought to constitute too great a departure from the historic sense of theistic concepts to count as appropriate. But this cannot be a final way of judging the matter. Many interpretations of traditional theistic claims and concepts offer themselves precisely as revisionary exercises in the light of the presumed failings in traditional thinking. It is only by falling back on a functional criterion that we can judge that such revisionary exercises fail in the initial requirement of providing an appropriate object for theistic discourse. Appropriateness in this instance may be a matter of whether the fundamental and distinctive role religious symbols play in human life can be preserved in any account of what the governing intent behind theistic symbols is or ought to be. Only this level of analysis will allow us to provide a rationale for 'transcendence' as a criterion for divinity.

Our first steps in defining 'transcendence' and in discovering its rationale as a criterion of divinity might begin with a well-known paper of Ninian Smart: to say that God is transcendent is to assert a causal asymmetry between God and all other things (perhaps excluding abstracta). All things depend continually on God for their existence, but God does not depend on anything else for God's existence (Smart 1966: 482). 'All things' here equals the physical cosmos: the set of things in space and time. This definition entails that God would exist even though there were no cosmos. Allowing for the sake of argument that God has properties, it follows that none of God's essential properties (none of God's properties if all God's properties are essential) need the physical world to exist, or to have a certain character, in order to be realised. God, then, exists beyond the mundane world. Realism is a matter of whether theistic discourse intends to, or does actually, refer to such an object. Such a criterion of transcendence gives us an object of reference which is epistemically and ontologically independent of us.

Life and realism, however, are not that simple. There is a good argument for saying that we should not tie realism in theism to the belief that God would have existed even though there was no physical cosmos. This notion is not a necessary condition for transcendence. For it is possible to find otherwise traditional, orthodox forms of theism which hold that, God's altruistic goodness being what it is, God had to create a universe.

We cannot get a more orthodox theist than St Thomas Aquinas. Norman Kretzmann has argued that the metaphysics of the *Summa Contra Gentiles* entails that God had to create the universe. Kretzmann contends that Aquinas is committed to the Pseudo-Dionysian principle that 'Goodness is by its very nature diffusive of itself and (thereby) of being' (Kretzmann 1997: 224). He finds this principle at work in *S.C.G.* I where Aquinas links the diffusive nature of God's goodness with the fact that God is the cause of being. Aquinas is committed, according to Kretzmann, to a necessitarian explanation of God's willing of other things than himself. God's free choice intervenes only in a limited way between the fact of God's being and goodness and the fact that there is created world. It only operates in God's choosing of which particular kind of world to create (Kretzmann 1997: 225).

It does not matter whether Kretzmann's interpretation of Aquinas is correct. All that matters is that it points to one interpretation of theism whose entailments are that God's very existence is a sufficient condition for the existence of a material universe, and thus that the existence of a material universe is a necessary condition for God's existence, and thus that God depends on the universe for God's existence. If we throw in the thought (merely for the sake of argument) that this is the best possible universe, then such a version of theism would hold that the existence of this particular universe is a necessary condition for God to exist. We then have a theistic system whose focus provides a clear violation of Smart's criterion of transcendence. Its God would not and could not exist if there were no creation. It is not transcendent in the sense of being logically independent of the existence of a created universe. Of course, we might try to distinguish the causal dependence/independence of God's existence and essential attributes from the Spartan notions of necessary and sufficient conditions. We might then contend that the logical dependence of a necessarily creative God upon the cosmos does not amount to the ontological dependence of God upon creation. Just how we might do that remains to be explored. I shall not attempt that here, since I will describe below accounts of God which suggest that God depends in a substantial way upon there being a universe for some of God's important attributes. Some of these views would suggest that God and the world must be co-eternal: if there was ever a time when the universe was not, then there would have been no God. They do not look to be anti-realist accounts of God for all that they postulate a clear measure of ontological dependence of God upon creatures.

We have not produced a precise definition of 'transcendent'. Matters seem more daunting when we consider the range of theisms we would need to test any such definition against. We have met two simple cases. Braithwaite's theism is anti-realist because it does not matter for his interpretation of God-talk whether such talk refers at all. Feuerbach's is anti-realist because 'God' in his system refers to human nature and its potentialities, with the result that if there were no human beings there would be no God. But consider the most literal, metaphysically bold readings of Hegel's philosophy of *Geist*, whereby *Geist* is a genuine cosmic reality existing over and above human nature. On such readings it would still be true that *Geist* needs there to be human beings with cultures and national histories to become absolute (realise its true nature and fulfil its potentialities). For *Geist* needs to alienate itself, project a world from its being, in order to know itself. Does that entail that if the *Geist* notion is the best a Hegelian can do by way of interpreting 'God', she or he is thereby a theistic anti-realist? Well, I do not feel like giving an automatic 'Yes' to that question.

Pantheistic and panentheistic religious systems in general provide borderline problems for defining theistic realism. The God of Hartshorne and other Process thinkers has a consequent nature which makes it dependent on there being a world of experiencing subjects to become all it might be. The divine realities postulated in pantheisms such as Spinoza's, Herder's or the Stoics' require a material universe for those realities to exist at all. For what pantheism asserts is that there is a god in the sense of there being a Unity in all things which is divine (Levine 1994: 25). Note that in the case of Stoicism this divine Unity is conceived materialistically. Stoics denied the existence of independent entities with a non-bodily nature (Gerson 1990: 145). The universe is animated by *pneuma* and *pneuma* is composed of fire and air (1990: 148).

The point of the above examples is to suggest the difficulty of using transcendence, in the sense of independence of the mundane, physical world, to define the appropriate object of a realist construal of theistic talk. Such examples (which could be multiplied) *seem* to be different from the four-square anti-realist interpretations of 'God' of Braithwaite, Cupitt or Feuerbach. Perhaps the difference between

Feuerbach and co. and Hegel and co. could be summed up like this. What makes Feuerbach an anti-realist in the interpretation of theism is that he so interprets 'God' that it does not refer to an entity with causal power beyond those entities with causal power in principle describable by the natural and human sciences. The measure of transcendence for an appropriate realist referent for God is that the referent, if real, would possess power beyond that which can figure in scientific descriptions of the world. Put another way: there is teleologically guided power acting upon or in the universe beyond that possessed by finite rational creatures. Recall the Stoics: they regard human beings as manifesting reason, *logos*, in their behaviour and products. But they are also proponents of the argument from design (see Book II of Cicero's *The Nature of the Gods*). Their design arguments move from part to whole. What obviously animates part of nature (that is the order and design produced by intelligence and reason in human beings and their products) animates the whole (that is the order and design produced by the intelligence immanent in nature and its products; Gerson 1990: 158). They have a theology, can give a use to a concept of 'divinity', because the unity which they see in all things is a teleologically guided unity. Their source of unity is also the source of a providential order in the world.

Suppose we accept that there can be realist conceptions of divinity which do not respect Smart's fundamental principle that a transcendent divine entity would exist even if there were no world, while the world would not exist if there were no divine entity. We go along with Byrne's suggestion that transcendence has to be understood in terms of the possession of power for order and for good beyond that possessed by human beings and natural things. Then we will count theism interpreted through the categories of, say, Hegel as a candidate for a realist interpretation of core concepts of divinity. Having got thus far, we do face a paradox. Hegel's system, and many of the others mentioned above, entails that if there is a divine reality there must be a non-divine reality. So the existence of non-divine reality is a necessary condition for the existence of divine reality. Some of them, like Hegel's system, entail that the existence of human beings (or at least, finite persons) is a necessary condition for the existence of divine reality, or at least for its possession of key parts of its nature. We are then accepting that realist accounts of the divine can leave us with the consequence that the divine is not ontologically independent of the world or of us. But we started out with the thought that a realist interpretation of theistic discourse had to make divinity epistemically and ontologically independent of us. We are now admitting that some postulated transcend entities would nonetheless be ontologically dependent on us. Here we need to make a distinction between ontological dependence and distinctness. Feuerbach's programme in *The Essence of Christianity* leaves talk about the

divine as talk about human nature. 'God' in that system is not distinct
from the human. Hence we properly style it reductionist. But we want to
leave open as a proper subject of debate among realist, non-reductionist
accounts of the divine what degree of unity or connection there is
between the divine and the non-divine. Orthodox theism makes God's
being and nature wholly independent, ontologically, from that of the
non-divine. There are, by contrast, varying degrees and modes of
dependence of the divine on the non-divine in the systems of Hegel, the
Stoics or Process philosophers. Such systems still make the divine to be
distinct from human beings. Talk of the divine is not simply another
way of repackaging thoughts about the human. To admit the existence
of the divine is to admit the existence of a source of providential power
and order beyond that found in human beings considered in isolation
from the categories of the religious system in question.

A minimal theistic realism could then be defined as follows. It is any
interpretation of theism which holds that the governing intent of core
theistic concepts is (or ought to be) to refer to a reality which is
epistemically independent of human beings, ontologically distinct from
them and transcendent.

I suggest that an account of what it is for a system of thought to
have a providential picture of the relation between a putative *theos* and
the world can be given by exploring the relation between religion and
the notions of good and evil. Stoicism should provide us with a good
test case for determining when a form of theism really deserves that
label or is to be dismissed as too revisionary. Stoicism does not
postulate a personal God who is apart from the world (in Smart's
sense of being capable of existence even if there is no world). But it
would be an obvious mistake in view of the examples cited above to
identify theism with personal theism. Seeing God as personal is but
one amongst many possible and actual conceptions of divinity. Stoics
are pantheists. They see all things as constituting a unity (in their case,
the unity of an organism) and they see this unity as divine. The
divinity of their principle of unity for all things (*logos/pneuma*) relates
to its being a supreme source of plan and purpose and a supreme
source of value. This need not be a reductive account of divinity. By
contrast, Huxley's account of Father, Son and Spirit as referring to
non-human nature, to human ideals and to human life is. Huxley's
account provides us with no conception of a providential order in
nature. There is no source of teleology beyond that provided by
human plans and purposes.

Huxley sets his interpretation of religion in the context of
'evolutionary humanism' (Huxley 1957: 236–7). This assumes that
the evolution of living and conscious beings from the stuff out of
which natural things are made was solely or mainly controlled by the
mechanism of natural selection (1957: 214). Religion plays an

important role in our lives in so far as it is one of the key ways in which how we live can be organised. It is the proper job of religion in human life to interrelate the goals and springs of conduct with each other and the full experience of outer reality (1957: 188). It deals in three categories of fact which it must organise: the powers of nature, the ideal goals of the human mind, and actual living beings in so far as they embody such ideals (1957: 188). These facts are not to be treated as isolated. As they are apprehended by the human mind they 'are reality embodied in human experience' and so become organised and unified (1957: 189). Once we see through the errors of regarding 'God' as the name of a supernatural person, then we should use the word to refer to the unity of the three great categories of fact which impinge on the human mind (1957: 190). It is important for our purposes to note that the unity is created by the experience of these facts by our minds. Huxley does not reject a personal God in order to argue that there is an impersonal ground of being or a general spiritual force behind all phenomena (1957: 49). This would be to breach the fundamental naturalism which characterises his position. Huxley does speak of 'the cosmic process' and of the role of human beings as the key products of evolution enabling the cosmic process to become aware of itself (1957: 236). But there is absolutely no reason to think he intends to add to the powers and capacities science describes in talking thus. Talk of the cosmic process seems to refer to no more than the powers and liabilities of natural things thought of as belonging to one evolving world system. There is no reality behind that world system. The system only acquires things capable of acting for ends when human beings emerge in it.

We can make our picture of what counts as a providential theism more precise by referring to Kant's account of what religion is designed to do. It is there to answer the question 'What may I hope?' (Kant 1997: A805/B337). According to a Kantian view, religions are sets of symbols associated with appropriate actions, attitudes, feelings and the like arising out of a certain need or problem and in presenting religious practitioners with a certain vision of the real.

The need or problem is that of finding a response to evil. In particular, they arise out of the human perception that the apparent order of the world around them is not a moral order; it is indifferent to the achievement of human happiness and the realisation of human goodness; it presents itself as blind and indifferent to justice. It is the job of a religion on this account to offer human beings a theodicy. By this is meant not necessarily a set of *doctrines* about goodness and reality, but a set of symbols presenting to human beings an order of reality beyond or behind the apparent, given order. Such a set of symbols works as a theodicy if the order of reality presented by religious symbols is: through and through moral; thought of as the *true* order of things, as the *ground* of the order which immediately surrounds them; and thought of as something to which human beings can be related to in thought and action. In particular, a religion presents right action as that which is guided by religious symbols and which consists in living in proper relationship to, in harmony with, that which is most real. Religion thus guarantees and assures that good for human beings is attainable despite the contingencies and hostile features of the given world. It is in this way that it answers Kant's question 'What may I hope?' What we can hope for is that the human good is achievable.

In brief: a religion is any set of symbols (and associated actions, attitudes, feelings and experiences) providing human beings with a solution to evil by way of a theodicy. We can give sense to 'religion in general' by these means as well. Religion is that propensity in human beings (however grounded) to respond to evil by seeking the kind of meaning (to engage in the kind of actions, exhibit the kind of attitudes …) associated with the enterprise of theodicy.

The above suggests that religious systems which employ the concept of a *theos* need that concept to have a transcendent reference for two reasons. First, as responses to the problem of evil, they need to invoke a moral and providential causality in the world which transcends both the forces inherent in nature and the power in human action to promote the good and fight against evil. Second, their vision of the good is correspondingly relational. They conceive of the human good as a matter of living in right relation to the source of the providential, moral order postulated as response to evil.

The argument about religion, good and evil has further consequences which need exploring. It suggests a programme for the proponent of religious realism. The defender of the realist interpretation is set the task of showing that avowedly anti-realist interpretations of theism, such as Cupitt's, have no answer to Kant's question about human hope and no satisfactory response to the problem of evil in human life. This defence might extend to trying to show that the accounts of good and evil in anti-realist versions of theism are incoherent. Further to this, the defender of realism has a task in checking whether versions of revisionary realism stay within the realist fold. They will do so if they continue to affirm a teleologically grounded mechanism for the realisation of human good and the overcoming of evil in human life. (Hick's revision of theism, for example, comes out as still realist on this criterion. For all that his Real is shrouded in mystery, it continues to serve the crucial purpose of guaranteeing a 'limitlessly good end-state' (Hick 1989: 179) which is the ground of a cosmic optimism about human fulfilment.)

As a final and welcome consequence of the moral approach to the definition of theistic realism, we may note that it offers to solve our problem about how to state a sufficient condition for transcendence.

This condition will then be helpful for distinguishing an appropriate referent of religious discourse from an inappropriate one. An interpretation of, or derivation from, theism preserves a picture of the *theos* as transcendent if its god or god-substitute is capable of exercising a moral causality in the world which in turn is capable of defeating evil and guaranteeing the human good in the long run. A system retains a sacred, transcendent reference if it posits a kind of causality that: extends beyond the efficient causality in natural things; is over and above the moral agency provided by human beings; and assures us that the apparent gap between the world of facts and the world of values is not finally real. We may acknowledge that this root idea can be fleshed out in all manner of ways and that it remains for different variants of it to debate amongst themselves as to the merits of their accounts of the *theos* and its relation to the world and human history.

The link between moral causality and transcendence is not one of logical equivalence. The above condition is not necessary for transcendence. The god of deism, as deism is defined in the textbooks, is one who made the world and then left it alone. It exercises no providential control over it. It may be deemed transcendent in terms of the causal-asymmetry criterion discussed above.

A final point to add to the initial definition of minimal theistic realism: not all of the concepts of a mode of discourse have to be taken to be referential (in intent or in fact) for it to be interpreted realistically. The definition of realism from Devitt with which we opened has a 'most' in it in order to make this point. We can interpret scientific discourse realistically even though we recognise that many terms in past theories referred to nothing outside of the human mind and even though we acknowledge the same will turn out to be true of many present scientific concepts. We can be realists while accepting that many current concepts are not intended to be truly referential, but rather serve to introduce convenient fictions and idealisations. A similar point must apply to theistic realism, but it cannot be cast in quite the same way. To interpret theistic discourse realistically it is not necessary that most concepts of past and present theistic systems be understood as referential in intention or in reality: only the central ones, perhaps the one key concept of God. So I am assuming that anti-realism does not arrive if a contemporary Christian denies a referential intent to concepts of angelic substances or to the concept of the devil. There will properly be differences among contemporary Christians (and among Muslims and among Jews) as to how much of the lush religious ontology of previous phases of religious thought can be abandoned. However, there might be agreement that even a vigorous weeding out of traditional religious ontology does not entail abandoning realism provided the central concept of the divine remains. (The weeding may be wrong for other reasons.)

A Realist Interpretation of Theology?

In exploring the possibility of a realist interpretation of theology, we need to explain how it is possible to give a realist verdict on theism while leaving open as a separate question whether a realistic interpretation of theology is possible.

Theism is belief, action and attitude centred around symbols referring to a *theos*. Theology is the theoretical, systematic exploration and adumbration of such belief, action and attitude. We may perfectly well judge theology, say as practised in the academies and seminaries of the contemporary Western world, to be anti-realist in its thrust, while judging theism in the opposite sense. This possibility is demonstrated by the overall argument of Chapters 19 and 20 of Hick's *An Interpretation of Religion* (Hick 1989). Hick's argument as a whole accepts the realist intent of talk about the Ultimate in various religions. It is also plain that he thinks there is an occupant of 'sacred space' which serves as the referent of this talk. But in these chapters in Part V of his book he maintains that the precise questions human beings have asked about the character and purposes of this referent are unanswerable. The answers human beings have proposed to transcendent questions of this kind cannot be relied on as containing true information about the divine, rather they serve a pragmatic purpose. They are not valuable to members of the appropriate believing community by way of giving them reliable beliefs about the detailed nature and doings of the referent of religious discourse, but serve the purpose of directing them in the right (that is, salvific) attitudes and actions toward this referent.

Whether Hick's views are at all acceptable does not matter for our purposes. The fact that they are intelligible suffices to show that when we face the question of the realist character of theological discourses we have a new *object* and a new *mode* of assessment in view. Our object is not merely the main referring expressions of religious systems. We are not merely assessing whether in intention and/or in fact these expressions are directed to the right kind of referent. The object of our questionings is the discursive elaboration of belief in an Ultimate. And what we are endeavouring to assess is whether those discursive elaborations look as though they might add to the stock of reliable belief about the ultimate in question. We are asking, too, if those discursive elaborations can plausibly be seen as controlled or shaped by cognitive contact with that Ultimate.

These questions will be considered at length in Chapter 7.

Chapter 2

Global or Non-Contrastive
Anti-realism

What is Global Anti-realism?

I have defined theistic realism in Chapter 1 as a doctrine about the *intent* behind theistic symbols. The theistic realists maintain that some of these symbols at least are used with the intent of referring to an appropriate mind-independent reality. This reality would be extra-mental, extra-linguistic and transcendent. Let us follow Searle (1995: 153) and gloss 'extra-mental, extra-linguistic reality' as 'reality independent of our representations'. He draws a fundamental contrast between social realities which are constituted by our beliefs (and are thus intentional) and non-social realities whose existence and properties are not dependent on human beliefs. Money is an example of the former, the North Downs of the latter. That the pieces of paper in my wallet with the Queen's head and other pictures on them constitute £5 and £10 notes depends on facts about human beliefs and actions. They are pieces of money because they are constituted as such in a human institution. The collective intentionality of the British means that these pieces of coloured paper count as money, as a means of exchange. If there were no people, in particular no British state, they would not be money. If the relevant institutions ceased to exist, these objects would cease to have the status of money. They would cease to exist as money. Their reality as money is a function of the existence of human representations, particularly beliefs and conventions.

The North Downs are different. It makes sense to say that the North Downs would have existed if no human beings had ever existed. (They are formed by a chalk escarpment made up of sediments from the remains of millions of sea creatures thousands of years ago.) The process that formed the Downs took place long before there were any human beings on the planet. No human activity was involved in their fundamental geology. By the same token, if perchance all of humanity was wiped out in some global catastrophe, the Downs would still exist.

What exists independent of our representations may nonetheless be dependent on us in other ways. A journey through a highly populated country like England reveals a landscape most of which has been shaped by human hand. Leaving aside the built environment, organic features such as field, hedgerow, wood and forest have been planted, or shaped by human activity. Nonetheless, the hedgerows, orchards and the like are not constituted by human intentionality. They would not cease of a sudden should there cease to be a human society in this part of the earth. Things can be people-dependent in a more radical way still without being representation-dependent. If Byrne has asthma, his asthma ontologically depends on Byrne in a most radical way (destroy Byrne and Byrne's asthma ceases of an instant), but its existence does not depend on Byrne's *belief* that he has asthma. He may mistakenly believe he suffers from asthma or mistakenly believe he does not.

Most of the furniture of the world, we think, is independent of our representations. This thought flows naturally from another: we consider ourselves to be physical things, flesh-and-blood human beings, in a physical world. The vast majority of people in the modern, Western world consider this physical world to be much, much older than the human race. They also consider the history of the human race to extend much further back in time than recorded human history. Human beings with their beliefs, representations and intentional states are thus late arrivals in the cosmos and on the Earth. We who exist now are the product of a history that is very long. Most of it is and must remain unknown to us. We can form no reliable beliefs at all about the happenings in spatially and temporally remote regions of our world. Even if we confine our reflections to the history of our species, the actions and circumstances of most of the generations of *homo sapiens* remain forever hidden from us. All this entails that we have the conception that there has been and is much to reality existing beyond our representations.

External realism, as the stark thesis that reality is not constituted by human representations of it, thus follows from the fundamental thought that *people* have representations: physical beings having a history set in a physical cosmos with its own history. But Searle is right to contend that external realism does not entail this fundamental belief about our existence as people. External realism is not committed to there being a physical reality (in which flesh-and-blood people are the bearers of representations), merely to a reality which is not constituted by (or logically dependent on) our representations (Searle 1995: 155–6). Forms of idealism which state that reality is constituted by non-physical stuff (such as our sense-data or a non-physical absolute such as *Geist*) are nonetheless world views postulating a reality which exists independently of our beliefs about it. Idealism holds that there is a truth about the world which is not determined by our beliefs about the world. Contrast: the fact that the paper in my wallet is money is determined by the conventions, beliefs and representations of a group of people. If I adopted the world view of personal idealism, I would think of all reality as having the character of Byrne's asthma. It would not exist if there were no human minds. But it would not depend on the beliefs those minds have. It is perfectly possible for an idealist to have a correspondence theory of truth, whereby what makes beliefs true (reality) is distinct from what bears truth (human representations).

From the fact that external realism does not entail that there is a physical world, it follows that it is not equivalent to that which Devitt defines as realism: 'Tokens of most current common-sense, and scientific, physical types objectively exist independently of the mental' (Devitt 1997: 23). Philosophical idealists or pan-psychists can dissent from Devitt's realism. So will certain types of philosophical sceptic. But all these philosophers may be external realists, indeed one would expect them to be realists. They have theses about the nature of reality as it exists independently of our representations of it. Indeed, the radical, philosophical sceptic tells us that our beliefs about reality are quite mistaken as to its true nature or at best lack any objective certainty. Throughout *Realism and Truth* Devitt treats his realist thesis as a plain empirical theory, but the truth of external realism is not an empirical matter. Offering theories and supporting them by evidence about the character of representation-independent reality presupposes external realism, because it assumes that there is a truth about reality independent of our beliefs. Devitt's realism entails external realism, but external realism does not entail it. Devitt's realism entails the further claims about our being people with a history and ancestry in a physical world with its own lengthy history, but those claims do not entail Devitt's realism. Those claims are compatible with a high degree of scepticism about the details of current scientific theorising and thus with a denial of Devitt's realism.

From the territory surveyed so far we can define a minimal metaphysical stance which is richer than the stark external realism introduced by Searle because it constitutes a denial of an idealist world view. We shall call this innocent realism (after Haack 1996: 304ff.). Innocent realism builds upon the fundamental thought that there is a distinction between how the world is, on the one hand, and the character of our representations of that world, on the other. Innocent realism states that there is one real world which exists largely independent of us. It is not completely independent of us. We are part of it and we shape it and interact with it. Some of the time what we say about this world is true; some of the time it is false. Whether it is so or not depends on whether the judgements we make, with the senses we have given them, are accurate accounts of how this one, real world is. Even where we make judgements about us and our states, as parts of this one, real world, whether they are true or not is not dependent on how any one of us thinks. Within the one, real world Haack then distinguishes real but external realities and real but internal realities (1996: 305). The former are facts about the world independent of how any one individual thinks and indeed of there being human beings at all. The latter are facts about the world independent of how any one individual thinks but not independent of how we collectively think or of there being human beings at all. Included in such facts are ones about people's mental states and about socially constructed realities. Innocent realism asserts the existence of external realities and thus constitutes a denial of personal idealism. It has a general picture of human beings as late arrivals who make a limited impact on a world which predates them. Most of the facts of the world are independent of us because most of the things and stuffs which make up the world exist independently of us. It is close to Devitt's common-sense and scientific realism: mind-independent tokens exist for a good number of the common-sense and scientific types we employ.

Innocent realism thus holds that for the most part the states of affairs which make up the one real world are external realities and thus mind-independent (excluding any divine mind). Whether they obtain or not is in no way determined by the thoughts human beings have. The obtaining of these states of affairs does not depend on the very existence of human beings. The human, internal states of affairs that make up part of the one, real world are mind-independent in a weaker sense: they are independent of how any one individual thinks them to be.

Innocent realism seems to be a sufficient background for taking theistic realism seriously. Innocent realism allows people to make diverse judgements about the furniture of the world, but supplies the background assumption that there is a body of furniture which, for the most part, is epistemically and ontologically independent of us. In the absence of specific reasons to the contrary, we ought to take at face value the intent of some to talk about a divine object. If such an object exists, then that would be a mind-independent (in the strong sense) denizen of the world (thought of as the sum total of what exists, not as the cosmos, the universe). Our statements about it would be true or false to the extent that they corresponded with mind-independent states of affairs. This is all that theistic realism requires.

Innocent realism deals in a real world independent of our representations of it and, for the most part, of our existence and characteristics. It speaks of 'one' real world because it respects one of the fundamental truisms about truth: all truths are compatible, no two truths can be related as contraries. Any true account of the world and what exists in it is a coherent account. It is important to note that innocent realism is not committed to stronger claims. Here are some which are frequently and mistakenly linked with it:

- There is one, true finite description of all there is.

- There is a fixed totality of mind-independent objects.

- There is a single theory about reality from which all true descriptions of it can be deduced.

These stronger claims will be seen to be at issue when philosophers (such as conceptual relativists) attack innocent realism. At their core lies the idea that there is a single true theory to describe all that is true about mind-independent reality. However, despite the popularity of the charge that realism entails these theses, we shall argue in this study that it does not. This is part and parcel of the idea that the one, real world contains a variety of states of affairs. The innocent realist knows (truism about truth) that all truths about the world are compatible. But the realist can leave as an empirical matter the extent to which all truths so far discovered can be incorporated into a single theory of the world and be related to other truths by mutual entailment or implication. In the last analysis the construction of a single theory to describe reality depends on a fact about the one, real world the realist says we live in, namely how diverse or complex it is. There is a substantive judgement to be made about the success of efforts to unify our reliable beliefs about what entities and properties populate mind-independent reality. It is precisely in the spirit of innocent realism *not* to let this matter be judged in favour of the one single-theory view *before* human experience of reality yields its testimony.

Some realists will argue that whether there is a single true theory of the world to be discovered is not an empirical matter. There may be no finite set of truths to be discovered about the world, not just because it may be infinite in spatial or temporal extent or in its variety, but, more deeply, because there may be no end to the aspects of it that different human languages, conceptual schemes and perspectives can bring out. Innocent realists may be struck by the fact that the world can be described using a variety of vocabularies and from a variety of points of view (see Kirk 1999: 149–51). There are proper metaphysical issues here on which innocent realists may hold divergent views.

Global anti-realism can now be defined as the rejection of innocent realism. It denies that the world is, for the most part, both epistemically and ontologically independent of us. Forms of personal idealism will count as expressions of global anti-realism on the definitions offered so far. In contemporary thought, however, global anti-realism is much more likely to be countered by philosophical theories which state that the world is constituted by our representations (our symbols, our beliefs, our activity as language-using subjects and as cognitive agents). Such theories highlight the epistemic dependence of the world upon us. Ontological dependence follows as a consequence.

The notion that the world is constituted by our representations or our symbols, or beliefs, or our activity as language-using subjects and cognitive agents can come in at least two forms. A stronger form states that there is literally nothing beyond representation or language. Reality is through and through constructed by language or by cognitive activity. A weaker version allows that there is an *indeterminate* reality independent of representation, contending that reality only becomes determinate in and through human linguistic and cognitive activity. What is outside cognition and language, on this view, is formless.

It is hard to find someone who holds global anti-realism in the strong form. It may be thought that Don Cupitt in *Creation out of Nothing* comes close to it. He does speak of 'a kind of creation of the world ex nihilo by language' (Cupitt 1990: 12) and of the world being all words (21). But he also speaks as if reality is given *form* by human representations. There is something logically independent of representational, cognitive activity: it is chaos, the void, a flux. It is shaped and made into a nameable, knowable reality by language and representation (see Cupitt 1990: 21–2). This is what Devitt calls 'weak or fig-leaf realism' ('so weak as to be uninteresting'; Devitt 1997: 23). It is the doctrine that something exists independently of our representations, but that every concrete feature it possesses is down to our construction. Robert Kirk styles it more colourfully the 'cosmic porridge' conception (Kirk 1999: 52). As delineated by Kirk, it holds that all that exists apart from our representations is an indeterminate something. It has no features of its own. Human representations impose features on it, make objects and qualities out of it:

> Sticks and stones, atoms and electrons, stars and clouds are our constructions in the strong sense that there is no more to their existence than the fact that we have imposed those particular concepts on the otherwise indeterminate stuff, the cosmic porridge itself. [Kirk 1999: 52]

The above quotation seems to capture perfectly Cupitt's anti-realism. The cosmic-porridge view tells us that the-world-as-known is constituted by our theorising about it. It is an idealist view of the-world-as-known. Innocent realists adopt nidealism (to use Haack's term) as a view about the-world-as-known. To do that they must hold that there is something true in scholastic realism as defined by Haack. What is true in scholastic realism is that there is some differentiation in the world before we came to experience it. There is shape and structure to the world. It contains, independent of us, distinct and different things.

The cosmic-porridge view, if not the stronger 'all reality is created *ex nihilo*' by representations, would seem to be entailed by any robust version of conceptual relativism. A view which states that truth, and hence reality, is relative to a conceptual scheme must hold that human conceptual activity creates what is real as it creates conceptual schemes. Things exist, are real, only relative to a conceptual scheme. So conceptual scheming must provide a shape to reality that was not there before. Such views can be impressed by the fact that there is something given to human conceptualising activity. Human beings have experience. Experience, for the most part, comes to us as from without. But it only gains form and shape from conceptualising. The object *qua* known, *qua* experienced is not independent of us but constituted by the human mind's conceptual activity. (These contentions will be found in Runzo 1986 and 1993.)

The cosmic-porridge view might seem to be so extreme as to be capable of being found only outside the mainstream of contemporary philosophy. Not so. Hilary Putnam endorses it in some of his attacks on what he styles 'metaphysical realism', as when he states: 'Objects do not exist independently of conceptual schemes. *We* cut up the world into objects when we introduce one or another scheme of description' (Putnam 1981: 52). This statement implies that there is something independent of our cognitive activities, something on which we get to work with our concepts, but that this something is formless. Prior to our applying the cutters which are our concepts there are no determinate objects in the world.

Something like the cosmic-porridge view is also implied in Michael Dummett's anti-realist semantics. Dummett's leading idea that statements are neither true not false in the absence of an effective means of showing them to be true or false produces the conclusion that reality has no determinate features prior to our establishing the truth of the claims we make about it. Dummett takes his lead from Intuitionism in mathematics, which holds that mathematical statements do not have determinate truth values prior to the discovery of proofs and disproofs of them. Intuitionists hold to a moderate constructionism: 'it is *we* who construct mathematics; it is not already *there* waiting for us to discover ... Our investigations bring into existence what was not there before, but what they bring into existence is not of their own making' (Dummett 1978: 18). Dummett then commends the application of this moderate constructionism to other areas of reality. We do not need to embrace 'subjective idealism' or the view that 'we create the world' but we abandon realism nonetheless (Dummett 1978: 19, see also xxviii–xxix and 229–30). These thoughts make sense if Dummett is stating that we do not create the world literally out of nothing, but do provide the cosmic porridge with its determinate features.

One of Dummett's followers, Michael Luntley, has made matters clearer for us. Anti-realism calls for 'a fundamental change in our concepts of object and knowledge' (Luntley 1988: 144). Objects cannot be thought of as having determinate characteristics beyond our capacity to recognise and discover those characteristics. So we must 'forgo the notion of a world determinate beyond our capacities to know of it as the object of our cognitive enquiries' (144). Rather, objects have determinate features only in so far as our experience gives us warrant to affirm knowledge claims about them. In the absence of effective means of determining whether statements are true, or whether their terms do refer to anything real, we must abandon the notion that there is a determinate reality of which they are true or to which their component terms refer (244–5). The realist is castigated for believing that there is a world 'populated with entities that exist irrespective of our ability to know anything about them' (246). Overall, these assertions give us the thesis that it is *only in relation to human representations* (here, warranted claims to knowledge) *that reality has determinate features*. Dummett's and Luntley's anti-realism must entail that if there had been no cognisers there would have been no determinate features to reality at all.

Global anti-realism of this kind has implications for understanding the intent of theistic talk. If there is no determinate reality independent of our representations of it, it cannot be the case that we use the word 'God' or its cognates to refer to an entity independent of our representations of it. It seems natural to assume that theists of whatever hue are global realists. They think that reality exists, and in a determinate form, independent of human representations of it. They contend for the truth of a referential claim about this reality. Different versions of theism offer rival referential claims and all versions are contradicted by the naturalist claim that the only realities which are real (that is, have causal power) are thoroughly mundane ones. So only if global realism is true can the fundamental realist intent of theism be sustained.

We must note that global anti-realism, even if it is all of the kind committed to the cosmic porridge, is capable of being taken in radically different ways. It is clear that Cupitt's porridge can be freely moulded in different ways, by different languages or sets of human representations. His global anti-realism entails a radical relativism. Languages differ from epoch to epoch and from culture to culture. They are shaped by human interests: 'our knowledge systems ... are period pieces' (Cupitt 1990: 14). Since language shapes the world it follows that there is nothing called *the* world only '*our*' world, a cultural product' (1990: 22; cf. Cupitt 1984: 20). Thus Cupitt's anti-realism entails a kind of Promethean constructionism. We really are free to mould the porridge one way or another as pressing interests or ideals invite. In a similar way, the conceptual relativism of Runzo comes with the implication that different conceptual schemes bring different accounts of what is real. It is in part designed to make us tolerant of diversity in accounts of the what really exists (see his 'pluralist ontology principle', Runzo 1986: 60).

Dummett's and Luntley's porridge does not flow so freely. Recall Dummett's remarks quoted above on the lessons to be drawn for reality in general from the Intuitionist arguments against an independent mathematical reality. They show that he rejects what he styles an extreme form of constructivism such as he sees in Wittgenstein's *Remarks on the Foundations of Mathematics*. We do not construct mathematical reality as we go along (Dummett 1978: 18) where that means we are completely free to do it one way or the other. Nor do we so construct other types of reality. Dummett clearly thinks that there are proofs in mathematics which show that some mathematical statements are definitively true. His famous essay on 'The Reality of the Past' (Dummett 1978: 358–74) sets out the anti-realist view that the past does not consist of determinate facts antecedent to our attempts to prove what happened in it, but it nowhere implies that the past is a free construct of ours. What prevents it from being such is evidence and public criteria of warranted assertibility. Matters are clearer in Luntley's exposition of anti-realism, which continually speaks of *experience* as something which provides an objective test of whether a knowledge claim can survive. Knowledge consists of the possession of experienceable truths (Luntley 1988: 144).

It can be argued that Cupitt is the more consistent thinker here. Luntley (and by implication, Dummett) seems to be committed to the idea of a given, that is determinate experience which is the basis of knowledge claims. But this determinate experience cannot be based on determinate objects interacting with a determinate cognitive nature in us, and cannot therefore be guaranteed to be universal and constant across all cognisers. For the essence of the mistake anti-realism tries to expunge consists in believing that there is a world of determinate objects and properties prior to and beyond what experience yields as evidence one way or the other. An anti-realist epistemology rejects the positing of a 'class of objects as the ground of our experience' (Luntley 1988: 144). But why then assume that there is determinate experience shared by human beings? If there is no determinate reality prior to and beyond our investigations of it, why assume that reality-as-investigated-by-me must be the same as reality-as-investigated-by-you? The same criticism can be levelled at Putnam. He denies that he is a relativist (see Putnam 1990: 118). He asserts that there are some facts waiting to be discovered and which are not legislated by us (1989: 114). In *Reason, Truth and History* he advises those who think that any conceptual scheme goes to choose one that says that human beings can fly and then jump out of window. They will soon be taught a lesson (1981: 54). But we must then ask where do the constraints come from that prevent us choosing what conceptual schemes we like? If the cosmic porridge will not let human beings jump from heights without hitting the ground with a bump, there must be a fact here which transcends any human representations. And we are entitled to ask what the fact consists in and posit features of our world such as gravity to explain it. The cosmic porridge cannot then be totally characterless.

The precise point here is that *our experience* appears to have features which no amount of conceptual chopping and changing can alter. The postulation of a reality beyond it which is determinate explains this. Anti-realists like Dummett and Putnam are forced to accept that there is some constraint on our experience and our theorising while having no account of the source of this constraint (see Devitt 1997: 230; Putnam avoids relativism 'by fiat'). Radicals such as Cupitt throw over the idea of restraint and attempt to deny that our experience is shaped and moulded by something independent of our conceptualising. This is a heroic consistency.

The freedom anti-realism gives us in moulding the cosmic porridge depends, therefore, on whether it does or does not posit a given. In Dummettian anti-realism there is an alleged given. It is constituted by logic and experience. In Cupittean anti-realism there is no given. On the surface, the Dummettian anti-realism can therefore give a sense to the notion of proving, establishing or discovering that there is a God and some sense to the notion of God as other than a free creation or projection of the cognising subject. These ideas cannot be, and are not, accepted in the later writings of Cupitt. On his account, we set out to choose a fundamental belief such as there is a God (Cupitt 1984: 19) and it follows that the word 'God' can have no reference to anything other than a construction out of our representations. The moderate anti-realism of Dummett and his followers places the notion of God (and all other notions with a putative objective reference) under a much subtler metaphysical cloud. But it is not evident that such moderate anti-realism is sustainable.

Can Global Anti-realism Be Refuted?

That there is a world existing independently of our representations and symbols is something presupposed in great swathes of our thought, speech and practice. It is entailed by our shared perception that we are so many human beings occupying a common world of objects. It is entailed by the particular story told above of our being flesh-and-blood creatures who are part of a physical world with a history. In terms of that story, it makes precious little sense to speak of human beings constructing their world or the objects in it. Human beings do literally construct some things in the human world. But artefacts nonetheless are made from human-independent materials and once made they exist independently of human representations of them. Human beings can and do, of course, construct stories, myths, theories and hypotheses about the world in which they dwell. This activity is unproblematic.

Such things are constituted by human symbols. Human activity makes and unmakes symbolic structures. Some of the world they live in is a social world inhabited by institutional objects (such as laws, road signs and traffic lights). Institutional objects have a reality that is partly constructed by human representations, since they exist as things with meaning derived from human conventions and beliefs.

My simple story about our place as historical beings in a physical world with a history, if true, is enough to refute the subtler anti-realism of Dummett and his followers. Physical things in a physical world have determinate characteristics prior to human investigation of them – save in those extreme cases where (as in quantum mechanics) the physical processes of observation and measurement so causally interact with the objects of investigation as to alter them. On a Dummett-type view, as objects and events recede from the present toward the remote past, they would cease to have determinate properties to the extent that the human ability to decide effectively on the truth value of claims about them decrease. This mind-boggling picture is clearly at odds with my simple story. On that story, I exist now only because of the activities of ancestors remote in time who lived as I lived in a given physical environment. Count back in time sufficiently far and you will reach epochs in which it is impossible to determine any specific facts about my ancestors. But the simple story tells us that there must be lots of determinate facts about them. By the same token, it entails that there must be determinate facts about regions of the physical cosmos that are physically inaccessible to us. (For example, each of the myriad of sea creatures whose remains helped to form the North Downs must have had determinate characteristics and a determinate history, despite the fact that what the characteristics and history consisted in is quite undiscoverable now.) The idea of a remote corner of the cosmos and of the past acquiring characteristics as human powers of discovery reach them is truly baffling. What, we want to know, can a human act of discovery do to the agents in a past event to shape, construct or determine them?

Luntley states that the price of accepting anti-realism is merely that of giving up 'certain myths and metaphors' (Luntley 1988: 256). But that cannot be so. What has to be given up, for the majority of us who are not committed to some species of idealism, is our conception of a physical object and a physical cosmos. What has to be given up is our belief that we and the world around us are the products of history, for that is the conception of them as the result of the causal activity of things and persons which existed in the past, things and persons which thus had to have determinate characteristics even if we could never effectively discover what these were.

A simple way of putting the common-sense objection to any version of the view that human beings construct or determine reality through their representations or cognitive activities is this: it gives a fantastic picture of the limits of human power. There are lots of things human beings can do in relation to the North Downs. They can form concepts of the Downs, tell stories about them, plant them, graze them with sheep and cattle and build on them. But they could not create a chalk escarpment of that size. In particular, nothing they could do with symbols could bring the Downs into being. The view that human symbolising constructs reality is committed to a magical view of the relation between words/ideas and things.

The above remarks serve to bring out the extent to which talk of constructing reality from a cosmic porridge is (a) hard to understand and (b) at odds with common sense. The arguments for global anti-realism will be considered in greater detail in later chapters and will be found to be extremely weak. If those arguments are indeed weak, then the fact that anti-realism conflicts with fundamental common-sense beliefs which ground our normal ways of talking and thinking will be found to be sufficient reason for rejecting it. In the meantime, can we find any arguments which provide knock-down refutations of anti-realism? I pursue this point by examining the case against anti-realism in Searle.

Searle's arguments are not an attempt to provide a strict proof of global realism, but rather to show that any attempt to communicate presupposes its truth (Searle 1995: 184). This would be enough, however, to refute all philosophical attempts to espouse and argue for global anti-realism, since the public espousal of a philosophical thesis is a form of human communication. The first step in Searle's argument is simple. Communication takes place in a public, that is shared, language. Understanding claims made in a public language assumes taking expressions in such claims referentially. Agreement or disagreement with a claim in a public language presupposes that the speaker and hearer take the referring expressions to pick out items in a publicly accessible reality and agree which specific objects the speaker is trying to refer to. Agreement/disagreement presupposes mutual understanding and that presupposes that 'we take it for granted that the utterances are about a publicly accessible reality' (Searle 1995: 186). No publicly accessible reality equals no communication.

Let us accept this conclusion: a public language, and communication within it, presupposes a shared, publicly accessible world. Does it follow that anti-realism must be false? Searle gives the global anti-realist one reply and then refutes it. The reply is: socially constructed phenomena can be publicly accessible. 'I have a £5 note in my wallet' is true in virtue of a socially constituted fact. Outside of a human institution, with its beliefs and conventions, the £5 note would not exist as that. But though humanly constituted, the £5 note is publicly accessible. It is something which can be the object of reference for more than one speaker. It is something which is objective, in the sense that there is a right and wrong way to describe it. If you take it to be a £10 note you make a mistake. As Searle notes, such objects are constituted by human representations yet exist in a public world independent of individual people and their representations (1995: 190). For all that such realities are constructed within human institutions, they constitute publicly accessible realities concerning which there are objective facts, which some can get right and others wrong. This is what the global anti-realist must say about reality as a whole. It is constructed by representational activity (by conceptual schemes, by language, by our activities as knowers) but is independent of particular users of language and thus can be an object of common reference and enquiry.

Searle accepts that anti-realists can thus escape his first argument, only to contend that they face a more serious charge. Anti-realists, he argues, liken reality as a whole to the money in my pocket. Money exists as money because it is a non-socially constructed stuff (paper or metal alloy) which in the light of human conventions and beliefs assumes a certain status and role. But then it must generally be the case that there is something out of which socially constructed reality is constructed. Socially constructed reality cannot be the whole of reality. There must be some non-social stuff in order for there to be social stuff:

> Because the logical form of the creation of socially constructed reality consists in iterations of the structure X counts as Y in C, the iterations must bottom out in an X element that is not itself an institutional construction. Otherwise you would get an infinite regress or circularity. [Searle 1995: 191]

Searle is telling us that social construction cannot be creation *ex nihilo*. Two responses to this are in order.

In the first place, it is surely not the case that all socially constructed realities are like money or traffic signals: physical things invested with social meaning within an institution. People can inhabit myths, stories. When they do so, what they take to be real may have no reality outside their myth making. If the myth is shared, then the myth will give the appearance of providing public objects of reference which exist independently of any one individual's thought and speech. This is one way of reading Berger and Luckmann's statement that 'The world of everyday life is not only taken for granted as reality by the ordinary members of society in the subjectively meaningful conduct of their lives. It is a world that originates in their thoughts and actions, and is maintained as real by these' (1967: 33). As Kirk notes, Berger and Luckmann may only mean that the world *as people conceive it to be* originates in their thoughts and actions (Kirk 1999: 50). Thinkers like Runzo who take the world to be constituted by conceptual schemes presumably do think that the world is a myth which has been given the necessary publicity and objectivity by shared character of the conceptual activity which produces it.

A second response to Searle's argument comes through noting that the anti-realist is not bound to be a believer in creation *ex nihilo*. We have seen that anti-realists are liable to think that there is an *ur*-stuff and that human cognition is responsible not for the existence of a public world as such but for its shaping. There is an X – the cosmic porridge – that in the circumstances of linguistic representations being applied to it comes to count as a world containing mountains, seas, trees and people. Of course, we have pointed out that this is very hard, if not impossible, to understand as a story of how the real comes to be, but it does not appear to have the particular contradiction that Searle claims to find in it.

I conclude that Searle has no cogent argument for concluding that anti-realist, 'constructionist' accounts of the real make public communication impossible and thus are refuted by the very existence of that which figures so largely in many of the philosophical theories in which they are embedded: language. Nor is it the case as Searle hints (1995: 194–5) that anti-realists must fall back on the option of solipsism, which can then be easily rebutted. The solipsist states that the only reality which exists, or which I can be certain of, is me and my representations. Reality is absorbed into the individual knowing subject. Global anti-realists will actually find it hard to espouse such a position. The philosophical resources which would allow an ontology to have a robust conception of the individual subject are lacking in the various versions of global anti-realism we encounter. If cognition, representation or language constitutes what is real out of some absolutely undifferentiated metaphysical stuff, then it likewise constitutes human subjects. They come into existence as spoken of or known about. In this connection, we are indebted to Cupitt for spelling out the implication of anti-realism: we are spoken by language; we are products of the Symbolic Order (Cupitt 1990: 37).

Global anti-realism is initially dualistic. There is the cosmic porridge on one side and there is representation, cognition, language on the other. But one half of the dualism is by definition unknowable (since it has no shape and form). Formed stuff is constituted by representations. In a world where the only formed reality is representations, there is no room for a strong conception of the subject. I am suggesting that anti-realism is like some versions of logical atomism. According to atomism reality is constituted by sense data, but then so are the subjects who have sense data. Streams of sense data bundled in one way give us material objects. Bundled another way, they give us the mental lives of the subjects who perceive those material objects. But in reality these are just two different ways of cutting the same cake. We have a species of metaphysical monism. Contemporary anti-realism is also a species of metaphysical monism (once the cosmic porridge has been set aside). Reality is constituted by symbols. One way of ordering the symbols gives us a public world; another way gives what we style the consciousness of human beings. This is not solipsism, because it provides no subject to be the primary locus of reality or certainty.

If we do have a minimally dualist view of the real in which there are enduring subjects of consciousness who interact with a world which does not depend on them for their existence, then we cannot be global anti-realists.

In the light of the discussion so far we can set out a variety of realities that we might posit in our world. States of mind, such as my depression, are ontologically dependent on subjects. They are nonetheless epistemically independent of any human subject. My depression might exist even though no one recognises its existence. Some bodily sensations (for example, tickles and pains) seem to be both ontologically and epistemically dependent upon subjects. No subject means no sensation. And it hardly makes sense to suppose that I have a tickling sensation without recognising the fact. Socially constructed realities like the money in my wallet are ontologically dependent on subjects and epistemically dependent on a sufficient number of subjects recognising them as realities, even while they are ontologically and epistemically independent of any individual subjects. Features of the physical world such as the North Downs seem to be ontologically and epistemically independent of all subjects (leaving aside their possible creation by a God). If there were no subjects to have representations, it would still make sense to say that the North Downs existed.

Innocent realism thus gives rise to the view that there are truths about the world which are independent of any human subjects and their cognitive activities.

'There are truths about the world which are independent of any subject': this claim of innocent realism has been castigated as incoherent by Alvin Plantinga. Truths, he affirms, cannot exist save in minds that think them. Propositions cannot exist unless there are minds to grasp them (Plantinga 1982: 67). To suppose otherwise is to embrace an extreme Platonism which holds that abstract objects can exist independently of any subject whatsoever and this is realism 'run amok' (Plantinga 1982: 68). The only way truths could exist independently of us, argues Plantinga, is if they existed in the mind of God. Truths can only exist if they are believed by some mind or other (68). The idea that there are truths out there waiting for us to formulate and discover entails that there must be a divine mind in which they are lodged.

But realism does not entail Platonism. Plantinga fails to distinguish truth-makers from truth-bearers. To say that there are truths independent of human subjects is to say that there are facts and states of affairs which do not depend on us. Our cognitive activities are not necessary for the existence of these truth-makers. Truth-bearers are, of course, produced by cognisers. They are statements or mental representations (such as beliefs). Undiscovered truths are facts and states of affairs that we have yet to either formulate in propositional form or propositions we have yet to verify. In one sense truth is dependent on intellects and their activities and in one sense not (cf. Plantinga 1982: 68–9). Truth is a relation between cognitions and states of affairs. It exists actually when there are representations (beliefs, propositions and the like) which exist and which do present what is indeed so. It exists potentially when what is so remains to be conceptualised and/or verified by us. There is no argument for anti-realism in the point that minds are needed to formulate propositions or to have beliefs. That simple thought in no way supports the claim that the world depends on human representations. Plantinga's claim that truth only exists if it is believed by some mind is seen to be bedevilled by an equivocation between truth-bearers and truth-makers.

There is a viable conception of the world-minus-us. Realism depends on there being such a conception. Realism then allows us to ask the question of whether this world contains a God which is independent of us. We have seen that question to be beset with complications. There are many conceptions of transcendent sources of moral order which require there to be a human race in order for the divine to exist or to develop all of its important attributes. And on such views there is an ontological co-dependence between God and (human) creatures. Despite these complications, we can still make sense of the question of whether the world-minus-us contains a *theos*. Where a conception of the divine specifies an ontological co-dependence between the human and the divine, God would be still be epistemically independent of us. If God is real, God would not be constituted by our cognitive activities. Further, even in these cases we have noted the need to make a distinction between ontological dependence and ontological distinctness. Conceptions of deity which regard deity as ontologically co-dependent on the human and the world, can still intend to refer to a *theos* whose properties and powers extend beyond those possessed by human beings or by the natural world considered in isolation.

Putnam and Metaphysical Realism

The account given up to this point affirms that we can divide the world into two broad kinds of reality/fact. There are those realities which are ontologically and epistemically dependent on human beings and those realities which are independent of human beings. Socially constructed realities are paradigmatic of the first and the realities discovered by such disciplines as physics and geology are paradigmatic of the latter. In a series of writings from the early 1980s to the mid-1990s Hilary Putnam challenged this distinction (his views have evolved since, and were not uniform during this period in any event). According to Putnam, both innocent realism and those forms of relativism or idealism which state that the world is a product of human representations rest on a mistake:

> ... to ask which facts are mind independent in the sense that nothing about them reflects our conceptual choices and which facts are 'contributed by us' is to commit a 'fallacy of division' ... To try to divide the world into a part that is independent of us and a part that is contributed by us is an old temptation, but giving in to it leads to disaster every time. [Putnam 1992: 58]

Putnam means to criticise both traditional realists and relativists. Both views, in different ways, embody impossible attempts to view the world from nowhere (Putnam 1990: 28). The idea is this: the realist compares our language with reality and says that much of it captures the way things are independent of language and concepts. The relativist or constructivist compares our language with reality and says that it does not capture how things are independently of us but merely reflects our interests and conceptual schemes. Both stances embody a common error of trying to view our language 'from sideways on' and judging its correspondence or lack of correspondence to an external reality (Putnam 1994: 297). Both realism and relativism crave for an absolute view of things, that is, a judgement about our language and theorising that is outside them and is able to conclude that they do or do not match an external reality. But of course any conception we have of our language and theorising comes from within it and thus cannot note its correspondence, or lack of it, with something external to it. Innocent realism and its opposites, such as the cosmic-porridge view, are metaphysical positions that no one can in truth occupy. To deny that the world is a projection of our concepts and interests, and to affirm that it is, both presuppose that we can distinguish the world and our language about it and stand on ground from which we can compare the two.

The above represents the official (at least for a time) Putnam position of 'a plague on both your houses'. It must be conceded that, while he has many criticisms to make of innocent realism, Putnam offers many strictures on relativism and constructivism. Putnam clearly thinks that relativism, if stated clearly enough, implies that there is no constraint on theorising. But it is obviously false that if we choose a conceptual scheme the world will bend to our concepts. Some conceptual schemes will be falsified by the sheer givenness of the world (Putnam 1981: 54). If relativism equals 'anything goes', it is just plain false. He offers a trenchant critique of Nelson Goodman's claim that we make the world through conceptual construction, contending as he does so that many words have extensions determined not wholly by our decisions but by things external to us (Putnam 1992: 114; I will return to Putnam's excellent critique of Goodman later).

Despite Putnam's disavowal of the view that we make the world through our conceptual schemes, there is much in his critique of innocent realism which implies that it is we who impose form and shape on a formless world and thus it is we who construct reality. Far from standing apart from the alleged doomed enterprise of distinguishing external from humanly constructed parts of reality, Putnam appears to tell us that all reality is of the latter stripe. This puts him in the same boat as the relativist or constructivist and leaves his reader baffled.

We have already quoted Putnam as telling us that objects do not exist independently of conceptual schemes and that we cut up the world into objects when we introduce one or another scheme of description (Putnam 1981: 52). The following statement also implies that our language shapes the world: '... elements of what we call "language" or "mind" *penetrate so deeply into what we call "reality" that the very project of representing ourselves as being "mappers" of something "language-independent" is fatally compromised from the very start'* (Putnam 1990: 28). The suspicion that Putnam does come down on the side of those who say that reality is a construction from our representations is heightened by his hint that there can be incompatible truths. Two statements can be incompatible (judged by the standards of 'classical logic and classical semantics') but nonetheless be true of the same situation (1989: 115–16). Putnam adds a qualification 'because the words are used differently' which would take away the force of 'incompatible' if he intends 'have different meanings'. But then that would make his initial remark pointless. In *Reason, Truth and History* he asks us to accept that there can be incompatible but equally coherent and empirically adequate conceptual schemes, adding 'If truth is not (unique) correspondence then the possibility of a certain pluralism is opened up' (1981: 73). The notion of plural sets of truths which are incompatible with each other makes sense if what these truths are true of is realities which are different – because they are shaped by different systems of representations. This thread in Putnam also fits in with an inviting reading of this claim that truth is idealised rational acceptability (1981: 55). If Putnam means by 'idealised rational acceptability' idealised rational acceptability to some community of human language users, then truth could alter from one language or conceptual scheme or type of cognising subject to another. We would have plural truths because there are plural sets of truth-makers. There would then be plural realities because of the way in which different sets of fundamental concepts shape realities.

This much is clear in Putnam interpretation: he attacks 'metaphysical realism' in the name of 'internal realism'. What he styles 'metaphysical realism' is defined by a number of alleged erroneous commitments, most notably: that there is a fixed mind-independent reality; that truth consists of correspondence to this reality; that truth as correspondence is unique (if a proposition corresponds, then no proposition incompatible with it corresponds); that accordingly there is one true, complete theory of the world (see Putnam 1994: 352; 1981: 49; 1989: 107). Putnam links these errors in realism with the notions that: there is a God's-eye view of the world, to which fact and truth correspond; there is a fixed totality of objects in the world and the one true, complete description of reality captures the intrinsic (that is, mind-independent) properties of these objects (1981: 49; 1994: 305).

Putnam loads a great deal on to 'metaphysical realism'. We will return to the question of how far all that he includes in metaphysical realism hangs together, as opposed to being arbitrarily linked by the critic in order to make his target easier to hit. Let us note the extent to which innocent realism faces Putnam's strictures. Innocent realism holds that there is one real world which exists largely independent of us. What exists in it and what properties those things have is independent of what anyone thinks, unless we are talking about those portions of the world which are ontologically or epistemically dependent on human judgements. It is natural to associate such a stance with a correspondence theory of truth (though, as noted above, a correspondence theory does not entail innocent realism). People utter statements and hold beliefs about how this world, existing largely independent of us, is. Those statements and beliefs are true to the extent that the way they represent how things are is as how things indeed are (see White 1970 for an elaboration of this account). How things indeed are is, unless we have in mind those parts of reality which belong to the human world, quite independent of any concepts we might have or languages we might devise. There can be no incompatible truths. It is interesting to explore Putnam's motives for styling innocent realism as 'metaphysical'. It can only be because he sees realism as impossible unless it arises from a metaphysical stance. This would be a stance of pretended transcendence, one in which we thought we had, quite impossibly, stepped outside of our language and inspected it and its relation to the world ('sideways on'). This would then explain why Putnam associates realism with an impossible God's-eye view. God would be able to view the relation between human language/concepts seen *in toto* and the world. We cannot, so we cannot affirm metaphysical realism.

This characterisation of realism is picturesque but wholly inaccurate. The main plank of innocent realism – that the world consists of things and properties which exist quite independently of us and our representations – is not a claim arrived at from an impossible transcendent point of view. It arises internally, from the very content of our statements about the world. Innocent realism follows from the content of our empirical claims. Its rivals are inconsistent with that content (see Nagel 1997: 87). Take an example. I affirm that chalk is a sedimentary rock while granite is an igneous rock. My statement, if true, is about a subject matter, a segment of reality, which has nothing to do with human representations. My statement has nothing to say about human representations. If true, it states a fact about the world-minus-human beings. It says nothing about how the world appears to us or how it looks from some standpoint or perspective. If true it is an absolute, non-perspectival truth. We can thereby contrast with it statements such as 'The green light means "proceed"', which are statements about how things mean to us. Innocent realism merely reflects on the content of our empirical claims, notes that most of them do not speak about how the world looks from a human perspective and concludes that the world, its things and properties, is for the most part independent of us and our representations.

Putnam tells us that we cannot ask which facts are mind-independent and which are contributed by us. We cannot divide the world into a part that is independent of us and a part that is. We cannot divide reality into those parts which are the genuine furniture of the world and those parts which are mere projections of us. But we can – and without trying to occupy a God's-eye point of view. What are the reasons for thinking that the facts that chalk is sedimentary and granite igneous are human-independent facts? They are their content and the reasons we have for thinking that chalk is sedimentary and granite igneous. Those reasons do not deal in any matters to do with human concepts or representations, in contrast to the considerations which tell us that a green light means 'proceed'. They deal in facts about the formation of rocks. Contrary to Putnam, we have innumerable indications of what belongs to the furniture of the world, independent of our human projections. They are all those things which tell in favour of our common-sense and natural scientific beliefs. It is Putnam's internal realism which endeavours to occupy a transcendent, metaphysical position. He wants, as Nagel points out, to get outside of our beliefs about the non-human world and think of them as the expression of a point of view, thereby recasting their content (into descriptions of the world-as-seen-though-our-concepts). But we simply cannot do that and take their content seriously at the same time (Nagel 1997: 89).

It is a strange fact that Putnam provides a powerful argument for the stance just enunciated in close proximity to his standard denials that it makes sense to divide the world into a human-dependent and human-independent part. He is discussing Nelson Goodman's claim (see Goodman 1980) that we make the world through our theories (Putnam 1992: 111–15). Did we make the Big Dipper through naming it? We certainly did not put the stars belonging to the Dipper into the sky. But we did give this arrangement a name. And it is a fact about us, and our perspectives, that we see this group of stars as having a significant shape, reminiscent of a big dipper. That there is a Big Dipper is a fact redolent of human perspective, but that there are stars is not. That there is a Big Dipper records how things look to us and there is no more significance to the existence of the Big Dipper than that there are some stars which, when seen from Earth, look to some people like a big dipper. The term 'Big Dipper' is wholly conventional in meaning, functioning like a proper name. Its extension is fixed by giving a list. That there are stars – clouds of glowing gas driven by thermonuclear reactions – is not redolent of human perspective. This fact does not record a human perspective, but rather something that is quite independent of human interests. What counts as a star is determined by us and by nature. We decide on the meaning of 'star'. We decide to use this word to refer to clouds of glowing gas in the heavens with the key properties we discover unite them. But nature then determines the extension. We cannot settle the extension by human decision or convention. It is a matter of non-human fact that the Sun is a star. As Putnam so clearly puts it, there are conventional elements in the meaning of the word 'star', but that it applies to this rather than that is a matter independent of us (Putnam 1992: 114). Stars are thus part of the furniture of the world and not a projection of our interests or concepts.

We can make the distinctions between types of reality Putnam's internal realism says we cannot make by dint of reflecting on the counterfactuals kinds of fact license. The fact that the green light means 'proceed' would not have obtained if there had been no people to establish the relevant patterns of intentionality which lie behind it. The fact that these stars form the Big Dipper would not have obtained if there had been no people to see this pattern in them and liken it to the shape of a roller coaster – though of course the stars would still have been there. The facts that stars are clouds of gas and that granite is an igneous rock would, however, have obtained if there were no people to mark them. This is not to say that decisions of this kind are easily made in every case. In notable instances, such as judgements of value, we may be eternally puzzled as to how to decide whether a fact about beauty, for example, is a fact which is about, or reflects, the human world, or whether it would have obtained if there were no human beings to discern it. What makes such questions possible, on my view, is that we can make an intelligible distinction in many instances between what is true of the world independent of human representations and what is true of the world only given human representations. We do not, for example, have to occupy an impossible, transcendent standpoint to make Searle's distinction between socially constructed and non-socially constructed realities and fill it out with many instantiations. (These remarks are an implicit critique of Heal's distinction between 'mirroring' and 'quietist' realism: Heal 1989: 23–4).

Putnam's critique of Goodman implies the innocent realist picture. There is a world of human-independent objects and facts. Our words apply (or do not apply) to these objects. Our statements are true (or not true) of these facts. How can he then draw back from the obvious into the obscurities of 'internal realism'?

One argument in favour of internal realism is based on the observation that there is no way in which human beings can discern facts without relying on human values and interests. Putnam is particularly keen to urge this point when attacking those philosophers who claim that facts are one thing ('out there') but values another ('our projections'). His counter is that in order to discern what the facts are in even the most hard-nosed natural science we have to rely on values: 'without the cognitive values of coherence, simplicity, and instrumental efficacy we have no facts' (Putnam 1990: 139). These values are said to be part of our conception of human flourishing. The claim appears to be: since we have to rely on the values implicit in our conception of human flourishing to live the life of reason which enables us to discern facts, then the idea that our true propositions correspond to a world of independent facts is out. Discovery and discernment even in physics is intentional activity guided by our conception of the good and thus what is discovered is not metaphysically external to us, rather it reflects those values (1990: 139). The notions of fact and rationality are interrelated and what we take to be rational reflections are values (Putnam 1981: 201).

So here is one motive for Putnam's rejection of innocent realism. The notion of correspondence between language and a largely mind-independent world in standard realism is implicitly that of something imposed by reality itself, something 'out there' rather than being a matter shaped by human values. Putnam urges us to abandon the idea that the world itself singles out a correspondence between our words and the furniture of the world (1990: 173). He repeatedly attacks all ideas to the effect that the relation between singular terms and their referents and general terms and their extensions can be fixed through routes which do not go through human judgement. Reference and extension can never be purely physical matters. Even if we go along with fashionable causal theories of the relations between words and things we will still find ourselves having to make judgements about which things are the causal grounds of which patterns of usage (see, for example, 1994: 290–91).

We can surely accept the initial burden of both these points: judgements as to what are the facts are guided by our epistemic and rational values, and the relation between words and things is never a wholly external one. The latter point means conceding that there is a link between how the extension of 'Big Dipper' is fixed and how the extension of 'star' is fixed. The former's extension is fixed by a list we stipulate. The latter's extension is not. We give 'star' a meaning and discover what range of things it applies to. But even then the world does not literally tell us what the extension of 'star' is. We have to make judgements as to what does and does not satisfy the criteria for being a star. We have to do this for the component parts of its definition ('gas', 'thermonuclear' and so on). At no point can we escape such judgement by finding that the world has done the job for us. If we did think that the world could determine reference in this way, then we would indulge ourselves in the illusion that the language we spoke (perhaps in privileged disciplines such as physics) was not our, human language but the Language of Nature itself (Putnam 1994: 302 and compare Luntley 1995 on the ideas of 'the world's own story' and 'the cosmic register'). Now we may see how Putnam might think that innocent realism is an impossibility. It aims to distinguish those truths we know which describe the facets of the world independent of human representations, putting to one side facets of the world which are parts of or reflections of the human world. But to do that it would have to distinguish those parts of our discourse which capture the Language of Nature (where truth, meaning and reference had been fixed by the world itself) from those other parts infected by human values and decisions. This is just the enterprise engaged in by the Logical Positivists. The natural sciences were given the accolade of speaking the language of the world and dealing in genuine items of furniture. Ethics, aesthetics, theology and the like were condemned to speak no truths but only to give expression to human emotions.

Such ideas made sense in Positivism because the movement inherited from Wittgenstein's *Tractatus* the belief that meaning flowed up through language via a set of terms which had it imposed on them by the world. Protocol or basic statements were in one-to-one correspondence with reports of experience. Terms within such basic statements were given meaning by virtue of their standing for sensory items. This kind of foundationalism provided an anchor for both certainty and for meaning. The positivist critique of non-scientific discourse as cognitively meaningless depended on mixing empiricist theory of knowledge with the *Tracatus* conception of meaning as depending on simple propositions which were made from names for simple objects. Sensory qualia became the simple objects Wittgenstein had been looking for (no matter that exclusionary relationships between qualia meant they could not quite fit Wittgenstein's bill).

The brief excursus into Positivism shows us that if we have a conception of a favoured mode of discourse the meaning and truth of whose statements is guaranteed by the world, then we can make a distinction between what facts and objects belong to the world-minus-human-beings and what facts and objects belong to, or depend on, human representations. Putnam's critique of realism clearly envisages that the entailment goes the other way: only if we have this conception of the Language of Nature can we make the kind of distinctions innocent realism promises us we ought to be able to make. The notion of the Language of Nature explains why Putnam associates realism with the thesis that there is one true, complete description of the world. The world of social reality is not the same for all. Patterns of human institutional activity vary from time to time and place to place. Facts that are clearly dependent on human perspective are thereby variable and relative. Hence, the variability in the way cultures divide up and name the visible stars or features of landscape. But if there is a theory of the world expressed in the Language of Nature and capturing 'the world's own story', it will not be subject to changing patterns of human intentionality. The aspiration to discover this theory and speak this language will be one to escape from the limiting effects of human culture and interests altogether. If we could speak the Language of Nature, then we could escape the point made earlier in this chapter that we should not expect there to be a finite set of truths to be discovered about the world because there may be no end to the aspects of it that different human languages, conceptual schemes and perspectives can bring out. If we succeed in speaking the Language of Nature we can escape from those different languages, schemes and perspectives.

To achieve the one true, complete description of the world in the world's own language would indeed be to capture the God's-eye view of things that Putnam has told us goes along with metaphysical realism. The question is whether our innocent realism entails all the manifold claims Putnam packs into metaphysical realism. Note that if innocent realism does entail all this baggage then it entails no less than a commitment to the Enlightenment Project as it is now styled: the attainment of a standpoint upon the world, with associated modes of discourse and theories, which is free of all cultural taint and possessed of absolutely certainty. If the Project were successful we would have aligned our modes of enquiry and speech with the Language of Nature, the cosmic register. Yet all that innocent realism starts from is the claim that for the most part the world exists, with determinate things and properties, independent of us and our representations. That minimal claim is compatible with rampant scepticism and the belief that we know nothing about that part of the world existing independent of us. Innocent realists will typically go on to assert that we know many things about the world-minus-us and they will contrast those things with truths about humanly constructed reality. Hence, we get our contrast between claims about coinage and traffic lights, on the one hand, and about matters geological and astronomical on the other. In between this contrast the innocent realist can place statements about the non-human world which represent a particular human 'take' on it: for example, the discernment and naming of star patterns or of mountain tops. Innocent realists do not have to pretend to a stance whereby all truths can be assigned to one class or another. There need be no sharp boundary between the world-minus-us and the world we construct socially. It need only be that, judged by reference to the content and grounds of different claims, we can make many sound statements about what the world would have been like if there had been no human judges of it.

Wittgenstein's early philosophy in the *Tractatus* is a major source in the twentieth century of the belief in a language of the world. In the semantics of the *Tractatus*, meaning flows up from simple objects to simple names and thence to elementary propositions. It is equally the Wittgenstein of the *Philosophical Investigations* (up to §242) who is responsible for the devastating critique of this belief that words could derive their meaning from the world. The essential point in that critique is well summarised by Jane Heal as follows (Heal 1989: 145–8). Wittgenstein begins from the diagnosis of the errors in thinking that understanding might consist in the possession of, for example, a mental image or sample corresponding to a word or concept. Such possession, we might be tempted to think, underlies our ability to use a word or our possession of a concept. But it cannot: for any image or sample can be variously applied and understood. Nothing of this kind can be inherently meaningful or representational, because it only has meaning or represents something *in so far as it is used one way or another by human beings*. It cannot determine how it will be taken or used by human beings. It has meaning only as taken by them, used by them, in a certain way. Locally in the *Investigations* this point serves to refute those who argue that association with mental imagery is what gives life and meaning to signs. This view is false, for it is only use that gives life to imagery. Hence, we make a redundant move when we seek to explain the life that signs have through their use by us by grounding their life and use in mental imagery. We miss the point that our use of the signs is of itself sufficient to give them life and meaning.

Wittgenstein also makes it plain that the point about use, life and meaning does not alter if we substitute physical, public objects (such as samples of colour or drawn diagrams) for mental images and mental samples (see Wittgenstein 1963: §§85 and 86). Physical samples and objects can be misunderstood. Nothing is inherently representational. Only things as used by human beings are representational, can have the meaning of signs. A radical point follows from this. A human sign cannot have a meaning which consists simply in its correspondence to something in the world. A thing in the world cannot be the meaning of a word. Granted that nothing in the world is inherently representational and that representationality comes with the use and application of meaning-bearers by human beings, then mere confrontation with things in the world cannot give signs their meaning. Meaning cannot consist in a simple tie-up between language and the world.

The above now gives us a clearer picture as to why there can be no language of the world. It also entails Heal's point that merely being confronted with objects in the world cannot force possession of a concept upon us (Heal 1989: 146–7). Any physical item or set of items can always be taken in various ways. That means they can be brought under different sets of concepts. The world cannot force a description of itself upon us. It will always lie open to different sets of human concepts. Here we are back in the familiar territory of Putnam's insistence on the possibility of conceptual diversity. There is no need to dissent from these points. Nor is there need to tie innocent realism to one facet of the view Heal rejects as 'mirroring realism': 'the claim that the world, if properly attended to, does determine one and only one (set of) thought(s)' (Heal 1989: 147). Thus we are accepting that the world can be described in a variety of ways because the concepts we use in those descriptions are not determined by the world. The world is not a sign or a set of signs. The concepts we use do not mirror the signs in the world – the Language of Nature. The concepts we use reflect human interests in exploring the world one way rather than another.

But none of this means that we cannot make distinctions between the kinds of facts and properties our words pick out. We can do so, as noted above, by reference to the content of our concepts and the nature of the evidence that shapes the claims we make about the world. Statements about traffic lights, about the Big Dipper and about sedimentary and igneous rocks all reflect human interests, but they do so in different ways. We can distinguish between talking about institutional facts within the human world, talking about how the appearance of the world strikes us and talking about the characteristics of rocks which explain their behaviour. It does not follow from the Wittgenstein-derived point that there is no Language of the World that our language does not pick up features of the world or that our language creates the features we talk about.

Realists can cheerfully admit that there is no way in which the world imposes reference or extension upon our words. Even the simplest ostensive definition can be misunderstood or fail to give words a meaning. With the point about the need to exercise informed judgement about what is true and false of the world, this entails that there is no guarantee of an absolute kind that our theories about the world-minus-us are true of it, capture the facts. *In that respect* even our best theories in the hardest of hard sciences remain an expression of us. The theories are parts of the human world, the embodiment of a human language and the expression of human interests. Yet, *to the extent that we think they are true*, then they record facts about the world independent of us. That reflects their content. It is always possible for someone to doubt their import, their referential success or their truth. There is no proof of them that will silence the absolute sceptic. But, if we espouse them, we espouse them as true accounts of the world-minus-us. Our regarding them as human, and therefore uncertain and limited accounts of what is so, means that we do not equate them with a God's-eye view of reality or with a complete and true description of the world. Many things we take to be true would in the light of God's eye be at best partial and at worst false, though of course we cannot know which things. Other kinds of investigators would uncover other facts about the world. But all truths are compatible and some truths are truths about the world independent of the things created by human representations or human intentionality and independent of personal or local slants on the world.

For the above reasons, we can with justice deny that innocent realism equates to an attempt to escape the human character of language and of claims to truth. By the same token it does not entail acceptance of the aspirations of the Enlightenment Project.

Innocent realism cannot be threatened by Putnam's assertion that human values are required to judge what is a fact. Realists can admit that coming to the conclusion that chalk escarpments are formed of the remains of millions of sea creatures is an exercise of human judgement which relies on values of reason and good inference. Realists can accept that scientific knowledge is maintained only in so far as values of reason are kept alive. Scientific knowledge is thus a human enterprise. That we need human values to discover the facts does not at all entail that those facts are constituted by the values. Claims about chalk hills and their formation say nothing about human doings. None of the evidence for the current geological understanding of the formation of chalk landscapes cites facts about us and our values. The realist here invokes a distinction between epistemology and ontology. This is a distinction which can be made internally – by reference to the content of the claim made and the evidence which supports it. The distinction stands, even though for us to come to accept the claim, via appraising the evidence in its favour, involves us exercising choices informed by values. It may be objected that this is question-begging: Putnam will allow no sharp distinction between the question of what makes statements true and the question of how we can judge that truth is present, since he links truth to idealised rational acceptability. To this the realist must reply that the distinction between what guides our judgement that 'chalk is formed of sediments of sea creatures' is true and what that judgement imports is given by reflection on the content of the propositional claim itself and of the evidence for it. The onus of proof is on those who would overturn this obvious fact.

Putnam's yoking of realism to the notion of there being one true and complete description enables him to launch another missile at his target.

We are aware of conceptual relativity. In particular, according to Putnam, we know that there are different ways of dividing the world up into objects and that only convention can be appealed to in choosing between the different ways. Putnam gives artificial and real examples to make this point. A typical artificial example is the following. Imagine a world which consists of just three atoms. How many objects really exist in this world? You can say three but you can also give higher numbers: the three originals and the various aggregates of two or more atoms which the mind can form into wholes. The question of how many objects there are is entirely relative to how we describe the facts and is not given by facts in isolation from ways of describing them (Putnam 1992: 120; and compare 1989: 111–13; 1994: 304–5). The real examples come from alternative modes of describing reality current in scientific theorising. Putnam asks us to consider a physicist representing a given physical system once in the language of particles and once in the language of fields (1992: 121). Or consider two styles of geometric representation: according to one, points are identified with sets of convergent spheres; in another, points can be taken as primitive and we can identify spheres via sets of points. A further example: space-time points can be taken as concrete individuals or as abstract entities, as mere limits (1989: 112 and 114). The upshot is the conclusion that 'what objects does the world consist of?' only makes sense within a theory or description (1981: 49). So the world cannot consist of a fixed totality of mind-independent objects.

Does the fact of conceptual relativity entail the demise of innocent realism? There are weaker and stronger facets to Putnam's arguments. The force of the argument from his artificial examples is decidedly weak. The sum and substance of the point arising from atoms, objects and counting is this: the word 'object' supplies no counting principle. So it is indeed arbitrary how I answer the question 'How many objects are there in the universe?' In the same way, 'event' supplies no counting principle. How many events took place when I brushed my teeth this morning? The answer is wholly relative to the degree of detail I use to describe what happens. That does not mean that the nature of what took place changes as I move from coarser to finer descriptions of what happened. 'Object' and 'event' are in truth formal notions. We assign a concrete sense to them according to need, purpose and context. Many other concepts we use are not formal. If it is arbitrary how many objects there are on my desk, it is not arbitrary how many table lamps or paper clips are on it. In Putnam's three-atom universe it is arbitrary how many objects there are but not arbitrary how many atoms. His question of how many objects exist in that simple world can then be given a ready answer: 'Three atoms, but of course you can count them under the heading "object" in a whole host of ways' (compare Moore 1997: 91). If our stress is on objects (or events), it is indeed true, but trivial, to say that there is no fixed totality of mind-dependent objects in the world. But there is a fixed totality of mind-independent paper clips.

Putnam's argument gets greater weight from some of his examples of real conceptual choice. Innocent realists had better accept that there are elements of convention in geometrical notation and description. Thus there may be an element of choice in what precise geometry we use to describe the world. This is far from saying, however, that the world is plastic to our touch. Likewise we can admit elements of convention and idealisation in physical theory. That would seem to be the best way of coping with Putnam's example of the different ways of taking space-time points. Let us agree that the world does not tell us whether to treat space-time points as physical or as abstract entities. The concept of a space-time point, we can concede, is part of the theoretical apparatus of physics which serves a heuristic purpose. Concepts like 'virus' or 'star' or 'tectonic plate' are not like this. Viruses, stars and tectonic plates have natures and characteristics which we must discover rather than determine by what is convenient for us. I cannot get the nature of space-time points wrong in the way I can get the nature of stars wrong.

We cannot deal with the choice between describing sub-atomic goings-on in the language of particles and the language of fields in the same way. Here we might be more tempted to speak of the facts as being ambiguous. Or we might concede that our ignorance of this sphere of reality is such that we can use alternative models for it without being able to reconcile them or find data which come down decisively in favour of one of the models. We can note in relation to this fact that innocent realism thrives on the notion that there is much about the world that we do not know. It is no defeat for it, rather it is a confirmation, to acknowledge that we cannot get the world to yield unequivocal answers to all our questions.

It may be said that we have not taken Putnam's fundamental concern about conceptual relativity seriously enough thus far. William Alston sees Putnam's most forceful point behind these remarks from *Representation and Reality*:

> We can and should insist that some facts are there to be discovered and not legislated by us. But this is something to be said when one has adopted a way of speaking, a language, a 'conceptual scheme'. To talk of 'facts' without specifying the language to be used is to talk of nothing. [Putnam 1989: 114]

Putnam would admit that the question 'Are there stars?' gets a non-arbitrary answer. (Perhaps he would concede that in this respect it is different from the question 'Are space-time points to be treated as physical entities or as mere limits, as abstract?') But the question and answer presupposes that we have a mode of description and the mode of description embodies conceptual choices and thus is not a simple mirror of a world independent of our language. Alston enables us to give substance to the idea of conceptual choices employed in such reflections. He reminds us of the deep disagreements between the conceptual constructions of philosophers when it comes to describing the world. Our language of stars and viruses is Aristotelian. It divides the world into enduring substances and then specifies their qualities and interactions with other substances. If we employed a Whiteheadian mode of description we would portray the world as fundamentally a collection of events. What we now call things, objects, we would then describe as societies of 'momentary actual occasions, each of which perishes in the moment of self-creation' (Alston 1996: 172). The very vocabulary we use embodies conceptual choices and it is only in the light of them that the world has stars and viruses. The world only yields objects and facts to us consequent upon such conceptual choices. This is why Putnam can affirm that elements of what we call 'language' or 'mind' penetrate so deeply into what we call 'reality' that the very project of representing ourselves as being 'mappers' of something 'language-independent' is fatally compromised from the very start (Putnam 1990: 28).

Let us accept that this is Putnam's fundamental point: in the light of clashes between different metaphysical systems (conceptual schemes) in philosophy, we see that description and discovery of what is independent of us presupposes modes of description which in turn inevitably implicate us in substantive decisions about the character of reality. How does this relate to innocent realism? Innocent realism states that reality for the most part exists independent of human representations. But Putnam, we are supposing, is telling us that no reality can be accessed by us save through our representations and that our representations come loaded with some substantial conceptual scheme or other. What fundamentally exists for us relates to the basics of our ontology. Our basic ontology comes with our language. It is only after we have committed ourselves to the ontology via the use of the language that it makes sense to consider what particular things exist.

Innocent realists should meet this revised Putnam challenge by pressing the question as to whether ontological disagreements of the kind illustrated by the choice between Aristotelian and Whiteheadian conceptual schemes are real or not. A real, substantial disagreement should affect our notion as to what in particular exists. Substantial disagreements of this kind pervade the history of science. It is surely right to say that we know much more about what things and stuffs make up the world now than we did 300 years ago. We know that the humours of Renaissance medicine do not exist but the viruses of modern medicine do. We know that the phlogiston of eighteenth-century chemistry does not exist but that oxygen does, and so on. If there is an argument against realism in the Alston reading of Putnam, then it depends on concluding that the facts and methods which led to the discovery of viruses do not confirm the Aristotelian conceptual scheme in terms of which we describe that discovery. If the facts and methods behind the exponential increase in reliable beliefs about what exists found in natural science did confirm our basic ontology, then they would disconfirm rival ontologies (Whiteheadian or Berkeleyan). The world would then be (indirectly) telling us that it contained enduring things and substances. If these scientific facts do not confirm/disconfirm any philosophical conceptual scheme or ontology, then it must be the case that they are neutral between them because they can be described in the vocabulary and terms of *all* of the relevant schemes selected. That means the *content* of the facts and methods can be expressed in the different *forms* provided by different conceptual schemes. That further means that there is no *substantive* difference between the schemes, at least if 'substantive' pertains to empirical content and what will come to light in empirical investigation. But if there is no difference in substance between such schemes, then the innocent realist can rest content in the claim that the world is for the most part independent of our representations of it. Though we have choices between how to represent it, that does not entail that its substance varies with our modes of representation. That means we are still happy in our contrast between the human, social world and the greater part of the world that is non-human, non-social. The substance of institutional facts and realities does change with changes in human representations and intentionality (think what happens when a nation adopts a new coinage).

There is another way in which innocent realists can turn the force of Alston-Putnam. Suppose the argument just given is set aside. We then accept that there can be substantive differences between rival conceptual schemes which are empirically indiscernible. The differences are not metaphysical-equals-verbal, but metaphysical-equals-deep. Innocent realism can then say: there are deep facts about ontology which we just plump for in adopting a language. Empirical investigation cannot justify us in postulating those deep ontological facts. But these admissions are quite compatible with realism, if we go on to state that this reveals the agnosticism about the true character of reality in all its fundamentals which is the natural bedfellow of realism. It is a fact about the world whether it has enduring subjects in space or time or consists in societies of momentary concrescent occasions, but this factual question is not one that we can resolve. Realism is still intact at the cost of some metaphysical scepticism.

The above brief survey of Putnam's strictures on 'metaphysical realism' has found points of value in his critique. His account provides a powerful warning against any conception of there being a language of the world which our talk somehow mirrors. The world does not consist of a set of signs and our words do not have meaning because they correspond to the world's signs. He also draws attention to the possibility that there *may* be deep, substantive conceptual-cum-metaphysical choices involved in ordinary vocabulary. None of this, however, amounts to a refutation of innocent realism.

The one aspect of Putnam's critique that we have not explored in depth is his attempt to outline an epistemic conception of truth. This aspect of Putnam will be treated in Chapter 4 when different members of the family of epistemic accounts of truth will be discussed.

Chapter 3

Scheming

Innocent realism, we noted in the last chapter, both seems like the merest common sense and to be presupposed in our ordinary talk, judgement and action. In this chapter, we shall look at the challenge to innocent realism from conceptual relativism. The key idea behind the various forms of conceptual relativism is that innocent realism fails to take account of the fact that human beings are concept users. Their ability to talk about the world depends on their being able to use and apply concepts. In so doing, human beings make, construct and fashion the world. The judgements human beings make are not true or false of a world independent of them, because in some way or other states of affairs are brought into being by human practices of using concepts. This world constructing is usually conceived after the fashion noted in Chapter 1. The real world is regarded as formless. It acquires form and shape through conceptualising activity. It is in this way that no definite states of affairs exist independent of human beings. Since it is human activity which thus fashions states of affairs into existence, then truth for the relativist has to be something to which there is a significant human contribution. This is not simply a matter of human beings making judgements, giving statements their sense and by these means establishing their correspondence or lack of it to what is so. Rather *truth-makers* as well as *truth-bearers* are shaped by human activity. Truth becomes relative to a set of concepts, for without a set of concepts there are no definite states of affairs to which judgements and statements might correspond.

A particularly clear presentation of conceptual relativism is to be found in Runzo's *Reason, Relativism and God* (supported and taken further by the arguments in *World Views and Perceiving God*). I will show the falsity of conceptual relativism by refuting the main arguments and contentions of Runzo. Since his case is particularly directed toward proving that truths about God (and indeed the very existence of God) are relative to human conceptual schemes, there is special reason to examine his contentions here.

Runzo's Schemas

Runzo's rejection of innocent realism and embrace of relativism shows in the three culminating principles of his argument: the diversity principle, the dependency principle and the pluralist ontology principle. The diversity principle states:

> There exist distinct and mutually incompatible world-view conceptual schemas, and each schema delimits a set of possible world orders which is incompatible with the set of possible world orders delimited by any other, mutually incompatible schema.

The dependency principle states:

> The truth of any statement, P, depends in part on the conceptual schema from within which P is formulated and/or assessed.

The pluralist ontology principle states:

> Each, and only each, distinct world-view conceptual schema, which adequately delimits a set of possible world orders, delimits an actual world, and no two schemas delimit identical actual worlds. [Runzo 1986: 58–60]

The sense and justification of these claims require exploring.

The diversity principle starts from a commonplace: human beings use different sets of concepts to interpret and understand their world. This commonplace is a well-established fact in the study of history and human society. Human modes of thinking vary and change. Innocent realists need not be embarrassed by this fact taken by itself. They are under no obligation to believe that the fact that there is one real world existing independently of human representations of it entails that there is no room for human beings to develop varying and changing sets of concepts to describe it. Innocent realists can accept that the world is a complex place. Different modes of description can be used in the attempt to capture its multiform character. And, in any event, it is of the essence of innocent realism to insist that the world is one thing, human representations of it another. Our representations do not determine or shape the world; no more does the world determine human thinking about it. The one, real world allows human beings who come into contact with it to develop all manner of ways of thinking about it – many of them of course false and inaccurate. Runzo makes two moves that transform the commonplace of human conceptual diversity into a potent basis for relativism. The first is the reifying of sets of concepts and the second is the transformation of concept users into world makers.

The second of the two moves Runzo makes is the more obvious one. It is apparent in the formulation of the dependency and pluralist ontology principles. Innocent realists are quite happy with the thought that concepts make a contribution to truths and to ontological claims, if all that is meant is as follows: the meaning of statements (the content of truth-bearers) depends on our concepts and the meaning of ontological claims likewise depends on the concepts we use. But the nature of our concepts does not affect truth-makers or what actually exists – unless our statements are about our concepts or assert the existence of things in the conceptual realm.

So, Runzo's second move is the most dramatic. But before exploring its character in detail let us pause over the first move. Recall Runzo's diversity principle: there exist distinct and mutually incompatible world-view conceptual schemas, and each schema delimits a set of possible world orders which is incompatible with the set of possible world orders delimited by any other, mutually incompatible schema. This takes the commonplace that different people use different concepts to describe the world and transforms it into the bold claim that people's concepts constitute *schemes*, that is, systems. These schemes/systems constitute world views. Each world view outlines a possible world-order. This is not a commonplace. It implicitly parcels out human thinking into so many metaphysical systems. Philosophers are used to thinking systematically. They produce world views tightly knit around a few key concepts (consider the systems of Spinoza, Leibniz or Whitehead). But the vast majority of ordinary thinking is not at first glance part of a world-view schema. The sets of concepts we use are much too rough and ready, much too fluid, for such characterisation to be apt.

The above point is not a trivial one. Runzo is playing an old philosophical game. We invent a piece of terminology, that of 'conceptual schemes' (or 'world-view schemas'). We assume now that there must be things corresponding to the terminology. So there are world-view schemas out there. They must be implicit in people's thinking if they are not visible on the surface. Having discovered a class of entities with the aid of our new terminology, we feel free to devise hypotheses and theories about these entities. So we can pursue such questions as: do world-view schemas shape what is true and what exists? The very fact of writing in Runzo's way about the concepts people use to describe the world plays down the fact that what people think of as actual and possible in part depends on (and is thus continually altered by) what reality throws at them. Thinking of concepts as belonging to systems implies the opposite: that concepts are used by people solely because they belong to humanly devised systems.

We might naïvely think that if there are such things as conceptual, world-view schemas, then there should be some criteria for their identity. It should matter what the counting principle for such entities is (how do I know how many world-view schemas are before me?) It should matter what the principle for reidentifying such schemas is (how do I know when a schema is the same as the one someone held ten years ago or different?) Runzo's response to these questions is to deny their legitimacy. There are lots of entities which we usefully talk about but for which we have no precise criteria of identity. Runzo cites the state of baldness (1986: 55–6). He states that where there are 'slight differences' between schemas we simply have to make a decision to treat the instances as if they were one schema or two (1986: 56). But this will not do. For where something hangs on drawing a borderline, then we need a reflective basis for drawing it that stands up to examination. And something does hang on the borders Runzo's relativism needs to draw. What depends on where the boundaries between world-view schemas lie are no less than questions as to what is real and what is true.

Runzo indicates that the counting principles for schemas do not follow those for natural languages. Two people can share the same natural language yet inhabit different world-view schemas. Runzo's example of this phenomenon is the English-speaking astrophysicist and the English-speaking spiritual healer-cum-astrologer (1986: 53). Let us consider how our points about the criteria for identifying schemas apply to this example. There are certainly going to be ramifying differences in the outlooks of two such people. At first blush, we want to say that they have multiple disagreements about what is true and real. But note that the impact of applying Runzo's dependency and pluralistic ontology principles makes that impression false. The dependency principle relativises truth claims. Let us suppose that the healer-cum-astrologer believes that there are astral influences and the astrophysicist denies this. They do not contradict one another on the Runzo analysis. According to that, statements of the form 'it is true that P' are to be understood as elliptical for 'it is true within $S's$ conceptual schema, C_1, that P' (1986: 35). This allows it to be both true and false that there are astral influences, by dint of making the statement 'it is true that there are astral influences' multiply ambiguous. What the statement asserts changes for each C_n that we care to specify. Now something very important has happened. If the healer-cum-astrologist and astrophysicist judge aright they will not see each the other as disagreeing in what they believe. In fact, they can agree with one another on the matter of whether there are astral influences. Once the statement and its denial are relativised in the manner of Runzo, both parties can agree that it is true taken one way, false taken the other. The pluralist ontology principle likewise enables each to agree that in the reality created by the one world-view schema there are astral influences, but in the reality created by the other world-view schema there are not.

These are very substantive consequences to draw from world-view schema relativism. They do not arise at all if the two parties in Runzo's analogy view themselves as making different, incompatible assertions in the one language and set of concepts about the one, real world. The astrophysicist holds views which entail the following: that judging what will happen in the future and what will causally effect it by the positions of the stars and planets as viewed from Earth is based on a deep illusion. The illusion arises because these positions are relative to our point of view on a moving planet. The relevant alignments, so called, would not exist if viewed from elsewhere. Therefore they can have no causal significance. Here is a substantive disagreement, though not to be sure over a particular matter of fact which can be considered in isolation from other things. It is the marker for a ramifying set of disagreements about what is and is not true. But such genuine disagreements exist and they call for appropriately complex modes of discussion and argument. These just cannot get off the ground if the fact of ramifying differences between theories, outlooks, is taken as sufficient for saying we have two world-view schemas.

The fact of ramifying disagreements between outlooks does appear to be central to Runzo's criteria for counting and reidentifying schemas. Two criteria are important for him. First, that one putative schema involves 'whole categories of things' not included in the second schema. Second, the conceptual structure of one schema entails the truth of propositions which contradict the propositions entailed by the conceptual structure of the other (1986: 190). There are differences in world outlooks of this order. As to the first criterion, viewpoints on reality can diverge over what kinds of things exist as well as over which particular things exist. As to the second, outlooks can differ over fundamental assumptions about what is possible and actual, assumptions which will have powerful entailments further down the line. Yet the facts about world outlooks which Runzo's two criteria point to are perfectly compatible with a very obvious, platitudinous conclusion. It is that, as well as having disagreements about particular matters of fact, we find some disagreements between individuals and societies on wide-ranging theoretical matters. People have different theories about the world and the chasms between some pairs of theories can be very broad indeed. Nothing like Runzo's dependency and pluralist ontology principles follows from the fact that there are theoretical disagreements. All that follows are the platitudes that what is true and real is sometimes the object of deep theoretical disagreement and that it is correspondingly difficult to sort out these disagreements about the true and the real.

Consider another example of divergent schemas, one which bears directly upon religion: Runzo cites the conceptions of deity in Spinoza, Whitehead, Hume and Thomas Aquinas as belonging to different conceptual schemas. He says that each conception can be seen as true relative to the corresponding conceptual scheme (Runzo 1993: 75). In saying that they can each be true relative to schemas he of course takes away his initial introduction of them as 'mutually incompatible conceptions'. We can see some obvious sense in declaring that these philosophers produce a conception of deity belonging to a unique system. The philosophies of these thinkers differ markedly. Yet before we conclude that they articulate a notion of God in a unique schema, we should note that they appear to disagree with one another. Whitehead accepts while he also rejects aspects both of Spinoza's pantheism and of Thomas' theism. In section 9 of his *Dialogues concerning Natural Religion*, Hume contends against one of Thomas' and Spinoza's main claims: that the divine being/substance necessarily exists. There, Hume is naturally taken as putting forward arguments and contentions that later defenders of these metaphysicians must rebut. All these thinkers, in other and plain words, are part of an intellectual tradition. Seen in that light, it is not at all obvious that they articulate different conceptual schemas, where that has the implications for what is true and real which Runzo wants.

Because the philosophical systems listed by Runzo stand in a tradition, there will be some overlap between them. Dialogue and debate will be possible despite conceptual differences. The same is true of Runzo's astrologer and astrophysicist. A shared language and many shared beliefs about the world will mean that debate is possible here too. One might have thought that this point about the fuzziness of conceptual schemes and the overlaps between them would spell grave problems for Runzo, but in fact he himself admits and welcomes these facts (see Runzo 1986: 56). He wishes to object to any account of human thought which traps subjects in watertight systems of concepts and which, in turn, prevents them from shared understanding and perception with others. He rejects the postulation of a shared world, to be referred to and perceived, as the assurance and basis of shared understanding. This is to put the cart before the horse. It is to presuppose that we could have access to a common reality or perceptual given independent of our conceptual schemas (1986: 189). Rather, it is the very fact that portions of our conceptual schemas overlap with portions of others which enables us to perceive a common world to the extent that we do and which enables understanding and dialogue between upholders of different conceptual schemas (1986: 189–90). Hence, incommensurability between schemas is prevented.

Note two facts about Runzo's welcoming of overlap between conceptual schemas. In the first place, this is something of a mystery on his account, because there is no reality possessed of any concrete shape or form the mutual experience of which would predispose human beings to share concepts. (In fact, Runzo does use the idea that there is some external constraint on our conceptualising, for all that it is unclear how this could possibly arise on his system. See below for discussion of his appeal to the noumenal.) In the second place, overlap would seem to create manifold problems for Runzo's theorising. What Runzo envisages by way of overlap is that, while two individuals might hold different world-view schemas, a concept or set of concepts may be shared between them. This allows genuine disagreement, understanding and dialogue and defeats the claim that the schemas might be simply incommensurable (Runzo 1986: 187). But it also means that the one set of concepts could be used to make true claims in one schema and false in another (refer to realities in one schema and have no referential force in another). So matters of truth and reference with respect to the same set of concepts fundamentally change, depending on which of perhaps many schemas we view them as part of. This looks like anarchy. Moreover, the fact of overlap raises the possibility, indeed likelihood, that any one individual will have a concept or set of concepts which are common between two schemas she or he adheres to. I presume that we cannot rule out one individual adhering to different schemas. Runzo does not want to say one individual's world outlook equals one schema. He denies that schemas get their identity through ownership by one human being. World-view schemas are social constructions (1986: 49–50). A society is bound to hand on different schemas to individuals. Runzo's astrophysicist will have absorbed the schema of modern science but may also have been brought up a Christian or a Jew. There are some cosmological concepts (for example, 'creation') common to both physics and Christianity and Judaism. Now, if what is true and real depends on which world-view schema I am thinking in terms of, I had better know which schema the concepts I am using to frame truth and referential claims fall under. I certainly need a criterion for counting and reidentifying world-view schemas for that. Without it relativism is useless as a doctrine.

One way out of this critique might be this: there are some cases of intellectual disputes in which disagreements seem so deep and ramifying that no appeal to observational data will settle them and where it is impossible to prove an incoherence in the rival conceptions. Each seems able in the end to interpret every fact which the other throws up. Many disputes in metaphysics answer to this description. Consider the dispute between, on the one hand, our customary 'Aristotelian' way of conceiving the world as containing enduring things and substances with properties and, on the other, a Whiteheadian metaphysics according to which reality is made up of events, 'occasions'. Runzo tells us that Carnap was right to suppose that our choices between rival schemas are pragmatic: not decided by observation or logic (1986: 218–19; more on Carnap on existence questions in Chapter 4). Well, we might come to the conclusion after pursuing some theoretical disputes that observation and logic give out. The questions at issue are not decidable. We must make a pragmatic decision to follow the conceptions and vocabulary of one theory rather than another. It is in this case precisely that we can say: here we face a choice between rival world-view schemas.

Let us grant that in some cases of deep intellectual or theoretical dispute we despair of finding anything in logic or observation which will settle them. It does not follow strictly that reason is silent on them. It may be that we need instead to broaden our conception of reason (an appeal to the pragmatic may be then too lazy or too narrow). It does not follow, further, that we explain the fact of such apparently unresolvable disputes by saying that they show the presence of two world-view schemas. That would require that we had some working conception of a world-view schema independent of the fact that we wished to explain. Part of such a working conception would be some means of counting and reidentifying schemas. A simple explanation of the phenomenon of unresolved disagreements of a metaphysical kind (such as that between theism and atheism itself) is this: some rival theories of reality deal in matters of great generality and abstraction. They are of their nature hard to rebut because they have no clear predictive consequences and their explanatory scope is so broad that they can be held to explain everything.

I return to an earlier reflection on conceptual scheme relativism. It is an instance, in my view, of that philosophical vice which starts from inventing a terminology, moves to thinking that a new type of entity has been discovered by that act of invention and then offers a bold theory about the type of entity. It is useful to talk in a rough and ready way about world views, world outlooks, theories, conceptual schemes. But we have not thereby discovered a set of things in the human world which could determine truth or reality, because we have not thereby discovered entities with determinate properties. This amounts to saying that we should not accept Runzo's diversity principle. It contains the truism that human beings use different sets of concepts to describe the world, but mixes it with a series of false presuppositions about schemas. It thus cannot be endorsed.

Runzo and World Making

Suppose that Runzo is correct in asserting that our thinking takes place within world-view schemas which determine what we can recognise as possible. Suppose further, as he claims in both *Reason, Relativism and God* (Chapter 9) and *World Views and Perceiving God* (Chapter 1), that all perception is propositionally structured and therefore shaped by our concepts. Thus all our thinking and experience would be structured by world-view schemas. Would his dependency principle and his plural ontology principle follow? Both have the immediate implication that world-view schemas shape not merely our thinking about and experience of the world, but the world itself. Truth-makers (states of affairs, facts) would be in some manner created by our concepts. Objects would in some manner depend for their existence on our concepts. The innocent realist will deny that claims about the dependence of our concepts on schemes or the dependence of our experience on concepts could have any such implications. It is an essential part of innocent realism to hold that human beings are members of the one, real world which for the most part does not depend on them for its existence and character. If we thought that, for example, the fact that we used these rather than those concepts was due more to the shaping power of schemas rather than prompting from the one, real world, what would follow from within innocent realism would be scepticism. If there were minimal or no input from the world our concepts putatively referred to, then we would on reflection have to agree that the likelihood that our concepts did enable us to be informed about the character of that world was slim. It makes no sense on innocent realism to suppose that human representations have the power to change the greater part of the one, real world that would have existed even if there had never been any human beings at all. The transformation of the world by our concepts would be magic. Runzo's scheming plus realism equals scepticism.

We only escape this scepticism if we make concept makers into world shapers. World shaping plus Runzo's diversity principle is what generates the idea that truth is relative to conceptual schemas and that there are plural ontologies corresponding to different schemas.

Runzo is sometimes coy about regarding concept users as world shapers. Thus he states at one point that our schemas do not create experience or the actual world (1986: 63). This reluctance reflects Runzo's taste for cosmic porridge. He has a dualist view of reality: there is unconceptualised noumenal reality which we do not create and phenomenal reality which we somehow do. Conceptual schemas determine what is possible for their adherents (they describe or constitute general orders of reality). But what is actual depends on the interplay between conceptual schemas, the content of our experience and 'the noumenal itself (things in themselves, apart from perception)' (1986: 59). This appeal to noumenal reality is a mere fig leaf which will not hide Runzo's conviction that concept users are world makers (compare Devitt's account of 'fig-leaf realism', 1997: 23). That the fig leaf of noumena will not hide Runzo's constructivism is shown by the fact that he claims, as consistency demands, that noumenal reality is characterless. To offer any conception of reality is thereby to be conceiving of phenomenal reality (Runzo 1986: 131). Claims about noumenal reality as having a specific character are meaningless (1986: 246). We cannot therefore sensibly ask how far what exists is down to us and what is down to noumenal reality. *That* something exists is down to the confrontation between subject and noumenal reality, but that *this* or *that* exists is down to conceptual schemas. Something similar must hold for Runzo's conception of experience. He need not hold that we are responsible for having experience at all. He can thus recognise the distinction between seeing something and imagining it, the latter being the product of our volition. But the *content* of what comes to us unbidden in our experience must come from our schemas, for the attribution of content or shape to noumenal reality is meaningless.

Runzo's problems with world making are shown in his confrontation with the dinosaurs (1986: 243–4). Runzo feels the oddity of saying that human conceptual activity created the dinosaurs and the weirdness of the claim that if there had been no human beings to produce the relevant concepts, there would have been no dinosaurs. His response to this kind of worry is two-fold. First he contends that what a conceptual schema does (the schema with our concepts of the prehistoric) is define a set of world orders for us, that is, delimit a range of possibilities. This makes dinosaurs possible. But it is down to something 'independent of our minds' (1986: 244) whether anything actual corresponds to the possible reality we create. This response has already been sufficiently rebutted. Granted the characterless state of the noumenal reality independent of our concepts, it can play no role in determining what is actual. Our author's own clear statements, plus the logic of talk about the noumenal, entail that is meaningless to suppose that we may have discovered that there is something in noumenal reality corresponding to our concept of a dinosaur.

Runzo's second response is to stress the distinction between questions and facts internal to a schema and questions and facts external to a schema. Prior to constructing the appropriate system of concepts, the question of whether dinosaurs existed before human beings arrived on the planet makes no sense. Once the appropriate geological, historical and zoological concepts are created the question has a sense (and the answer 'Yes'). But all that means is that it is a truth relative to our schema that dinosaurs existed before us and were not created by us. Dinosaurs are phenomenally real entities, real 'within the way *we* conceive things' (1986: 244). Here we have the relativist playing a double game. Human representations create phenomenal worlds. These worlds with their occupants would not exist if there were no human beings with representations. They are ontologically dependent on us. But some of these phenomenal worlds are such that human beings (*qua* phenomenal objects) are latecomers in history. The world contains entities which are independent of the phenomenological human beings who also exist in the realm created by representations.

Innocent realists may respond to the above defence by suggesting that there is no way in which the relativist conclusion that dinosaurs *qua* phenomenal objects depend upon us can be prevented from filtering through into the very phenomenal picture of them as part of prehistoric and therefore human-independent reality. Realists will argue that Runzo gives the game away when he classifies relativism with other responses to conceptual diversity which 'share the basic assumption that the world we experience and understand is not the world independent of our perceiving but a world at least in part structured by our minds' (Runzo 1993: 201). The only thing wrong with this admission is the assertion that the world is *in part* structured by us. Structure can only belong to the human side of the contribution to reality/experience on a conceptual relativist view. There is no structure in the noumenal.

Runzo's remarks, however, raise a yet deeper issue about the very character of relativism, the phenomenal/noumenal distinction and the conception of human concept users as world makers. Runzo starts his articulation of relativism with the diversity principle. That principle records the facts that human beings use a variety of concepts to interrogate the world and that sets of concepts come and go. The facts about us as concept users can only be facts about us as phenomenal entities, in the terms of Runzo's relativism. Human beings as concept users, together with facts about the history of human ideas or about present cultural, conceptual diversity, are all on the phenomenal side of the phenomenal/noumenal divide. We cannot catch or describe human beings in the act of world making or of constructing general orders of reality which then interact with mysterious noumenal reality, for the only human activities we can describe are phenomenal ones, activities which exist only after some world making, reality shaping has been completed. What does the world making cannot be us, that is, human beings in history, because the world making must already be completed for us – *qua* human beings, *qua* beings who espouse different conceptual schemes in the history of ideas – to exist. This entails that no fact about us (human beings in history) can entail radical relativism. (This point will be seen in Chapter 5 to drive a coach and horses through the arguments of Cupitt's *The Sea of Faith*.) It also entails that radical relativism becomes nigh unstateable.

The relativist will have to say that, along with all facts and distinctions, the facts about us and our theorising and the distinction between us and the world, are the products of representations. Examine the problem at the heart of this section again. We ask: 'Did human conceptual activity create the dinosaurs? Would the dinosaurs not have existed if there were no human conceptual schemas to refer to them? Do we not exist in a world which is largely not of our own making?' What can words such as 'human', 'we' refer to in such questions? They can only refer to flesh-and-blood human beings in history. It is such things which developed the zoological, geological and palaeontological concepts from which talk of dinosaurs sprung. Thus the words must refer to phenomenal realities. We can only get at what these words refer to via a rich set of concepts. The facts about us and our concepts which enable us to reflect on how the theories in which talk of dinosaurs arose are every bit as phenomenal as the dinosaurs themselves. There is just no way in which we can catch and describe a subject in the act of making phenomenal worlds. Subjects and objects we can describe have to be phenomenal, that is delineated by concepts. This means that at the core of conceptual relativism lies incoherence. Consider Runzo's 'basic assumption that the world we experience and understand is not the world independent of our perceiving but a world at least in part structured by our minds' (Runzo 1993: 201). We must again ask 'What do "we" and "our" refer to here?' It cannot be to noumenal subjects independent of human beings. That would be inconsistent with Runzo's citing facts about human beings in history to support his case. Moreover, it would be inconsistent and pointless to describe the noumenal, or to suppose that the noumenal is divided into things which use concepts and other things picked out by those concepts. So, the 'we' and the 'our' can only refer to human beings. But human beings cannot structure the world, if that means 'add structure to a characterless noumenal world'. Human beings are part of a non-noumenal world. Some structuring has to have taken place already to give us human beings facing a world which they want to describe. The world human beings face has to be a phenomenal, structured world if it is to contain a set of subjects who speak languages, construct theories and devise concepts. The world making has already taken place and only noumenal subjects could do it. But, in the nature of the case, we cannot describe what they are up to. It is the purest nonsense to suppose that they use conceptual schemes which vary with time and place.

This passage of argument suggests that John Searle may be right in suggesting that the core of innocent realism, namely external realism (the view that reality exists independent of our representations), is necessarily true, since the attempt to work out alternatives to it proves difficult. Runzo himself acknowledges one charge of incoherence against relativism. It is the old chestnut that relativism devours itself by virtue of claiming as an absolute, schema-independent truth that all truths are relative, schema-dependent truths. His response to this is most unconvincing to my eyes. It consists in distinguishing first-order from second-order claims/truths. Runzo then limits conceptual-schema relativism to a theory about the relativity and dependence of first-order claims. Second-order claims about first-order theories and concepts are not subject to scheme relativity and dependence (Runzo 1986: 39–41). This response is suspiciously ad hoc. It depends on being able to demarcate first-order from second-order – Runzo supplies no criterion. But, at a deeper level, it is hard to see how any reasons which support relativism about the first-order should not support relativism about the second-order. Runzo's primary support for relativism about the first-order stems from noting the diversity of human concepts used to describe the world. There is a diversity of concepts and theories about theories and concepts. Epistemological and semantic theories and concepts exist in profusion. If diversity is a reason for thinking there is no one truth to be told about the world, by what right do we ignore diversity in conceptions of knowledge, language, reference and the like?

My own query as to the coherence of conceptual-schema relativism is after a deeper target: relativism cannot state what it wants to state, for it can only make points about the dependence of reality on thought which are couched in a language already containing a division between language and reality. This critique has echoes of comments of Putnam. As noted in Chapter 2, Putnam, in a number of places, states that the problem with relativism is that it tries to give a view of reality as a whole, stating what belongs to our conceptions and what belongs to reality as such. No such standing back is possible because we cannot escape from our language and the way it divides up things in order to make the relevant distinctions (see, for example, Putnam 1992: 120–23; 1990: 118–19). This implies my point. We cannot stand back from our language to make a statement about how language or the subject relates to reality, because we cannot but rely on our language to make that distinction and the concepts of subject and world it already contains.

Phenomenal and Noumenal

The distinction between phenomenal and noumenal reality, whether it is explicit or implicit, has been seen to play an important role in all those forms of anti-realism which hold that reality is humanly constructed. The initial implausibility in supposing that human representations create what exists is mitigated by the thought that representations shape a pre-existent material. Thus the concept of the noumenal as that which exists prior to all representations – the cosmic porridge – is ushered in. The concept of the phenomenal – of the world as it appears to or as it is shaped by us – is also helpful in getting the constructivist bandwagon rolling. Once again, Runzo's texts are exemplary for seeing how anti-realism functions.

We have noted (previous chapter) the utter implausibility in supposing that human concepts and representations create or construct the furniture of the physical world. This is an absurdly Promethian estimate of human powers. The concept of phenomenal reality enables a slide from sensible, arguable positions into this absurdity.

This is how the slide goes. First, we note that people use different conceptual structures to interpret the world. Second, we state that this means they experience the world differently. Third, we conclude that people who use different conceptual structures live in different experienced worlds, different phenomenal realities. The move from step two to three is supported by the transition from the vocabulary of 'experiencing the world differently' to that of 'the world as experienced is different'. And that transition is aided by a ready-made name for the world-as-experienced: 'the phenomenal world'.

Steps one and two in the slide are present in Runzo's diversity principle. That records the existence of diverse conceptual schemas and notes the way a system of concepts delineates what is possible and impossible for its adherents. We have noted already that Runzo takes all perception to be conceptually and propositionally structured. Thus the diversity principle automatically entails that human beings' experience of the world is shaped by their conceptual schemas: 'the phenomenological content of sensory experience consists in the "output" of the physiological sense-reception processes *qua* ordered or categorised by the mind, via the percipient's conceptual schema' (1986: 96). There are two ingredients in experience: raw unconceptualised 'data' from the sense organs and concepts which give the former content and shape. So as concepts change, experience must change. People with different conceptual schemas will experience the world differently.

Steps one and two may seem innocent, once we have accepted that experience is shaped by our concepts. But note that the realist will want, rightly, to deny that concepts and schemas *determine* what I experience. Two people may investigate the Loch Ness phenomena, each possessed of the concept of the Loch Ness Monster (a large aquatic reptile left over from prehistory). One may be convinced the Monster exists and thus perhaps be predisposed to see each pattern in the waves of the Loch as the wake of a huge reptile. The other may be a passionate Nessie sceptic. Mere possession of the concept does not make this individual at all predisposed to see manifestations of the Monster. Whether they do find any convincing observational evidence either way depends on what is there to be seen, not on their concepts. Hence, it is at best misleading, at worst plain false, to say that 'what we experience is inextricably determined by our schemas' (1986: 251). Our concepts will influence what we can notice and discern in the world around us, but what there is to notice and discern depends on the world.

Step three follows from steps one and two once we do a little hypostasising. We are told that 'in a certain sense' those who use different schemas live in different worlds (Runzo 1993: 68). The authority of Kuhn (Kuhn 1962: 109, 115–16) is cited to prove the fact that scientific schemas are constitutive of nature and that scientists who use different schemas live in different worlds (Runzo 1993: 125). The fact that you do not share the same schema as another means that the world you live is not the same as the world that person lives in (Runzo 1986: 59). 'The world as I experience and live in it' could just serve as an innocent turn of phrase to indicate the fact (to the extent that it is a fact) that how I experience and engage with the world is affected by the concepts I use. So interpreted, the phraseology is compatible with the obvious truth: *that my concepts change does not change the world those concepts apply to*. Here Devitt has it spot on in his strictures on Kuhn's statement that after oxygen was discovered scientists 'worked in a different world' (Kuhn 1962: 117; Devitt 1997: 240). What changed after the discovery of oxygen was the perceptions, beliefs and activities of scientists. But nature did not change. It contained oxygen before Lavoisier. It would have contained it even if there had never been any scientists or concept users at all. Nothing to do with the chemistry of combustion changed. The changes were confined to the world of human representations and the things it shapes (such as human behaviour). Only if 'the world I live in and experience' names nothing more than the manner in which I live in and experience the one real world can the 'world' change as my concepts and beliefs change. The phrases 'phenomenal world', 'phenomenal reality' are gifts for those who want some world to change or be constructed anew. Once we have such phrases to refer to the world as we experience it (that is, to how we experience the world), then we have a reality which can be created, structured by us as our concepts and experience change. Then we can, indeed must, postulate a noumenal reality which does not change as our experience changes. But of course the world of chalk escarpments, oxygen, Scottish lochs and planets does not change as our ways of conceiving it changes. It existed prior to us and will continue long after we and our schemas are no more. And yet the things it contains have to be placed on the phenomenal side of the line, since they are things we name and experience.

Relativism starts out as an epistemic doctrine. It is fuelled by reflections on the ingredients of human knowledge and on facts about human concept use. It turns metaphysical, transformed into an account of truth-makers (facts and states of affairs) and objects being fashioned by concepts. The language of phenomenal and noumenal fuels this transition. Once we start talking of phenomenal reality (in apposition with noumenal reality) we are speaking of an ontological realm which is constituted by our epistemic activities: it is the world as we know it. This shift is embodied in Runzo's account of one of the basic assumptions which, in his view, supports conceptual relativism. He first states this as

> ... there are no neutral 'facts' to which we have access, no facts which are utterly independent of minds, but which can be discovered by minds ...; rather, 'the world' is, in part, constituted of facts as we read them, in virtue of our schemas, *into* the 'world'. (1986: 36)

This, complete with scare quotes round 'world' is a bold metaphysical claim, using the language of world making with which we have become so familiar. Runzo associates this assumption with Kant and then, tellingly, states that it is part of the idea that all perceiving is theory-laden. Now the latter claim is epistemological. It is the view that there is no perceptual given, no perceiving without the aid of concepts. That epistemological view is just assumed by Runzo to include the notion that facts are not discovered but created, 'read into' the world, by our conceptual and theoretical activities. There is a huge leap here which is not seen as such. It is easy to show that 'all perceiving is theory laden' is utterly innocent of the metaphysical implications Runzo and other relativists see in it. In so doing we can show that there is quite another interpretation of the phenomenal, noumenal distinction than the illegitimate one which makes phenomenal reality into world we constitute by our concepts and modes of experience.

Let us accept Kant's dictum that intuitions without concepts are blind (Kant 1997: A51/B75). This contains our message that experience is concept-laden. Without concepts, that is, forms of judgement which enable discrimination and recognition, experience would be as nothing to us. Experience would certainly be incapable of being the foundation of empirical knowledge. It does not follow that facts, objects and states of affairs are conceptual creations. We must distinguish two ways of regarding the conceptual apparatus: as a filter and as a fact factory. Runzo regards it in the latter guise, hence talk of the phenomenal realm being constituted by our concepts. But 'experience is concept-laden' is just as easily compatible with the filter view. The filter view assumes that the world we experience has (apart from those parts of it consisting in human realities) a structure and an ontology independent of us and our conceptualising. We are only able to be aware of the structure and the ontology because of our conceptualising. The precise character of our conceptualising will determine how we experience, and what we know of, the world because our concepts act like nets or filters. We do not create objects and qualities, facts and events, but the only portions of the one real world we will be able to notice are the ones which our apparatus allows us to notice. The fisherman's catch sitting in the bottom of the boat was not created by the nets used, but those nets determined what would be hauled aboard and what would escape. By analogy, only in this sense is the character of how we interpret and experience the world determined by our concepts: they filter what we experience. To be sure, some people, some of the time, experience a world created by their concepts and theories. This is how illusions and myths are created. For all that our concepts allow us to be aware of only some aspects of reality, we can still distinguish living in an illusory world and living in the real world. There are lots of things people have thought existed in the one real world which we know do not exist. They include things such as fairies, astral influences, humours (as in premodern medicine), phlogiston, witches and so on. We know perfectly well in most cases how to pursue the question of whether something people apparently experience (such as Nessie) really exists.

The notion of conceptual structures as filters gives us a sense to the noumenal/phenomenal distinction which is harmless and useful. We can mark the fact that concepts function as filters which shape, in the precise sense given above, how we interpret the world by saying that we only know the world as it appears to us but not as it is in itself. It is a tautology, but one of those significant tautologies, to state that we know only appearances and not things in themselves. It is equivalent to saying that we can only know things as we know them (Schrader 1968: 173). The significance of the tautology lies in this: it reminds us that our way of knowing things is not the only conceivable way of knowing things, that other types of epistemic subjects may be able to discover facts that can never come our way, that there may be aspects of reality which we do not, and could not, have access to. On this understanding, 'things in themselves' is a place-holder. It is a means of signifying that there are bound to be aspects of nature we are not and never will be in touch with. 'Noumenon/noumenal object' can have a slightly more positive sense. We invoke by this terminology the thought that there could be other types of cognitive subject who will discern reality differently from us. We may indeed be able to flesh out this thought of other subjects. Kant was exercised by the fact that our cognitive apparatus depends on a 'sensibility', that is, on sense organs which receive 'intuitions' from independently existing objects. But we can conceive, in the instance of God, of an 'intellectual intuition', that is, a way of being aware of particulars through intellect alone, minus data from the senses. Since it is, in his view, our sensibility which ties us to experiencing the world in the dimensions of space and time, the conception of a noumenal reality (one known through an intellectual intuition) allows us to conceive that there may be aspects to the real which transcend the spatio-temporal (see Kant 1997: B307–9). In these varied ways, the Kantian language is a powerful reminder that our cognition is selective and what we know is unlikely to be coterminous with all that exists. This is a properly critical, negative use of the appearance/thing in itself and phenomenal/noumenal distinctions.

Once we construe the phenomenal/noumenal along these lines the metaphysical consequences relativists need to derive from the fact of human conceptual diversity vanish. Nothing is created by our concepts – save for things in our world, including illusions and myths. We are not world makers. We can accept the denial of all forms of constructivism while conceding that we are not given reality on a plate by our senses, because those senses and our concepts filter it to us. The only metaphysical consequence that follows is the useful but minimal recognition that reality is bigger and more varied than anything our concepts allow us to discern. This last point is a handy antidote to dogmatism. It is four-square, 100 per cent compatible with innocent realism. It is useful not least for underscoring this fact: innocent realism is not wedded to the view that there is a single, complete description of reality. 'We only know the world as it appears to us, not as it is in itself' tells us plainly that any true account we give of the world will always be a selective one. It will ignore those features of the world which creatures with our sensibility and conceptual resources have not discovered and perhaps never will discover. The full compatibility of innocent realism with a critical, regulative use of the phenomenal/noumenal distinction gives the lie to the idea that realism is equivalent to the thought that there is a God's-eye view of all the facts and that we can appropriate this. Realism is perfectly compatible with the recognition that our insight into reality is partial, limited and aspectual. Indeed, realism demands this conclusion, since it rests on the founding assumption that the world is in large measure not constituted by our representations of it.

The Relativist God

We may naïvely think that a relativist metaphysics and epistemology fits in ill with any form of theism. Theism in its many guises is an absolutist metaphysical doctrine. Paradoxically, Runzo defends relativism as the best metaphysics and ontology for theism. One set of arguments for relativism in religion is drawn from religious diversity and confrontation with the fact of diverse religious conceptual schemes. Relativism can avoid the exclusivist condemnation of rival traditions and conceptions of the divine. Yet it can also avoid the problems which come with pluralist responses to religious diversity. These last are taken by Runzo to be paradigmatically exemplified in John Hick's *An Interpretation of Religion*. Pluralist responses involve interpreting each religion as speaking only of an 'image' of the divine, while postulating an unknown divine reality lying behind those images (Runzo 1993: 207–8). Whereas pluralism thus regards the real God as noumenal, leaving the differing faiths with only unreal images as their immediate foci, relativism can identify the phenomenal God with the real God. It can close the gap between rival religious conceptual schemes and the divine by allowing differing sets of religious truth claims to be correct (Runzo 1993: 210) and each phenomenal focus to be real. Exclusivist responses to diversity are imperialistic. Pluralist responses are sceptical. Relativist responses are neither.

Runzo has a further important argument for making use of relativism in the articulation of theism. He contends that there is a long-recognised and fundamental problem in religious thought. It is that of reconciling the fact that all conceptions of the divine are human, and therefore conditioned and relative, with the fact that these conceptions purport to be of something divine, and therefore unconditioned and absolute. The problem highlights an ever-present human tendency: to identify limited and relative human conceptions with the divine itself. Runzo cites H.R.

Niebuhr and Paul Tillich as thinkers who have identified this tendency and its underlying seduction: that we will merge the human and the divine by giving our conceptions of the divine the absolute status which properly belongs only to their object, God (Runzo 1993: 67). Relativism solves this tension. It produces the humility which comes from recognising that 'the theological conclusions one reaches are relative, *human* conclusions' (Runzo 1986: 138).

Let us deal with this latter point first. The argument is that if we believe in an absolute conception of truth and reality, we will be prone to transfer the non-relative, absolute character of the reality we think we represent in our theories and conceptions to the character of those theories and conceptions themselves. This must be a mistake, since we know that our theories and conceptions are human products and as such conditioned and relative. In the theological case, this error turns into a form of blasphemous identification of the divine with the human. Runzo's claims for relativism bring to mind Hick's strictures on 'naïve' realism: the view that our conceptions of God (or whatever) can be literal, true-for-all-time pictures of reality. Naïve realism is incompatible with a recognition of the human character of all theorising. Only a critical realism which stresses the human, limited, fallible character of even those conceptions we regard as true is acceptable (Hick 1989: 175).

It is obvious what the realist response to these contentions must be: they are the reverse of the truth. Only a robust realism can save us from dogmatism. No true realism can be naïve.

Recall the main thrust of innocent realism: there is one real world which exists largely independent of us. Leaving aside that portion of the world which is the human world, reality is not constituted by our representations of it. Our representations (the truth-bearers) are one thing; reality (containing the facts and states of affairs which are the truth makers) is another. At the heart of innocent realism lies a stress on the notion that representations are but representations. They do not make the world. They do not constitute what is true. For the most part, reality would be what it is if there had been no human representations of it or if they had been utterly different. If we claim truth for some of our representations, that claim has to be justified by reference to facts independent of human representations. No representations, as such, can claim an absolute status. No facts about who holds representations or how many people hold them can make them true. Representations are one thing; the world is another.

Realism thus enforces a gap between mind and reality. It must, then, prevent any elision of the distinction between the human mind and its conceptions, on the one hand, and God on the other. By contrast, constructionism and idealism reduce the gap between mind and reality (by making the former that which shapes or constitutes the latter). Hick's naïve realists are folk who have forgotten the purport of realism since they think that accurate pictures of the facts are easily won. Runzo's theological strictures on those who give their religious conceptions an absolute, non-human status which belongs to God alone are proto-idealists. They cannot see that it is one thing for theologians to have theories of the divine, but quite another for them to be true. There is every reason on innocent realism to ask of any theological conception, no matter how long or widely held, 'But is it true?'.

The above highlights a simple truth: realism in general always gives room for the scepticism, since by its very nature it cannot allow for the closing of the gap between mind (human representations) and reality. Realism applied to religion must leave the door open for religious scepticism. Reflection on religious diversity can promote religious scepticism and Runzo is right to see the pluralist response to religious diversity of John Hick as a form of religious scepticism ('agnosticism' would be a more appropriate term). Religious diversity yields the fact that there are world religions with incompatible accounts of the divine. The fact seems to face philosophers of religion with a choice: either find some means of proving one such account to be more probable than the others, or produce a revised account of religious truth and certainty. Philosophers who espouse religious pluralism despair of the first alternative and embrace the second. Embracing the second involves accepting something like this: all (or most) world religions give partial, limited accounts of a religious ultimate whose true nature is hidden from them (see Byrne 1995b: 6). This is a severe form of religious agnosticism which does, as Runzo rightly notes, threaten to undermine actual religions through the promotion of religious scepticism. We know what Runzo's general response to conceptual diversity is: the dependency and pluralist ontology principles close the gap between human conceptions and reality diversity threatens to open up. They do so by giving different religious world views the power to create their own religious worlds and (phenomenal) gods (Runzo 1993: 212).

Having reached this point an easy retort to Runzo appears to be available: whatever the problems in exclusivist and pluralist responses to diversity, either one is much better than a story which tells us that human beings through their conceptual schemes manufacture God. It is of the essence of any religious view of life that it recognises deep problems in human existence centred on the fact of evil. It must postulate some trans-human source of power which guarantees that evil and finitude can be overcome (see Chapter 1 for this case). A God who is merely a member of a phenomenal realm, all of whose citizens are shaped by human representations, cannot be the source of such a guarantee. Such a God is created by us and expires with us. No such God can be the anchor for a theodicy.

This easy rebuttal of Runzo faces the complication that he appears to anticipate the problem that, crudely, a phenomenal God cannot save. He does so by making use once again of the phenomenal/noumenal distinction. He does postulate a noumenal Ultimate Reality behind the phenomenal religious worlds of the different faiths. He gives some hope that there will be some correspondence between the phenomenal gods and the Ultimate Reality. We can judge of better and worse correspondence by pragmatic criteria. If theists find that their religious outlooks succeed by some relevant standards, then they may have faith that their conceptual schema latch onto the noumenal divine. Religious allegiance is in the last analysis founded upon such faith:

> ... the greater the correspondence between our conception of the phenomenal and the character of the noumenal (whatever it is), the more our purposive activity, carried out within phenomenal reality as *we* understand it, will be successful and the closer – in principle – our understanding of the phenomenal will correspond to the noumenal. For the monotheist it is a matter of faith that, in this manner, one's *own* experience of the presence of 'The' God of history does increase, on the whole, one's understanding of God in Godself. [Runzo 1993: 212]

Runzo's ability to bring the noumenal cavalry riding to the rescue of his phenomenal but powerless God depends on him being able to take religious believers to be making reference to the noumenal God in and through their descriptions of phenomenal deities. He employs recent, non-descriptivist accounts of reference to aid him in that task (Runzo 1986: 246ff.). Thereby, the reference we make with a notion of God is not tied to the intensions of the words and phrases we use to make the reference. Let us not dwell on that point but yield it to him (for more on the possibility of referential success in religion accompanying descriptive failure see Byrne 1995b: Ch. 2). We must focus instead on his response to the charge that to speak of referring to the noumenal is out, since by definition the noumenal is characterless and that which is characterless cannot be referred to. Runzo's response to this powerful point takes us to the heart of the confusion I diagnose in his invocation of a noumenal God. We noted above that he concedes that it is meaningless to characterise the noumenal, for all characterisations come from a perspective, and anything which comes from a perspective can only delineate the phenomenal. But this does not mean he accepts the conclusion that we cannot refer to the noumenal: 'this confuses the claim to know that the noumenal has some specific character, with the bare claim that there is a noumenal, whatever its character turns out to be, which "lies behind" the phenomenal reality we experience' (Runzo 1986: 246). What is wrong with this reply is that it will not serve at all to ground the idea that we might refer to a noumenal *God* behind phenomenal reality. To use the word 'God' referentially, or one of its cognates, is already to characterise the intended object of reference. Even if we accept a non-descriptive account of reference in the case of 'God', we will have to agree that any entity to which 'God' successfully refers would have to belong to a rough type or kind (see Byrne 1995b: 44). The account given in Chapter 1 above implies that no one could refer to God unless they intended to pick out something which exercised a kind of moral causality over the world or something which was the world's creator. There is no point Runzo insisting on the importance of religious life being sustained by faith that the phenomenal God one worships is God in Himself (Runzo 1986: 253; 1993: 236) unless there is something at the level of noumenal reality which corresponds to our distinction between divine and non-divine reality. Yet to suppose there is something of that kind is to characterise noumenal reality, and we have been told (on very good grounds, given the central purpose in talking about the noumenal) that once reality is characterised it is phenomenal.

The point being urged against Runzo is not the epistemic one that faith in a correspondence between phenomenal object of worship and something noumenal would be absolutely groundless. Rather, I am arguing that such a faith lacks content. The very idea that a phenomenal object corresponds to noumenal reality involves an attempt to characterise the noumenal – such attempts are by definition illegitimate. The only world in which we can picture there being one kind of thing rather than another – mice, people and gods – is the phenomenal one. That is the world of types, kinds and distinctions. If there is a realm of reality which is unconceptualisable, then it is has no types, kinds and distinctions we can speak of. Any types, kinds and distinctions we can speak of are not in it.

Runzo's claims to the effect that our faith in a God beyond the phenomenal can be vindicated by the pragmatic results of the religious system we adhere to is a laudable attempt to introduce some constraint into his relativistic system. But we have noted a major problem with this mode of argument already: no constraints of any kind can come from noumenal reality because it is beyond characterisation. Only that which has some definite characteristics of its own could resist our moulding it as we choose. What has definite characteristics belongs to the phenomenal side of the divide.

It may be objected that all these strictures can easily be avoided if it is affirmed that the noumenal reality can have characteristics. It can then be supposed to consist of things with definite qualities, relations and so forth. All that the phenomenal/noumenal distinction gives expression to is the thought that the things and qualities we name are the result of our moulding of the world. The distinctions and characteristics of our world belong to our shaping activities. On these grounds we cannot be sure that the noumenal world has the characteristics of our world, but it is meaningful to suppose that it has some.

Why won't this tempting reply work? It goes against the whole thrust of 'scheming'. It affirms that there is a world which exists, with a definite shape and form, independent of human representations. It is like innocent realism in that respect. It does not affirm that distinctions and characteristics only come with our conceptual activities. In the light of this, it will rapidly lose the basis for its talk of our moulding the world. There is no cosmic porridge to mould. There is a world of definite kinds and things, but it seems that we know nothing of it, since our concepts and representations float free of it. Our concepts and representations are shaped by our activities and not by this independent world. This is not so much relativism as out-and-out scepticism.

Chapter 4

Realism and Verification

Realism and Scepticism

The innocent realism defended in this book leaves the door open for scepticism. Innocent realism states that we live in a world which is largely ontologically and epistemically independent of us. How the world is is one thing; how we represent it to ourselves is another. As Paul Horwich notes, this entails that, seen from one point of view, there is a tension in realism. On the one hand, realism holds that there are facts of science, history and the like which hold independently of us, which do not owe their existence to our awareness of them or even the possibility of our awareness of them. On the other hand, realism holds that we are able to acquire considerable knowledge of the world around us (Horwich 1996: 188).

The realist can venture naturalistic explanations of why we are able to cognise an epistemically and ontologically independent world. We are products of that world and could hardly have flourished as a species if we lacked the powers to observe it and reason about it. In the final analysis, however, innocent realism must accept the logical possibility that our judgements about the world are mistaken. Radical scepticism is thinkable. Stories can be told about evil demons or brains in vats which make radical scepticism coherent. The innocent realist's attitude toward radical scepticism should be that it is possible but boring. Countless states of affairs which are logically possible are not worth bothering about. Radical scepticism of the kind exemplified in Descartes' first *Meditation* illustrates a truism: our reasoning about what is so in the one, real, independent world is ampliative. The hypotheses and theories we construct about that world may be, and often are, based on solid evidence and cogent arguments. But no facts about the content of our experience entail the conclusions we reach about the independent world. This is a truism for the realist because the realist position is built on the hypothesis that most of the states of affairs which make up reality do not depend on our representations. So it is built on the postulation of a type-gap between statements describing our experiences and statements describing the world around us. And where there is that type-gap there will be the lack of entailment between statements about how things are represented by us and how they truly are.

Radical scepticism is boring because it is built around the logical possibility of error and because it celebrates the truisms described above. Scepticism about this or that branch of human knowledge will be interesting to the extent that it offers specific reasons why that branch of knowledge is bogus. But if it does that, it will be dealing in more than the logical possibility of error and will be involved in ampliative reasoning of the kind that radical scepticism shuns. Thus I am arguing that the innocent realist's attitude toward a radical sceptical hypothesis of the kind 'Perhaps the world came into existence five minutes ago with all the traces indicating it is much older built into it' should be: this is a logical possibility but there is not the slightest reason to take it seriously or to alter our intellectual and practical lives in the light of it. It merely illustrates the admitted fact that all the manifold evidence we have for believing in the past does not strictly entail the conclusions we reach about it. There is a type-gap between evidence and customary beliefs.

We noted in Chapter 2 that Putnam in one phase of his writing appears to reject innocent realism. He condemns it via incorporating some of its central theses in 'metaphysical realism' and arguing for the inferiority of that against 'internal realism'. Many of Putnam's arguments were criticised in Chapter 2. One of his arguments bearing on the possibility of radical scepticism now needs to be considered. We can summarise it crudely thus: metaphysical realism entails that scepticism is coherent; but scepticism is incoherent, therefore metaphysical realism is incoherent. The argument is based on the relation between theories and their interpretation and thus is often dubbed 'the model-theoretic argument'.

Imagine, states Putnam, we have constructed an ideal theory about some domain of reality. It is ideal in obeying all observational and theoretical constraints. All the observation statements the theory entails have been found to be true. It meets the theoretical constraints of elegance, simplicity, coherence and explanatory power. Metaphysical realism (and our innocent realism) nonetheless states that the theory could be false. Though the theory is epistemically ideal, it is not guaranteed true. But truth *can* be guaranteed for such a theory, Putnam affirms. It is possible to assign an interpretation for the singular and general referring expressions of a theory such that the resultant 'model' for the theory is internally consistent and makes every statement in the theory come out true: 'one can always find a reference relation that satisfies our observational constraints and also satisfies such theoretical constraints a simplicity, elegance, subjective plausibility, and so on, under which such a theory ... comes out true' (Putnam 1994: 353). Putnam's model-theoretic argument is used to support his claim that truth is a matter of ideal rational acceptability. Truth is not a relation between statements and a reality 'totally uncontaminated by conceptualisation'. Truth is instead a matter of what would be accepted in ideal epistemic conditions (Putnam 1981: 54–5). The notion of a fact or of a true statement is an idealisation of the notion of a statement that it is rational to believe (1981: 201). Putnam went on to deny that he ever intended to *identify* truth and some ideal epistemic state, or reduce truth to epistemic notions. His conclusion from the model-theoretic argument is better expressed by saying that it shows that truth and rational acceptability are interdependent notions (Putnam 1989: 115). What this means is not quite clear. It seems evident that the original argument had power by virtue of its critique of the idea that a theory meeting epistemic constraints could nonetheless be conceived of as false. The possibility that an epistemically ideal theory can yet be false is built into innocent realism. Innocent realism's natural bedfellow in theories of truth is a correspondence theory. It is of the essence of a correspondence theory to affirm that a statement is true when things are as it says they are. The correspondence theorist must hold that the connection between ' "Chalk is a sedimentary rock" is true' and 'chalk is a sedimentary rock' is one of strict, mutual entailment. The first statement is wholly sufficient for the second being true (and vice versa). But the second would not follow strictly from the first if truth partook of rational acceptability. If truth were even the highest degree of rational warrant, it would be conceivable (that is, logically possible) that 'Chalk is a sedimentary rock' is true but that chalk not be a sedimentary rock. This holds in the light of the points made above about scepticism, type-gaps and the lack of entailment between our evidence and the substantive claims we make about the world.

Innocent realism can give content to the thought that a theory which now meets, and continues to meet in future, all theoretical and observational desiderata is nonetheless false. It can do so through the hypotheses of radical scepticism. It can also do so via the reflection that human powers are limited. There may be observations to be made about the world which we cannot make, and never will make, which would show one of our cherished theories to be false in part or in whole. It is conceivable that there are beings with greater intellectual powers than ours capable of formulating theories to fit the facts we know but which explain those facts better. Such theories would be stronger candidates for truth. We know that in the past cherished theories have been rebutted by later observations or by the emergence of more cogent rivals. Even if a theory never receives such a rebuttal, it is conceivable that it will. Only if 'ideal' in 'epistemically ideal' actually means 'correspondence true', can epistemically ideal theories be guaranteed truth.

If it will not do to make truth dependent on ideal rational assertability, what then of Putnam's model-theoretic argument? Where are the flaws? Criticisms of it are legion (see Alston 1996 and Devitt 1997 for full surveys). I shall pick out three.

It can be shown first that the argument proves too much. Putnam's contention is that any ideal theory can be assigned a model, a mapping of its referential terms onto objects, such that its statements come out true. The contention rests on the Lowenheim-Skolem theorem in logic which asserts that any consistent theory can be assigned a model which makes its statements true. But then consistent but non-ideal theories can be assigned models whereby they come out true. Hence, Putnam's argument can show nothing about the connection between epistemically ideal theories and truth (see Glymour 1982: 175–6).

The first criticism of Putnam's model-theoretic argument suggests that, in proving too much, it does not establish that epistemic perfection leads to truth. The second criticism suggests a similar conclusion but from the opposite tack: the argument proves too little. All the model-theoretic argument shows is that it is possible to assign an epistemically ideal theory an interpretation which makes it come out as true. But that indicates only that it is logically possible for the theory to be true, not that it is true. The conclusion is quite compatible with the claim that the epistemically ideal theory is false (see Alston 1996: 138).

The third criticism comes from Alston and concerns the relevance of the Lowenheim-Skolem theorem to a discussion of the theories of natural science. The theorem's home is in discussion of the unin-terpreted formulae of symbolic languages. Such languages can be given an interpretation by specifying a domain of objects and hooking singular and general terms in the language to the objects in the domain. But the theories of natural science do not consist of uninterpreted formulae. We do not have to hook each singular and general term in them to objects. We do not assign references and extensions to theories by a purely extensional process. The terms used in our theories possess meaning. In virtue of their meaning, their use, they link up to objects in the world. As Alston notes, it is particularly galling for realists to be told that they need to assign references and extensions to the terms of a theory. Being realists, they will hold that what the extension of a general term is depends on the world as much as us. We give meaning to the term 'igneous rock' but it is up to the world what things, if any, are igneous rocks. We cannot assign an extension to this term. Alston argues, correctly, thus: we give meanings to the terms of a theory; thereby the theory becomes comprehensible and can be used to make definite statements about the world; whether the terms of the theory refer to anything and whether its claims are true, then depends on the world (1996: 146).

Innocent realism requires a very minimal set of commitments concerning the relation of language to the world. It postulates a world of things and properties. It states that people are part of that world.

Through thought and language, they can interact with that world and frame descriptions of it. Some of the descriptions are true and some of them are false. The terms of those descriptions must therefore be capable of picking out actual and possible things in the world. Realism does not require that this process be free of human judgement. The choice is not between the world dictating to us what our words refer to or of us assigning references to words in model theoretic fashion. We cannot thus save the truth of the claims we make by a complete freedom to assign a new reference to them. (For a full discussion and critique of Putnam's ideas on reference see Devitt 1997: Ch. 2.)

Positivism

It is perhaps with no great enthusiasm that a reader of this book encounters a discussion of the verification principle. Surely all those discussions belong to the history books. Alas, they do not. We will see in the next section that recent efforts have been made to use Rudolph Carnap's 'Empiricism, Semantics and Ontology' to clarify the debate about theistic realism. Further, and as shown in the final section of this chapter, contemporary debates on realism have to take account of Dummett's attempt to argue for anti-realism on the back of a revived verificationist account of meaning and truth.

The original Vienna Circle offered a verificationist theory of meaning and derived from that a verificationist criterion of the meaningful. The verificationist account of meaning held that the meaning of a statement was the method of its verification. The criterion laid down that no sentence was cognitively meaningful (that is, capable of making a true or false statement) unless it asserted something which could be verified. Numerous different versions of the criterion were produced, as positivist philosophers tried to make it fit their pre-given intuitions that the statements of natural science were cognitively meaningful but those of metaphysics were not (see Hempel 1952 for a survey of these different versions).

Upholders of classic verificationism took it that the method of verification for a genuine statement consists in the observational data that show it to be true or false. Statements that meet the terms of the criterion are entailed by observation statements or have observational consequences such that they can be confirmed or disconfirmed by the data of the senses. Necessary truths were allowed as the limiting case of cognitively meaningful statements, being regarded as having only formal, linguistic or conventional truth. It is clear that classical verificationism is the union of two philosophical stances. One links testability and meaning. It affirms that the meaning of a statement consists in the further statements which show it to be true or false. Or, at the least, it affirms that if a statement is not testable it has no meaning. The second component stance links testability and observation. The way to test genuine factual claims is by reference to the data of the senses. Verificationism thus unites a theory of meaning and of the meaningful to an empiricist theory of knowledge. These two elements are separable. It is conceivable that a philosopher might hold a testability theory or criterion of meaning – affirming that all meaningful claims about the world are decidable – while having a non-empiricist theory of knowledge. There are actual philosophers who have been empiricists while disavowing any link between meaning and testability. Thus Russell puts forward an empiricist theory of knowledge in *An Inquiry into Meaning and Truth* while explicitly rejecting any linkage of meaning and knowledge: 'truth and knowledge are different ... a proposition may be true although no method exists of discovering that it is so' (Russell 1962: 271).

Is the combination of an empiricist theory of knowledge and a testability theory of meaning neutral as between realism and anti-realism? Alston says it is (Alston 1996: 104–5). But that is because he defines realism in terms of a slimmed-down version of the correspondence theory of truth according to which it is true that *p* if and only if *p*. As he points out, there is no need for a verificationist to add further conditions for truth to such a minimalist correspondence theory. However, we have defined realism as a metaphysical doctrine. Innocent realism states that there is one real world which exists largely independently of us. We are late arrivals in this world and the majority of facts which make it up are neither ontologically nor epistemically dependent on us. Testability plus empiricism is a clear threat to this metaphysical outlook. Verificationism delimits the range of sentences which can state facts. Only those which are testable via the data of observation can be either true or false. Thus there are no facts which are not discoverable by human observation (verificationists differ over whether facts have to be discoverable in practice or merely in principle – see Hempel 1952: 166). This doctrine places limits around what is real and the limits make what is real dependent on *us*, specifically on the practical or theoretical limits to human observation. Such a conclusion is fundamentally at odds with the essence of innocent realism.

To avoid a fundamental clash with realism, verificationism will have to separate the notion of the observable from the notion of what is observable by us. Consider an example from Russell: 'there is a cosmos which has no spatio-temporal relation to the one in which we live' (Russell 1962: 262). A cosmos lacking any physical connection with ours would be by definition unobservable to us. Those who find Russell's supposition meaningful may nonetheless state that in principle observations could be made to confirm or disconfirm it if we hypothesise that a non-temporal, non-spatial God could do the observing. But this move will rapidly lead to the emasculation of the verifiability criterion. Progressive emasculation of the criterion is evident in the history of its formulations as more and more convincing examples of statements which were apparently cognitively meaningful but unverifiable were produced.

Another noted feature of the history of positivism is the progressive divorce of the verifiability criterion of the meaningful from the verificationist theory of what meaning consists in. 'The meaning of a statement is the method of its verification' has its home in an account of meaning which is a union of elements of traditional empiricism and developments in philosophical logic at the beginning of the twentieth century (see Quinton 1966 and Brown 1976). Traditional empiricism says that the building blocks of thought are ideas derived from sense experience. Applied to meaning, that gives us the contention that meaningful words are either names for sense data or definable in terms of such names. Wittgenstein offered a doctrine of the analysability of all meaningful sentences. If not an elementary proposition already, a sentence could be shown to be a truth-function of such propositions. Elementary propositions were concatenations of simple names in one-to-one correspondence with simple objects. Verificationists, leaving Wittgenstein behind, identified elementary propositions with reports of sense perception and took simple names to correspond to items in sense perception. Meaningful names had then to correspond to sensory items. Meaningful propositions were either direct statements about the observable or truth-functions of such statements. A basic statement's method of verification was its correspondence to some actual or possible perceptible state of affairs. A non-basic statement's method of verification was given by its analysis into a truth-function of basic statements. Either way, we have a radically foundationalist account of meaning and truth. Both flow up from the confrontation of subject and experience. Radical foundationalism of this kind is contrary to innocent realism. As noted above, radical foundationalism closes the gap between human subjects and reality by making the range of possible facts dependent upon human powers and capacities. A mark of this closure is that it rejects the possibility of scepticism. Sceptical hypotheses of the kind entertained by Russell become meaningless.

The evolution of the verifiability criterion shows its gradual separation from the theory of meaning out of which it was born (see Brown 1976: 142–4). The theory of meaning soon met problems when it was shown that statements of unrestricted generality in science could not be a truth-function of statements about particulars. We might verify claims of the form 'All Fs are Gs' by looking to enumerate instances of form 'This F is G', but such claims go beyond any, necessarily finite, enumeration we can conduct. Not only does this show that unrestricted generalisations fall foul of strong versions of the verifiability criterion of meaning, it demonstrates that their meaning outreaches their method of verification. Moreover, as more holistic ideas about justification gained prominence in the theory of knowledge and the philosophy of science developed, it became clear that the notion that a statement has a single method of verification is a fiction. As theory and speculation develop, new ways are found of arguing for and against hypotheses, but they do not thereby change their meaning. We merely find new ways of confirming or disconfirming the same facts. Furthermore, the past and present of human theorising is replete with speculations which are made in advance of there being a method for verifying them. Atomic hypotheses about the structure of material things were produced in Greek and Hellenistic thought. Only with much later developments did the means arrive for testing the extent to which they were true. The crucial notion in verificationist theories of meaning that knowledge and sense flows upward from its secure anchorage in the confrontation of basic statements with sensory reality met with problems. Verificationists noted the problems in producing basic statements which were pure descriptions of sense data. Our vocabulary for describing the content of sense perception is dependent on that for describing material objects. In fact, so-called basic statements in ordinary life are not verified or falsified by pure phenomenological reports. The evidential relations that we grasp in ordinary life and in science are between statements about material things and substances. Such statements are not conclusively verifiable by observation. Even ones employing humble concepts have a surplus of meaning giving them ramifications beyond observable properties. (Cf. 'Here is a dog': something may look and sound just like a dog but that does not entail that it is.) It came to be generally accepted that quite humble statements about observable objects are justifiable only in a holistic way. They are verifiable only against the background of standing assumptions and can be thrown into doubt by changes in surrounding beliefs. Justification flows down as well as up. These points about the holistic character of verification were reinforced by the realisation that many concepts used to describe the observable are theoretically laden and that means of observation themselves depend on theory. Thus when a biologist 'sees' a virus by means of an electron microscope, the observation confirms the presence of the virus only if the theory in which the concept of virus is embedded is sound and only if the theories behind the use and construction of electron microscopes are sound.

All the above shows that the idea that meaning and knowledge are derived from basic statements which in turn derive their truth and meaning from confrontation with a verifying state of affairs is a fiction. It is false to suppose that there is, generally, a verifying condition, a method of verification, for each of our statements. It is false to suppose that meaning flows up from statements and words which label what we can observe. The collapse of verificationist theories of meaning brings with it the isolation of verifiability criteria of meaning from that which would give them their justification. Verifiability criteria then lack a rationale (as Brown notes: 1976: 143). When shorn of their connection with radical foundationalist/empiricist accounts of meaning and knowledge, it is not at all clear that verifiability criteria of meaning provide any threat to theistic realism. Consider as an example A.J. Ayer's version of the criterion. In *Language, Truth and Logic* it is stated thus:

> ... it is the mark of a genuine proposition, not that it should be equivalent to an experiential proposition or any finite number of experiential propositions, but simply that some experiential propositions can be deduced from it in conjunction with certain other premises without being deducible from those premises alone. [Ayer 1971: 52]

The criterion thus stated has lost all pretence to be based on a theory whereby the meaning of non-basic statements is a function of its relation to reports of experience. It bids the theist merely to point to the possibility that the claim that there is a God is relevant to observational data. Manifold problems have been found in Ayer's formulation of the verifiability criterion (see Hempel 1952: 171–2). Setting those aside, there is the further difficulty that there is no lack of possible data to which the hypothesis of God's existence is relevant. The problem with verifying the theistic claim is that there is too much. The observation of order in the world is certainly evidence for the existence of God, traditionally conceived, whilst the observation of undeserved suffering is evidence against. There is a host of other facts about the world as we know it relevant to the issue. The problem lies in the lack of *decisive* evidence one way or the other.

When it comes to the critique of theological language, Ayer displays a noted tendency to depart from his weak version of the verifiability criterion in favour of a strong version that is dependent on the theory that the meaning of a statement is the method of its verification. He notes that order in the cosmos may be taken as strong evidence for the existence of God, but states that 'if the sentence "God exists" entails no more than that certain types of phenomena occur in certain sequences, then to assert the existence of God will be simply equivalent to asserting that there is regularity in nature' (Ayer 1971: 152). Of course, the theist will not say that the fact of order is the only thing 'God exists' entails. But Ayer moves on from this misrepresentation of his opponent to allow the theist to make the following very sensible suggestion: talk about God is talk about a transcendent entity which can be known through its empirical manifestations but cannot be defined in terms of such manifestations (1971: 152). This sensible suggestion is immediately knocked on the head with dogma:

But in that case the term 'god' is a metaphysical term. And if 'god' is a metaphysical term, then it cannot be even probable that a god exists. For to say that 'God exists' is to make a metaphysical utterance which cannot be either true or false. And by the same criterion, no sentence which purports to describe the nature of a transcendent god can possess any literal significance. [1971: 152]

Ayer's critique depends on equivocation of mind-numbing proportions. Utterances are metaphysical by Ayer's weak version of the verifiability criterion if they purport to be factual but have no observational consequences. On this story, no stigma attaches to a theory about matters of fact which postulates entities which are not observable but which can be known through their empirical manifestations. Thus the theist who is prepared to go along with the verifiability criterion merely has to show that some things could count as empirical manifestations of the divine. Yet Ayer will not play the game according to the rules he has laid down: postulation of a God who manifests in the spatio-temporal realm but exists in some transcendent space is metaphysical (bad, meaningless) because the being of that God transcends its observational manifestations. By this ruling, any theoretical postulate is metaphysical (bad, meaningless) if it is not reducible to its empirical manifestations. That kind of critique is only acceptable if we espouse what Ayer has admitted we cannot espouse, namely the thought that it is the mark of a genuine proposition that it should be equivalent to an experiential proposition or a finite number of experiential propositions. Only if the meaning of a statement is the method of its verification, does it follow from the fact that a proposition is accepted on the basis of empirical observation that its meaning is reducible to talk about observable things.

My point that verificationism is a toothless tiger unless it is espoused in the cruder forms which its proponents long since rejected can be added to the list of defences of theistic language against positivist attacks (see Swinburne 1977: 21–9; Heimbeck 1969: *passim*; Plantinga 1969, 156–69). Verificationism should be a dead duck in debates about theological realism. Some recent writers have tried to persuade us that Rudolph Carnap's 'Empiricism, Semantics and Ontology' is the source of a worthwhile case against theological realism. It is to that attempt that I now turn.

Frameworks

It was the aim of the logical positivists to dissolve many of the traditional problems of philosophy on the ground that they were metaphysical. Such problems are not solvable by recourse to empirical reasoning. If they were, they could be handed over to natural science. They cannot be resolved by demonstrative means. Answers to them cannot be proved or disproved as theorems in mathematics can be proved or disproved. So the dispute, for example, between realists and nominalists over the reality of qualities is to be regarded as a pseudo-problem. The protagonists in the dispute are confused in the same way Ayer alleges participants in the debate over the reality of God are confused. Ayer asserts that since it makes no sense to assert that there is a God, it makes no sense to deny that there is a God or doubt that there is a God (Ayer 1971: 153).

It is evident that the philosophical argument between global realism and global anti-realism is liable to be treated in the same way. Global realism in the form of innocent realism is a metaphysical thesis opposed by some equally metaphysical thesis, such as the thesis that what we call 'the world' is ontologically dependent on human representations. The dispute does not appear resolvable by demonstrative proofs. It is not settleable by observation or by inductive or deductive inferences from observation. It will then be styled a pseudo-question.

Carnap's 'Empiricism, Semantics and Ontology' captures the positivist portrayal of traditional metaphysical questions about what really exists as pseudo-questions. Central to his argument is the claim that such existential questions cannot be resolved by collecting empirical data or by deduction from accepted axioms and are as a result purely pragmatic, concerned merely with the practical advantages or disadvantages of the adoption of terminologies. Such a view threatens to yield the conclusion that global, innocent realism is not the truth about our world. Further, the question over whether there really is a *theos* will become merely the question of whether it is useful to employ a theistic vocabulary or not.

The building blocks Carnap uses to reach the conclusion that traditional philosophical debates about what is real are in truth pragmatic disputes misunderstood appear at first glance to be simple. They are the notions of a framework and of internal and external questions we can ask about frameworks. A framework is an interrelated set of expressions governed by a set of rules (Carnap 1952: 218). In this sense, we can speak of the mathematical framework, meaning a vocabulary for talking about numbers and a set of rules for using the vocabulary. Once we have a framework we can ask existence questions. They are either internal or external to the framework. I can ask the internal question 'Is there a prime number between 3 and 7?', in which case my answer is to be given by consulting the rules which govern the use of mathematical expressions. These will allow me to produce a proof that there is indeed such a number. I can also ask an external question about the existence of 'entities' apparently referred to by the expressions in the framework. As an internal question, 'Does

the number 5 exist?' has a trivial answer, once we get over its oddity:
yes, there is prime number between 3 and 7. As an external question, it
means 'Are there really numbers at all?' And that external question has
no true/false answer, because there is no framework in which we can
answer it. It is the pragmatic question of whether it is useful to use the
number framework. It is not a theoretical question at all (1952: 213). It
can only be resolved by asking us to weigh the gains for the efficiency,
simplicity and fruitfulness of our thinking if we adopt the framework
(1952: 211).

For Carnap, only internal existential questions have true/false
answers, but not all such internal questions are trivial. In the case of
the number framework, the internal questions as to which numbers exist
are settled by the simple laying out of the deductive consequences of the
vocabulary and rules of the framework. By contrast consider what
Carnap styles 'the thing language' (1952: 211). We introduce the
material object framework, a vocabulary and rules for talking about
spatio-temporal things. Now we can ask 'Did King Arthur really exist?',
'Is there a white piece of paper on my desk?'. The 'thing language'
framework specifies that such questions cannot be settled trivially, in
contrast to the general question 'Are there material things?' which is
answered just in choosing to use 'the thing language'. Specific questions
in this framework are to be settled by observation because the
framework defines a particular notion of what it is to exist in it:

> To recognise something as a real thing or event [in 'the thing language']
> means to succeed in incorporating it into the framework of things at a
> particular space-time position so that it fits together with the other things
> recognised as real, according to the rules of the framework. [1952: 210]

So, in contrast to other frameworks, internal questions in this one
cannot be settled by simply looking at linguistic rules and their
consequences. Albeit this framework is different in this respect, it is true
of it, as of all frameworks, that acceptance of the framework as a whole
does not wait upon the resolution of theoretical questions. Someone
could decide not to use 'the thing language' but to use a phenomenalist
framework instead. They would not be wrong, theoretically speaking –
though we may think they were foregoing pragmatic advantages that
only came with the material thing framework (see 1952: 211).

Carnap's contentions have immediate application to the debate
between innocent realists and those who think reality is constructed out
of human representations. There is no theoretical question here. One
party thinks that it is pragmatically justified to indulge in talk of
undiscoverable facts. Innocent realists, for example, wish to speak of the
past as if it had a definite shape beyond our ability to discern what
actually happened in it. The other party prefers different ways of

speaking. The two sides to the dispute have different concepts of an object and an event (cf. Luntley 1988: 143–5). But the respective sets of concepts cannot be thought of as corresponding to how things really are. Only when we have set up a framework does talk of how things are make sense. The upshot of Carnap's case is to dissolve the traditional metaphysical disputes over what is real. Questions in metaphysics as to what is real are not theoretical questions (Carnap 1952: 211) and they have no cognitive content (1952: 213).

The Carnapian proposal has recently been applied to the dispute between theistic realists and anti-realists by Messrs Le Poidevin and Scott (Le Poidevin 1995, 1996; Scott 2000). This is how Le Poidevin applies it (1995: 488–9). To understand the question 'Is God real?', we introduce the idea of the theistic framework. This lays down the meaning of 'God' and associated expressions such as 'God is powerful'. Within the framework, methods are set out for deciding the truth of propositions about God, by, for example, specifying certain texts as containing authoritative accounts of God's doings. Some questions about God will then be analytic. That God is good will be settled by the meaning rules introduced when the framework was set up. Others will be contingent. To decide whether God spoke to Moses from a burning bush we will need to check whether this claim is vouched for in our authoritative texts. If we then ask the question 'Does God exist?', it will have two readings. As an internal question, it will have the trivial answer 'Yes', following analytically from fundamental propositions in the framework. As an external question, it has no true/false answer. For no one has laid down how it is to be answered independently of any framework in which the question can be raised. We can seek pragmatic reasons for adopting or rejecting the theistic (or Christian or Islamic) framework by enquiring as to whether the resultant form of life is more fulfilling than its alternatives. But this decision, however made, carries no metaphysical implications. It is the decision to adopt or to reject a linguistic framework.

As urged by Scott, the merit of Carnap's approach to existence questions is that it lays down the requirements for such questions to have a content. Carnap is credited with showing that long-standing disputes in metaphysics about what is real are vacuous (Scott 2000: 458). External existence questions, in contrast to internal ones, lack 'the required context of syntactic discipline and standards of correct use that *any* statement requires to be contentful' (2000: 465).

A just response to Carnap's contentions should not be so accommodating. I think we should enquire as to whether there is the slightest reason to take Carnap's dissolution of existence questions seriously. We should be 100 per cent suspicious of the introduction of the terminology of 'frameworks'. How can Carnap's decision to introduce this terminology change anything? It cannot be the case that the mere production of the terminology establishes the truth of the claim that all our thinking and discourse is done in one framework or another. Carnap's argument depends on the truth of the claim that frameworks are exclusive: a question of existence belongs to one framework but not to another. If a question appears to belong to two, then it must be ambiguous. Only thus do we get the result that an existential question is either internal or external, either settled by the criteria laid down by its relevant framework or raising the purely pragmatic matter of which linguistic framework to adopt. (Thus Scott is wrong to say that Carnap does not require frameworks to be objective, identifiable segments of language: Scott 2000: 471 n.11.) The framework theory of language must face all the (insoluble) problems besetting Runzo's attempt to divide up our thought between so many conceptual schema. We are looking at another example of that recurring philosophical vice of inventing a piece of terminology and concluding thereby that one has discovered a new species of object in the world.

The artificiality of talk about a theistic framework with its rules for deciding what are and are not facts about God is revealed in many ways. Is it Christian or Jewish? If Christian, is it evangelical/conservative or liberal? Such questions are germane because these different forms of theistic belief will have different ontologies, employ different axioms with reference to the divine and recognise different authoritative sources for settling questions about the being and nature of God. We should ask for the persuasive argument which shows that the differences between such forms of theism are but pragmatic. Further, we must remind ourselves that theistic talk is linked to other kinds of talk. Many authors, past and present, have thought that some facts revealed by science are best explained by theistic beliefs. Scientific theories, such as Darwinian evolution, have been held to undermine component beliefs of forms of theism. The introduction of the framework terminology implies that such thoughts about the links between religion and science are delusive. But if they are, we need arguments to show this. Terminological tricks will not do the job.

What is perhaps at the forefront of Carnap's thinking about frameworks is the introduction of new theories into scientific discourse. Such theories will have their own distinctive vocabularies and therefore will contain explicit or implicit definitions for a range of new terms. They may lay down methods for measuring and testing the quanta introduced by the new terminology. They look like Carnap's frameworks. Most importantly, Carnap appears to hold to the positivist mantra that there are no non-pragmatic ways of deciding between at least large-scale scientific theories. Laudan (1996: 18–19) points out the desire among Logical Positivists to find an algorithm for theory choice. Disappointed of that, they frequently opted for the alternative of denying that there could be a rational choice among theories. They saw only two options. Theoretical questions could be settled, on the one hand, by demonstrative or inductive means, or, on the other, they could be left to a choice guided by pragmatic considerations alone.

That Carnap thinks in terms of the restricted notion of rational theory choice outlined above is evident from the text of 'Empiricism, Semantics and Ontology'. The decision to accept 'the reality of the thing world' is not a cognitive question. The external question about the thing-framework is not a theoretical one. This is because it is not settleable by observation/induction or by demonstration. Factors like efficiency, fruitfulness and simplicity can guide theory choice but they are pragmatic and not indicative of truth (Carnap 1952: 211). Such factors relate to what Carnap styles the 'efficiency' of the thing language and are not confirming evidence for the reality of 'the thing world' (1952: 212). Now there is no reason to accept this account of the limits of reason and of truth-indicative factors and therefore no reason to accept Carnap's claim that theory choice is a pragmatic affair. (For justification of my claim see Laudan 1996, Mitchell 1973 and Wisdom 1953 and 1963.) What we have in truth in 'Empiricism, Semantics and Ontology' is an argument driven throughout by the crudest verificationism. The 'framework' terminology and the distinction between internal and external questions reflect this crude verificationism. It is plausible only to the extent that the verificationism is plausible.

That Carnap is motivated by verificationism is indicated in his opening theme: the problem which empiricists have with talk about abstract entities. It is hardly possible to avoid terms (such as words for numbers, properties, propositions and the like) which refer to such abstract entities, yet empiricism will hardly want to admit abstract objects into its ontology (1952: 208). By transforming, for example, the question of whether there are numbers into an innocuous because internal question or an innocuous because purely pragmatic question, Carnap reassures the empiricist that using number terms does not entail making any ontological commitments. In the very act of thus transforming the question 'Are numbers real?', Carnap makes it plain that he is privileging the theory of knowledge and the (implicit) ontology of empiricism. The metaphysical question about the reality of numbers is senseless because

> ... philosophers have so far not given a formulation of their question in terms of the common scientific language. Therefore our judgement must be that they have not succeeded in giving to the external question and the possible answers any cognitive content. [1952: 213]

Carnap hereby privileges language used to describe empirically discoverable entities and seems to have no qualms about their real existence. On almost every page of Carnap's paper we find tacit affirmations of the thesis that statements which are not testable are devoid of cognitive content. The preferred way to test statements is by matching them with observations. In a passage commenting on the empty character of the debate between nominalists and Platonists over the reality of numbers, Carnap cements his point by saying that 'I cannot think of any possible evidence that would be regarded as relevant by both philosophers, and therefore, if actually found, would decide the controversy or at least make one of the opposite theses more probable than the other' (1952: 225). He emphasises that the non-cognitive character of the external questions which he characterises as metaphysical pseudo-questions has been diagnosed by the Vienna Circle (1952: 220).

Failure to see that Carnap's argument relies on a verificationism about meaning bedevils Scott's attempt to restate it. Scott appears to think that Carnap provides a killer dilemma for any one wishing to pursue a question such as 'Does God exist?' as a genuine metaphysical question. The question is asked either before or after setting up the theistic framework. If it is asked outside of a framework, we must ask what the question consists in. Without agreed criteria for settling it, the question lacks a content. But if we specify what the question consists in by laying down the criteria, we reformulate the question by identifying or constructing a framework in which it could be addressed. Having done that, we have of course reduced the question to an internal one. In which event it is no longer the big external question we thought it was (see Scott 2000: 459 and 466). This argument ('Carnap's challenge') gets whatever plausibility it has by dint of depending on a crude form of verificationism. It relies on a confusion between rules for the use of a term and rules specifying how to collect evidence for the existence or non-existence of that to which the term might refer. Scott tells us that, in the absence of a surrounding framework, we lack 'the required context of syntactic discipline and standards of correct use that *any* statement requires to be contentful' (2000: 465). But if all that is saying is that, to understand an expression or statement, we need syntactic and semantic rules governing its use, it is trivial. Meaningful expressions have rules, syntactic and semantic, for their use. It does not follow that any meaningful sentence has a method of verification. If a framework contains nothing more than the syntactic and semantic rules for using expressions and sentences, then no one will dispute that all meaningful existential propositions must belong to frameworks. It just does not follow, however, that all meaningful existential propositions must have a method of verifying them. Scott has simply equated rules for use with verification.

Let us return to the hoary example 'There are atoms'. When this proposition was affirmed by Hellenistic thinkers they had, let us assume, no method of verifying it. It does not follow that there were no rules governing its use. A further assumption for the sake of argument: they understood by the Greek equivalent of 'atom' the smallest unit of matter. To assert that there were atoms was thus to assert that the process of physical analysis could not proceed *ad infinitum*. There are some physical entities which are not compounds of yet smaller entities. Now the question 'Are there atoms?' has a clear sense. At the least it means 'Can the process of physical analysis, decomposition, go on *ad infinitum*?' That sense is not taken away if parties disputing the question disagree how to settle it or if they have no clear idea as to how it should be settled at all. There are *criteria* for the use of the expression 'atom', but not as yet any idea how to collect *evidence* for the existence or non-existence of atoms (see Heimbeck 1969: 48ff.).

Once we diagnose the verificationism implicit in 'Carnap's challenge', as it is styled by Scott, it looks feeble. The question 'Is God real?' is not to be declared meaningless because we have not yet agreed a way of settling it. It may be a real but as yet undecidable question. It is a meaningful question if there are ways of explaining what the term 'God' means, if there are things we can do which count as teaching someone what it means, correcting them if they misuse the term, and so on. Reflection on the term 'God' reveals, of course, that there are many notions of deity. The pursuit of the answer to the question of the reality of God can thus take various forms. One reason why there are disputes within philosophy as to how to settle the question of the reality of the divine lies in these disagreements as to what is the appropriate conception of deity to use. So the concept of God will not come with anything as hard and fast as a Carnapian framework. This does not mean that Carnap has shown some great difficulty in establishing a sense to the dispute between religious realism and religious anti-realism (as Scott alleges: 2000: 467). The sense we give to the dispute will flow from our grasp of the particular conception of deity in question. To the extent that we understand Whitehead's concept of the divine, the question 'Does the Process God exist?' has a sense, even in the absence of a recipe for settling the question. The production of the recipe may involve the consideration and resolution of matters metaphysical and theoretical. But provided Whitehead's notion of God is comprehensible, it will itself give us an indication of what are the relevant metaphysical and theoretical issues we need to pursue (see the discussion of 'atom' above). Moreover, as noted in Chapter 1, it is possible to discern a generic concept of deity behind many different conceptions of God: the postulation of a transcendent source of moral order. Or as Aquinas puts it, whatever God is, God is that which exercises a wise providence over all things (Aquinas 1964: 1a, 13, 8). Such a root notion gives us a sense that some things are relevant to the question of the reality of God, notably the distribution of good and evil in the world, the nature of our moral awareness, and much else besides.

Thinking that questions about what is real must fall in one framework or another merely has the effect of distorting our reflection on what may be profoundly difficult questions. Scott notes that some may regard issues about what is responsible for the fine tuning of the universe and the consequent production of life in it as relevant to the question of whether God is real (Scott 2000: 467). This is not surprising given the root connection between the concept of deity and the notion of a providential order in things. Evidence yielded by natural science thus becomes relevant to the question of God's reality. But Scott maintains that making these connections is tantamount to analysing the question of God's reality as 'Is God's existence a probable hypothesis?' (2000: 466) and replacing the question of God's reality with that of whether maintaining God's existence is a respectable scientific claim (2000: 467). The equation of meaning with method of verification is in evidence once more. It is perfectly possible that evidence and reflections arising from natural science are relevant to the question of God's reality without that question becoming a scientific question (without locating the question in 'the scientific framework'). The question of whether God is real is a highly ramified one. Scientific evidence may be relevant to it, but so are moral reflections. It has nothing which is its one and only method of verification. Strait-jacketed thinking is going to get us nowhere in reflecting on the question.

I have suggested that Carnap's attempt to deflate all philosophical questions about what is real and to espouse a form of neutralism with respect to philosophical theories about the real fails. It does so because, amongst other things, it privileges an empiricist account of knowledge and a corresponding ontology in which observable realities are foundational for all else. Support for this view is provided by Le Poidevin's point that Carnap's framework theory cannot be neutral as to the existence of *me*, the being who uses the frameworks (Le Poidevin 1995: 497–8; 1996: 132–3). The notion of a framework requires the notion of a linguistic subject who produces and employs it. The account we give of the nature of that subject will then establish a privileged part of our ontology. If we say that the subjects who use frameworks are beings who exist in space and time – as Le Poidevin assumes we must – then we cannot be neutral or deflationist about the existence of spatio-temporal objects. A fundamental criterion of what is real is bound then to be whether something is related to us, the users and producers of frameworks.

Le Poidevin's argument against Carnap is sound. He is surely right to contend that the only candidate for the entities behind frameworks is us – beings enduring in time and located in space. His point will be built upon in later discussions of anti-realism in this study. It yields *a* criterion for what is real: what is related to the spatio-temporal framework we inhabit. So far, so good. We need to take issue, however, with a consequence that Le Poidevin draws from these unexceptionable points: talk about a God who transcends the spatio-temporal cannot be talk about something real. This swift dismissal of theological realism will not work. Here is how Le Poidevin effects it:

> If the fundamental concept of existence is that of spatio-temporal location, then when we ask 'Does God exist?' we mean 'Can we locate God in our spatio-temporal framework?' But if the theistic framework is one which emphasises God's otherness, his being utterly different from any familiar object, and in particular his being outside space and time, the answer to this question must be 'no'. [Le Poidevin 1995: 498]

An error underlies the first premise of the argument quoted from Le Poidevin. He assumes that the fact of relatedness to us in our spatio-temporal framework is an important criterion of the real entails that we can 'define "real" in terms of being located in the spatio-temporal framework' (1995: 497). This is that old devil verificationism at work again. Le Poidevin here seems to assume (as does Scott) that we are in search of a definition of 'exists' or 'real'. A criterion for deciding what is real provides us with the meaning of 'real' and 'exists'. Carnap is perhaps victim of the same confusion. But the question of whether God exists or is real is just the question of whether there is a God, of whether 'This is God' is true of something. The puzzle is not over the meaning of 'There is' in 'There is a God' but of what it means to talk of God and how such talk can be warranted. We do not need a definition of 'real'.

We cannot answer the question of God's reality by simply noting that if God is non-spatial and timeless then God is not real. It remains to be argued that, if this is the conception of deity we are employing, a non-spatial, non-temporal God could not be related to us, for example, by being the cause of the reality we inhabit. There may be reasons for thinking that the spatio-temporal word depends on a non-spatio-temporal reality for its existence (consider here the cosmological argument in its various forms). If such reasons are judged persuasive, then a fundamental criterion for judging what is real has been met. What Le Poidevin presents us with is a simple fiat, which dismisses the metaphysical question 'Can there be non-spatial, non-temporal realities?' and rules *a priori* that no such things are conceivable and no reasons for postulating them could arise. What he needs, but does not provide us with, is an argument for the contention that talk of causal relationships between timeless reality and temporal reality make no sense.

My last point does indeed raise a problem. There is a *prima facie* difficulty in conceiving of a real, causal relation between a non-temporal God and our world. A sceptic about the existence of this kind of deity may well wonder what content we can give to the notion of a causal agent which is not in time, given that our knowledge of what it is for something to be a cause is bound up with our awareness of causes as productive and active agents in a physical world. What sense can we give to 'depends' in an assertion that physical reality depends upon a non-spatial, non-temporal ground? It remains true, however, that Le Poidevin is not right to smuggle in an answer to these questions by dint of defining 'exists' in terms of what occupies a position in space and time.

There is a genuine worry which moves those such as Michael Scott who think that 'Empiricism, Semantics and Ontology' has something important to say about philosophical debates between realists and anti-realists. At least some of these debates seem empty. The notion of a framework and the allied notions of internal and external existence questions is one way of explaining this perceived emptiness in philosophical discussions about what is real. Scott quotes some remarks from Wittgenstein's *Zettel* to good effect (Scott 2000: 458). Wittgenstein makes the point that philosophical idealists and realists appear to be engaged in a substantive debate when the one says that material things do not exist outside the mind and the other says that they do. Yet if these philosophers educated their children in their views, we would find no difference in how these children talked or behaved. Ask the idealist child to pass the chair and he or she will respond just as the realist child (Wittgenstein 1981: §§413–14). We might add that something very similar will be true of children brought up to be mathematical Platonists or mathematical nominalists: they will count, add and multiply in just the same ways. Reflection on the apparent emptiness of such disputes may well lead us in the manner of Carnap to employ 'metaphysical' as a term of abuse and to speak of pseudo-questions.

Let us admit for the sake of argument that there is a problem about taking seriously all philosophical debates about what is real. It does not follow that Carnap's diagnosis of the problem is accurate or that his cure is better than the disease. The two examples given above are different. In the debate between idealists and realists over material things, we have a concept of material substance which is tolerably clear. The tree in my garden is a material thing, but a quality is not. The problem comes with the fact that the idealist's denial of the existence of material things is not the denial of the existence of trees. What comes with the denial is a revised form of philosophical vocabulary but no difference in behaviour or expectations. That inclines us to say the dispute is merely verbal. But that could be too hasty. Perhaps metaphysical disagreements of this sort may be real but theoretical, rather than practical. We would have to explore what other things in our theorising with which the alleged disagreement was connected. In the case of the Platonist-versus-nominalist dispute, the problem appears to lie with the fact that we speak about numbers but that our notion of a number is unclear. It inhabits a vague territory on the border of talk about substantial entities and talk about properties, concepts or relations. Numbers, if real, would be causally inert. They then look like candidates for unreality, but we can say such things as 'There is a number which divides into six three times, viz. two'.

Much more could be said about the puzzling character of metaphysical disputes of the kind considered. But let us note that they are *prima facie* disanalogous to disputes about the reality of God. It makes perfect sense (except perhaps to those in the grip of certain views in the philosophy of religion!) to say: 'I have no use for talk about God because I have become convinced that there is no God.' Becoming convinced that there is no God seems to involve perfectly intelligible things: giving up belief that there is a providential creator, realising that this world and this life is all there is, having no hope that good will triumph over evil in the long run. It makes sense to imagine someone who has no use for religious language. But consider: (a) 'I have become convinced that there are no material things, therefore I have given up talk about tables and trees' and (b) 'I have become convinced that there are no numbers, therefore I have given up talk about primes, evens, fractions and the like'. It is not clear what corresponds to the consequents of (a) and (b). Does the one who asserts (a) really no longer talk about tables? How could such a person survive and communicate? Do those who assert (b) really stop counting, adding, dividing and multiplying? The antecedents in both cases are opaque, especially that in (b). And whereas there is an intelligible link between becoming convinced that God is a fiction and giving up talk about God, there is no such link between deciding that numbers are fictions and giving up counting. Taking part in arithmetical operations does not seem to be connected with holding a theory about the reality of numbers. Taking part in religious talk and life does appear to be connected with holding a view about the reality of God.

Dummett's Anti-Realism

Students of contemporary philosophy of language will know that the root ideas of Logical Positivism are not dead. Some of them at least survive in the writings of Michael Dummett and his followers. These writings are held to provide a powerful case against realism. They are held to demonstrate fundamental problems in the key claim of innocent realism that truth-bearers and truth-makers are distinct. Innocent realism holds that most of the propositions we utter and the beliefs we hold are true or false of a reality which is in no way ontologically dependent on us. In particular, the reality they are true of is not constituted by or dependent on our representations of it. The independence of truth-bearers (beliefs, propositions) from truth-makers (facts, states of affairs) is violated by the verificationist claim that meaning is constituted by method of verification, or depends on a truth-bearer being testable. Such verificationist claims make possible facts, states of affairs, dependent on the state of human knowledge, on our ability to verify claims. Dummett's anti-realism asserts this dependence, and destroys the independence in anti-realism, by affirming that the meaning of any proposition is determined by the conditions under which it can be justifiably asserted. The limits of the world are then linked to the limits of human cognitive activity.

It is impossible in the confines of this study fully to expound and explore Dummett's arguments for anti-realism. Exposition of Dummett is widely acknowledged to be difficult. His views shift and change from publication to publication. In early writings (for example, Dummett 1978: xxxvii), he affirms that the meaning of a statement is given by, and is dependent on, our recognition of conditions which conclusively establish that it is true. In later writings he has come to see that, apart from *a priori* claims, propositions about the world are not conclusively verifiable and has therefore settled for a weaker notion of verification (Dummett 1991: 317). Moreover, Dummett has gone on to state that he was never putting forward a hard-and-fast theory about meaning, truth and reality to be accepted or rejected. His anti-realism is but a 'research programme' (Dummett 1993: 463–4). I believe there is a full refutation of Dummett's anti-realism in the literature (see, for example: Alston 1996; Appiah 1986; Baker and Hacker 1984; Devitt 1997; Horwich 1998a and 1998b; Kirk 1999). This refutation establishes that there is nothing in the Dummettian 'research programme' which should make innocent realists lose their confidence in the fundamental distinction between truth-makers and truth-bearers. For the sake of defending the innocent realism outlined in this book, all that needs to be done is to document the main points of departure between it and Dummettian anti-realism. Dummett's views are in fact a species of idealism. We noted in Chapter 2 that his general metaphysical picture is of a reality which is partly constituted by the human act of investigating it. The world we live in is, he states, partly indeterminate – like a novel with gaps. Its indeterminacy is related to facts about *us*: 'If our statements and our thoughts are not all determinately either true or false, then reality is indeterminate' (Dummett 1991: 318).

The first point of departure concerns Dummett's methodology. He takes it that the traditional disputes between realists and idealists are to be tackled by explorations in the theory of meaning. Behind the different metaphysical 'pictures' in these philosophical disputes lie different meaning-theories (1991: 339). Dummett lumps together many disputes in traditional metaphysics that can be presented in terms of a choice between realism and anti-realism. They include debates over the reality of the past, the status of mental contents and the nature of physical objects. All are presented as debates over the theory of meaning to be supplied for the relevant part of our language. If we transpose the disputes into 'a meaning-theoretical key', then these age-old metaphysical conundrums will dissolve (1991: 14–15). Innocent realists will dispute this way of representing the matter. There is no reason why they should see an underlying similarity between, say, disputes about the status of the mental events and those about the reality of the physical world. They will suspect that Dummett's initial move is question-begging. To think that disputes about what is real can be settled by pursuing a theory of how human linguistic representations work is already to be inclined to make the real dependent on human representations.

Another bone of contention now emerges. Dummett persistently represents the realist as committed to one particular theory of meaning (or meaning-theory, in later writings; see Dummett 1991: 22 for the difference). That theory explains the meaning of an (assertoric) utterance as given by its truth-conditions. A speaker's understanding of an utterance consists in the grasp of its truth-conditions. A speaker can grasp what the truth-conditions of an utterance are even when he or she lacks any means of telling whether they obtain or not (cf. Dummett 1978: 146). A theory of meaning is supposed to represent in explicit form the tacit knowledge a speaker must have in order to understand and use his or her natural language. Now it should be clear that innocent realists need have no theory of meaning and no commitment to a truth-conditions theory of meaning in order to assert the main theses of innocent realism. Innocent realists do need to be able to claim that we can make hypotheses about the one real world which transcend our ability to verify them. That claim flows from the general realist picture of the world being such that it contains many objects, events and states of affairs that have existed beyond human awareness and knowledge. But only the most primitive ideas about meaning are needed to maintain the claim, not a full-blown theory of meaning and not a commitment to the rigmarole that constitutes 'truth-conditional semantics'.

The realist can properly reject as misguided the attempt by recent philosophers of language and linguisticians to produce theories of meaning. There is no need to produce a theoretical representation of what users know tacitly when they understand English or some other natural language. This is because we can conceive of understanding English to consist in a complex range of abilities (verbal, behavioural, mental, social): a complex case of *knowing how* not *knowing that* (cf. Baker and Hacker 1984: 325 and Devitt 1997: 272–5). Coming to understand English is not coming into the tacit possession of a theory. Coming to acquire language in infancy cannot be coming to acquire any kind of theory, for the theory would have to be in a language and so its possession would already presuppose linguistic ability.

Dummet has an argument for his link between linguistic understanding and theory. Linguistic competence cannot consist merely in mastery of a practical ability, like knowing how to ride a bicycle or to swim. It makes sense to respond to the question 'Can you swim?' with 'I don't know, I've never tried'. But a similar response to the question 'Can you speak Spanish?' would make no sense (Dummett 1991: 94; cf. Dummett 1993: 94–5). I might ask you to have a go at riding a bike, though you have never tried before. But I could not tell you to have a go at speaking Spanish if you have no knowledge of Spanish. Dummett's conclusion: there must be something which constitutes knowing what it is to speak a language which is other than merely having a practical ability.

Those who find it easy to resist the temptation to produce theories of meaning in the Dummett style can cheerfully accept the concluding sentence of the above paragraph. There is something which knowing Spanish involves which is more than a mere practical skill. That something consists in knowing some Spanish vocabulary and knowing some Spanish grammar. This knowledge can be represented theoretically (in dictionaries, traditional grammars and teaching manuals for speaking the language). It is the fact that natural languages have vocabularies and grammatical forms that enables speakers to understand an indefinite range of sentences in them. This same fact enables me to understand sentences which I could never in principle verify. The sentence 'Where Byrne's house stands a sabre-tooth tiger once ate a mammoth' is now unverifiable. But it uses English vocabulary according to established English grammar and thus makes perfect sense. There is no greater mystery to these matters than this (cf. Horwich: 1998a, 155ff.; Swinburne 1977: 28). That I need to be acquainted with some Spanish vocabulary and grammar in order to speak Spanish explains why I cannot be sensibly asked to have a go at speaking Spanish.

Philosophers who produce theories of meaning want to say something profound in answer to the question 'What do English speakers know when they know English?' The trivial answer is: 'They have a lot of practical skills and a knowledge of English grammar and vocabulary'. There is in fact no one thing that knowledge of an English sentence like 'Snow is white' consists in. Knowing the meaning of a sentence can involve knowing how to explain its meaning to others, knowing how to correct others who misuse it, knowing its entailments and incompatibilities, and so on. The general, theoretical answer that it consists in knowing a theory which lays down the truth-conditions for this and other sentences is neither helpful nor informative. A major flaw in the truth-conditions answer is that many sentences are non-assertoric. Sentences expressing commands, questions and exclamations immediately pose problems which have to be dealt with by cumbersome epicycles in the theory of truth-conditions. (A sense/force distinction must be employed but is subject to numerous problems: see Baker and Hacker 1984: 48ff.) If we swallow this difficulty, another major one remains: it is impossible to give independent sense to the notion of a truth-condition. The notion of a truth-condition was formulated by Wittgenstein in the *Tractatus Logico-Philosophicus* to make a point about how the truth of compound formulae in the propositional calculus was determined. The truth-conditions of a compound formula were given by those combinations of its component parts which yielded truth for the whole. These could be set out in tabular form. In the compound p & q, setting out all the possible combinations for the atomic sentences p and q showed that the conjunction was true only when both p and q were true. Thus the conditions for the truth of the whole are laid down. Such a usage for 'truth-condition' yields no sense for the talk of the 'truth-conditions for "Snow is white"'. The standard way setting out those 'truth-conditions', derived from Tarski, gives us the innocuous '"Snow is white" is true if and only if snow is white'. When we catch philosophers talking of the 'circumstances under which a sentence is true', we quickly realise that attempts to specify such conditions *independent of understanding the meaning of the sentence itself* fail. Talk of truth-conditions is uninformative precisely because to grasp what it is for a sentence in a natural language to be true, to identify the circumstances in which it is true, cannot be done save by way of grasping its meaning. So, it makes no sense to say that we come to understand the meaning of the assertoric sentences of a language by means of deriving their meaning from a knowledge of their truth-conditions. We have no way of specifying truth-conditions independent of specifying meaning. Truth-conditional theories of meaning are empty (see Horwich 1998a: 71–4). When we come across truth-conditions theorists telling us what truth-conditions are, we find bathos. Devitt and Sterelny tell us that the meaning of a sentence consists in the meaning of its words and the syntactic structure into which they are fitted. Nothing earthshattering there: that is the familiar point that sentence-meaning depends on vocabulary and grammar. They then inform us that truth-conditions are determined by what the words refer to or apply to and how those things are related (Devitt and Sterelny 1987: 17–18). They do not tell us how those things are to be determined other than by understanding the sentence. The cynical might be forgiven for surmising that the only way to state a sentence's truth-conditions independently of its meaning is by constructing a lame paraphrase of it: a sentence is true if the words in it refer and if the things it refers to are related as it says they are related.

If we reject the search for a theory of meaning for a language and for a theory of meaning based on the notions of a grasp of the truth-conditions for the language's sentences, we are going to find the core argument for Dummett's anti-realism singularly unimpressive. For that argument takes its departure from truth-conditional meaning theory and suggests a modification to it. The core argument has the following form:

1 To understand a sentence is to understand what it is for it to be true, to grasp its truth-conditions.
2 But meaning is use: we must be able to display whatever knowledge of meaning consists in use. Knowledge of meaning must come to us from circumstances in which we learn meaning and displayable in circumstances in which we can manifest meaning.
3 From (1) and (2) it follows that knowledge of meaning cannot consist in knowledge of truth-conditions we could never encounter. If meaning is use, knowledge of truth-conditions can never be 'recognition transcendent'.
4 Therefore knowledge of meaning consists in knowledge of the circumstances in which we could verify, inspect or recognise that a sentence is true. Theory of meaning must employ a verificationist, not a realist or absolutist, conception of truth.

Truth is the key to unlocking meaning, but truth has to be understood in terms of conditions we can recognise as making something true. Truth is some form of justified assertability. (This core argument can be found with many variations in Dummett's corpus. See 1978: 358–9 and 1975: 133ff. for examples.) We have argued that we should not seek a theory of meaning, in Dummett's sense, and should not begin, if we did, with truth-conditions. Thus we will not begin by accepting (1) of the above argument. Much of the rest of the argument is common sense. Whatever theoretical comments we offer about meaning, they must be compatible with the fact that human beings learn meaning and manifest a grasp of meaning. Thus they must square with the facts that understanding a language involves grasping and manifesting some recognitional capacities. Who could doubt this? The jejune thoughts on the nature of understanding I have offered in this section are certainly compatible with the truisms that move Dummett's argument after step (1). However, we find that when Dummett describes how knowledge of meaning can be acquired and manifested his suggestions are behaviouristic and crude.

The above charges can be made good if we examine what Dummett understands by the notion of truth. We should note that Dummett is fully aware of the problem bedevilling truth-conditional accounts of the meaning of an assertoric sentence, namely that standard accounts of truth-conditions leave us with the paradox that one can only grasp truth-conditions when one grasps the meaning of the sentence. Grasp of truth-conditions cannot therefore explain grasp of meaning. He writes:

'If the equivalence of " 'Snow is white' is true" with "Snow is white",
and so on, constitutes the *whole* explanation of truth, then the concept is
useless in giving a theory of meaning' (Dummett 1993: 111). He is aware
that some will say that to grasp what it is for the sentence 'There are
intelligent beings on a planet in the Andromeda galaxy' to be true is just
to grasp what it is for there to be intelligent beings on a planet in the
Andromeda galaxy (1993: 145). Hence, the notion of truth is perfectly
useless in giving an account of what a knowledge of meaning consists in.
What this shows for Dummett is not that the philosophical enquiry for a
theory of meaning via the notion of truth was always misguided.
Rather, it demonstrates that a more fundamental understanding of
truth is needed in semantic theory than that provided by the standard
truth theorem: ' "p is true" if and only if p'. That more fundamental
notion is of truth as acceptance.

For Dummett, the root notion of truth is that of correct assertion. A
sentence is true just in case, if uttered assertorically, it would have
served to make a correct assertion (see Dummett 1991: 165–8). The
notion of establishing and accepting a sentence is the usable part of a
concept of truth in a theory of meaning (Dummett 1993: 144). Such a
notion provides what a theory of meaning needs: a connection between
meaning and understanding, on the one hand, and behaviour, on the
other (1993: 161). Truth as correct assertion enables us to see the link
between whatever grasp a speaker has of the meaning of an assertion
and the conditions in which the speaker learns and manifests knowledge
of meaning. Dummett avers that one can only learn a sentence by
learning what it is for it to be true (1973: 467–8). A knowledge of
meaning has to be something that is manifested once learnt. One
manifests knowledge of meaning by showing that one recognises when
the statement has been verified as true (or shown to be false) (1973: 467;
1991: 149). Grasping meaning must be a practical ability and it relates
crucially to being able to associate sentences with circumstances in
which they are correctly asserted. It is thus related to truth once we
understand truth in terms of correct and incorrect assertion. This is
behaviouristic in so far as it wants understanding to be displayed in
behaviour, the behaviour of accepting or rejecting sentences.

No one would doubt the claim that understanding of a language and
its component parts has some link with behaviour. There must indeed
be some things that a speaker of the language can do which manifest
that understanding. But it does not follow that the crucial thing a
speaker can do is correlate sentences with circumstances in which
sentences are used to make correct assertions. Language learning, in
particular, is not a matter of being confronted with correlations between
asserted sentences and circumstances of correct assertion. The flaws in
this account are listed by Devitt (1997: 282–3). Most of the sentences we
understand we never heard uttered by anyone. We understand them in

virtue of understanding their vocabulary and grammatical structure. Most of the sentences an infant hears uttered are not uttered in circumstances which justify their assertion. Infants hear very many sentences which are false or unjustified. The sentences still manifest linguistic competence on the part of their elders and can help infants acquire competence. By the same token, we manifest understanding of sentences in a greater range of linguistic behaviour than assertion, as in hypothesising, speculating or entertaining propositions. As noted above in the case of speculation about atoms, our theorising can run ahead of our ability to determine which hypotheses are true and which false. It is in the light of understanding a speculation that we are able to determine whether it can be verified or work out what it would take to verify it. Many things could manifest my understanding of 'There are intelligent beings on a planet in the Andromeda galaxy' beyond the ability to match it to conditions of correct assertion. These would be things which manifest my grasp of the sentence's vocabulary and grammatical form.

There are fundamental problems in tying the notion of truth to assertion conditions. One such problem is that we can predicate 'true' of non-linguistic items – notably of beliefs. I can hold a belief without ever asserting it. Dummett could of course argue that to say that a belief is true just is to say that an assertion of it would be correct. But we could equally lay down that to say that an assertion is true means that the belief corresponding to it is true. We need an argument to show that truth is essentially linked to linguistic behaviour in the first place. Further, the attempt to equate truth with assertability conditions flies in the face of the obvious fact that 'correct assertion' is an ambiguous notion. Many dimensions of assessment may be indicated by this phrase, involving many considerations other than truth (Appiah 1986: 28). It may be correct to assert that *p* on grounds of politeness even though *p* be false. Ditto, it may be wrong to assert that *p* even though *p* is true. In order to get round this point, we will need to specify those circumstances in which correct assertion is linked not to etiquette, politeness and the like but to *truth*. And that implies we have an independent notion of when an assertion can correctly be asserted *because it is true*. 'There are intelligent beings on a planet in the Andromeda galaxy' is correctly asserted in the relevant circumstances when the circumstances give grounds for thinking that 'It is true that there are intelligent beings on a planet in the Andromeda galaxy', which are circumstances which make it likely that there are intelligent beings on a planet in the Andromeda galaxy. In the absence of a grasp of what it means for the sentence to be true – which is nothing other than a grasp of what the sentence asserts – there is no way of distinguishing when I am asserting it merely out of politeness to the surrounding, highly-strung members of the Friends of the Andromeda Galaxy Society and when I am asserting it because I believe it to be true.

There is a yet further problem in Dummett's reworking of the concept of truth. It requires that those who understand a sentence be able to correlate it with circumstances of its correct assertion. But there may be no such determinate circumstances in the case of many sentences. Dummett's numerous critics point out that he neglects the fact that justification is holistic (see Alston 1996: 111; Devitt 1997: 277ff.; Kirk 1999: 126ff.). This is a point spelled out in our discussion of verificationism. Justification takes place in the context of webs of beliefs, of theories. What counts as evidence for and against a proposition may vary as the web grows, as theory develops. There is no correlation to make between circumstance and acceptance. Realists are not bound to meet the challenge of specifying the circumstances in which a statement is verifiable, because there is no determinate thing answering to the description 'the circumstances in which a statement is verifiable'. They are not bound to accept the conclusion of Dummettian anti-realist semantics: knowledge of meaning consists in knowledge of the circumstances in which we could verify, inspect or recognise that a sentence is true. Realists will therefore deny Dummett's suggestion that they are bound to think that sentences which are now undecidable by us have a determinate sense only if we can imagine a superhuman being who is capable of directly matching such sentences to reality (Dummett 1991: 345–6).

I have tried to show that Dummett has no strong case from the demands of 'the theory of meaning' for the assertion that reality is in some way constructed by human beings. This critical commentary on his anti-realism can be reinforced by noting the paradoxes his views throw up. Note in the first place that his account is mired in the problems faced by earlier verificationists. It leaves standard scientific assertions under threat of loss of meaning. Universal generalisations are an obvious candidate. While the assertion 'Some actions have an opposite and equal reaction' may have conditions for warranted assertion, 'All actions have an opposite and equal reaction' cannot be conclusively justified, and, on earlier versions of Dummett's anti-realism, comes out as meaningless. In the second place, there is strong reason to think that Dummett's views suffer from a fatal incoherence. He has criticised truth-conditional accounts of meaning. In part, the critique rests on the point that the standard notion of a truth-condition specifies something that cannot be grasped independent of grasping a sentence's meaning, and therefore cannot be used to explain grasp of meaning. Dummett falls into a similar trap. He bids us turn to conditions for the correct, that is, justifiable, assertion of a sentence. That means looking to the verification conditions of a sentence as the key to its meaning. But verification conditions are those factors which indicate that a sentence is true, conditions which make it more likely than not (see Psillos 1999: 15). Conditions which indicate that 'There are intelligent beings on a planet in the Andromeda galaxy' is true are conditions which indicate that there are intelligent beings on a planet in the Andromeda galaxy. This problem is another reflection of the futility of explaining meaning in terms of circumstances for correct assertion. We need to specify what 'correct assertion' amounts to. It is that which relates to the presence of evidence *for truth*.

A final paradox for Dummett is well aired by Alston (Alston 1996: 123ff.). It is the object of Dummett's theory to show that the meaning of a sentence is given by the conditions for its correct assertion (and the meaning of words by their contribution to the correct assertion of the sentences in which they occur). Correct assertion is a matter of verifying conditions, not truth-conditions thought of as existing independently of our capacity to recognise them. This apparatus means rethinking the meaning of assertoric utterances, especially those which purport to be about non-observable states of affairs. The sense of a sentence, Dummett avers, is given by the conditions under which we recognise it to be true (1973: 586; 1978: 17). But if the sense of 'There are intelligent beings on a planet in the Andromeda galaxy' is given by the conditions which govern its correct assertion, which justify it, then there can be no worry about it referring to a state of affairs we cannot in principle discover. If it is not simply meaningless, its meaning is given by its justifying conditions. The same will hold about assertions which appear to be about the remote past beyond human knowledge. Dummett's theory entails that such assertions about the past must specify putative facts which can be verified or falsified. But that further entails that such assertions have accessible truth-conditions. Dummett's theory must reduce the meaning of such apparently verification-transcendent assertions so that they describe verifiable states of affairs. But then the truth of such statements does consist in their one-to-one correspondence with states of affairs. In other words, they have a truth value in the good, old-fashioned realist way. In short, if Dummett has a verificationist theory of meaning (which he does), he does not need a verificationist theory of truth. His reduction of meaning makes his theory of truth redundant. Someone may think that truth attaches to a proposition independent of our ability to recognise it and yet they will never be in a position to find a possible truth which is verification-transcendent. All we can speak about is states of affairs which we can recognise as obtaining. If Dummett's theory of meaning is true, realism – as the belief in the possibility of states of affairs which obtain whether or not we recognise them as obtaining – is simply unstatable. The picture within innocent realism of human subjects being part of a world not of their own making and having properties or containing events which obtain quite independent of their thoughts is simple nonsense. We can only describe actual and possible facts which we can discover.

Thus: if the picture within innocent realism even makes sense, Dummettian semantics is misguided.

Chapter 5

Cupitt, Postmodernism and All That Jazz

The Postmodernist Turn

The writings of Don Cupitt are frequently taken to be the very epitome of theistic anti-realism. Whatever their philosophical merits, they have been enormously influential, to the point of spawning a movement – the Sea of Faith network – which has influence on parts of the Church of England. Cupitt's anti-realist interpretation of Christian theism was announced in *Taking Leave of God*, published in 1980. There has been an obvious shift in Cupitt's anti-realism from that work to later ones such as *The Sea of Faith*, *Lifelines*, *The Long-Legged Fly* and *Creation out of Nothing*. The movement is from a contrastive anti-realism in the interpretation of theism to a global form of anti-realism. My discussion of Cupitt's views will not follow this development in them. First, the arguments in the later works listed above will be discussed (I select them as a representative sample of the global anti-realism in late Cupitt). In the chapter which follows we shall explore the contrastive anti-realism of *Taking Leave of God*.

The importance of Cupitt for an examination of theism and realism lies in this: for many people interested in religious questions he has passed on and applied the thought of postmodernism. His post-*Taking Leave of God* books contain frequent references to writers such as Derrida. Some have questioned whether Cupitt is a true postmodernist (Ward 1997: xl), but I shall not pursue that question. Postmodernism is in any event not capable of precise definition. Let it be said for the moment to be a movement in Continental thought which is suspicious of all grand philosophical theories and which is committed to the application of a hermeneutics of suspicion to past and present theorising in the Western tradition. It is a branch of contemporary critical theory, usefully defined by Graham Ward thus:

> ... the presupposition of the critical tradition is that meaning is always historically embedded, is always caught up with the exercise of individual and historical 'will to power' ... The presupposition of the critical tradition

is that meaning is constructed ... contrary to being discovered, meaning is created and invested with value within certain cultural matrices – the critical tradition seeks to unmask the processes of such investment and their implications. [Ward 1996: 6]

It is part and parcel of postmodernist critical theory to reject the grand theory embedded in the so-called Enlightenment Project. It is a mistake, according to postmodernist ways of thinking, to expect science to produce a final theory of things or a language for describing reality which will match up to the Language of Nature (a language free of the taint of any *human* or *local* perspectives on reality). Scepticism about this 'meta-narrative' concerning the success of the hard sciences in particular has been argued to the defining feature of postmodernism (see Lyotard 1984: xxiii–xxv). We have seen in earlier chapters that many link such ideas about the arrival of a final theory and the ability to describe things in terms of the Language of Nature with innocent realism. We have argued that this link is mistaken. However, once the link is made, it is possible to move from the critique of this 'meta-narrative' to forms of relativism and constructivism.

The above movement of thought will be seen in Cupitt. Late Cupitt interprets contemporary critical theory as supporting a radical form of linguistic constructivism of the sort diagnosed in earlier chapters in this study. Hence, he provides arguments in the context of thought about God for a global anti-realism. Hence, the importance of giving him some space here. Furthermore, we can find, and will explore in a later section of this chapter, applications of the thought of Foucault in the philosophy of religion with a clear anti-realist message. We will find affirmations to the effect that the authority of Foucault is sufficient to ditch the idea that there are universal truths to be told about the world. The feminist thinkers discussed in that section think that truth-makers are somehow a function of our differing political interests. The upshot of this contention is that we can let our political interests properly determine what is true for us.

What we are discussing in this chapter is thus a selection of applications of postmodernist thought to ideas about the divine. The applications selected embody a constructivism about truth-makers. Cupitt's constructivism is primarily derived from ideas about the nature of meaning and the history of ideas influenced by postmodernism. That of Sharon Welch will be seen to be derived from the postmodernist idea that knowledge is everywhere a function of power. Neither will be seen to be capable of disturbing the key claims of innocent realism. Indeed, discussion of these two applications of postmodernism will confirm a leading theme implicit in earlier chapters. Opposition to innocent realism frequently involves a tacit commitment to magical modes of thought. It is characteristic of magic to suppose that what we do with our symbols can change reality, so that if I manipulate someone's name or image I can affect them. Cupitt and Welch have stories to tell about truth-bearers – human symbols and theories. They seem to hold that states of affairs and what is real are affected by the processes of symbol and theory construction. This is magical thought in action.

Language Creates the World

Cupitt's theistic anti-realism ceased to be contrastive with the arrival of *The Sea of Faith* (1984). These radio lectures preach the death of realist theism as a consequence of the death of the general prejudice that there is a world of mind-independent things and facts. They present a form of idealism as an obvious discovery of post-Enlightenment historical criticism, philosophy and cultural studies. The post-Enlightenment banishment of a real world over and apart from human beliefs about it is announced thus:

> We have come to see that there can be for us nothing but the worlds that are constituted for us by our own languages and activities. All meaning and truth and value are man-made and could not be otherwise. The flux of experience is continuous and has no structure of its own. It is we who impose shape upon it to make of it a world to live in. [Cupitt 1984: 20]

Cupitt's global anti-realism is evidently a species of the familiar genus 'linguistic constructivism': language and our symbolic forms in general create reality. It is hard to pin down the precise character of Cupitt's version of this idea. At times it appears to be a form of absolute, linguistic idealism, as if there is nothing – not even a subject – other than words or signs. ('The world's all words' Cupitt 1990: 21, and see 1990: 37.) Yet in places he refers to a formless something which language shapes and structures. In the above quotation we have reference to 'the flux of experience'. Cupitt also speaks of 'the Void' (1990: 5) and of a 'productive life energy underlying all things' (1986: 102). He toys with the idea that there must be a minimal metaphysics implied by his constructivism. Given that the life energy produces language – representation – there must be subjects in time capable of communicating. But he immediately states that 'this is only a myth and a heuristic device that we use to remind ourselves that we have no intelligible starting-point other than the supposition of a plurality of subjects in communication' (1986: 182). Overall, he appears to be a purveyor of cosmic porridge in the grand style: 'The world as such – if indeed we can speak of such a thing at all – is no more than a featureless flux of becoming which different cultures simply order in different ways' (1986: 133).

Some of Cupitt's many arguments for this radical conclusion will be considered in due course. But it should be clear now that we have already assembled the resources to see that Cupitt's radical anti-realism is yet another instance of the magical world view that permeates linguistic constructivism. The demonstration of its incoherence arises from a predominant strand of argument in *The Sea of Faith*. This strand begins with an unfolding of developments in the history of ideas in modernity, such as the dissolving of the teleological, Aristotelian world view by mechanistic science and the overthrowing of 'high' doctrines of the human self by Darwinism (see Cupitt 1984: 187 for a summary). But we know that there cannot be disproof of realism which begins by citing facts about changes in human thinking. The premises of such an argument can only remind us that human beings produce thoughts in history. But once we reflect on the fact that human beings are creatures in history, we realise that they cannot make the world of things and facts because they are a part of that world. If the facts about the history of ideas are facts, then they belong to a reality which we cannot change or wish away by changing our speech-habits. The propositions which record these facts are not true-from-our-perspective, but simply true. They record events which took place in the history of the one real world of which we are all a part (specifically events in the history of the planet Earth). Reflections on the history of ideas presuppose realism and cannot therefore undermine it. If all there really is is a featureless flux of becoming, then there cannot really be different cultures which order it in different ways. If there really are different cultures, then the world is structured. It contains human beings on a planet which has a certain geology and natural history.

'The world's all words': Cupitt has a number of ways of making that point. He tells us that reality is a beginningless, endless interplay of signs (1986: 2). He says that all meanings and truths are established in language (1990: 10). This leads to the embrace of 'a semiotic materialism' in which reality (as we confront it) is constituted by signs ('we insist there is only the signifier', 1990: 12). Let us remind ourselves of why this is incoherent. What lies behind the abstractions ('sign', 'signifier', 'signified', etc.) involved in the account of 'semiotic materialism'? It can only be the many and varied human languages. There are signs and the like only because there are words in the many and varied natural languages of the human past and present. Take any one such language, for example, English, and one realises that it is the product of flesh-and-blood people living in a material world. As a phenomenon it is unintelligible unless seen as an historical product. Its history is bound up with the geography, climate and natural history of the regions of the Earth occupied by past and present English-speakers. Thinking of the historical development of English ties the language to an even larger story of the emergence of *homo sapiens* and the historical geography and geology of the planet, of the solar system and of the galaxy and of the cosmos. Simple reflections along these lines make it plain silly to suppose that the world is all words or that 'there can be for us nothing but the worlds constituted for us by our own languages and activities' (Cupitt 1984: 20). We have seen that it is equally silly to suppose that how we speak and write changes the world of birds, rocks, planets and stars. To suppose otherwise is to be addicted to a view of reality which is not so much child-like but childish. This is the fundamental error of linguistic constructivism showing itself again.

Many segments of current English vocabulary can be seen to have arisen out of contact with the world. Think in this connection of our words for the birds of the British Isles, or of the names of the planets. Our vocabulary in these and countless other areas grows in interaction with a world which we do not create and have precious little control over. Our languages are one of the tools we use to explore this world and they are shaped by the outcome of these explorations. Cupitt is unable to see these obvious points. He is addicted to false opposition. He tries to rebut the common-sense truth that we use words to name things in a world beyond our language with this sally: 'Common sense assumes that words stick directly on to the things they name; that meaning is selfsame, atomic and referential. The meaning of a word is just the thing it labels' (1997: 21). So Cupitt has a dichotomy when it comes to meaning. Meaning is either differential and conventional, or it is referential and atomic. The latter view is absurd for two reasons. First it makes words into luggage labels – their meanings are just the things they name. Second it ignores the great truth announced by Derrida that the meaning of a word is a function of the play of relations between it and other words. Word-meaning is a function of the place of a word in a system. But, *contra* Cupitt, the dilemma he offers us is a wholly false one and his argument for its horns is weak.

Cupitt's dilemma in *The Long-Legged Fly* – either word-meaning is conventional and differential or it is atomic and referential – explicitly draws upon Derrida's claims that meaning is differential and infinitely deferred. Derrida's argument can be found in such works as *Writing and Difference*, *Positions* and *Grammatology*. It is based on a key thought in Saussure: meaning is created by the opposition of terms. This point can be illustrated by the colour vocabulary. The meaning of 'orange' in English is (wholly or in part?) given by its place in a system of contrasts: a surface is either orange, or blue, or green, and so on. To understand the word is to grasp that it is one item from a system of colour words and that orange contrasts with blue and green. Thus if, for example, someone had learnt to use 'purple' without knowing that 'violet' could be used for different tones of a blue-red kind, their understanding would change on being introduced to 'violet' as a possible description of colour. So the meaning of colour words is not atomic: it is at least in part dependent on the meaning given to other words.

So far, so simple. Derrida wishes to move from the above to the claim that meaning is infinitely deferred. This conclusion is meant at least to make the notion that words have a definite sense which can be grasped by users of the language problematic. It is, in consequence, meant to make the idea that words have a determinate graspable reference problematic. (Whether it entails for Derrida as for Cupitt that words have no referential function is open to doubt. In Kearney 1984: 123–4, Derrida denies that he ever meant to say that there is nothing beyond language or that we are imprisoned in language; cited in Jantzen 1998: 190.) The indefiniteness of sense is a function of the fact that meaning is infinitely deferred. The meaning of a sign is a function of its place in an unending chain of signs and there is no way we can escape from that chain and compare the sign with an extra-linguistic reality to test its accuracy or appropriateness. This is part and parcel of Derrida's attack on the 'metaphysics of presence'. This metaphysics operates at two levels. Those taken in by it wrongly think that the meaning of a word can be present to a user all at once and complete (as if, for example, the meaning of a term is given by some concept present to the mind which it immediately names). At the second level, this false metaphysics shows itself in the false thought that meaning can be guaranteed and immediately grasped because the word names a thing beyond language and the connection between word and thing can be given in a flash.

But what of the argument for the claim that 'meaning is infinitely deferred'? Derrida's argument for this contention turns Saussure's limited point about meaning arising at least in part from systematic contrasts surrounding a word to the much bolder claim that the meaning of any one word depends on the 'play' of differences between it and every other word in the language. This play is unending both synchronically and diachronically. The meaning of a word cannot be perceived in a single act. The use of any one word at any one occasion is affected by the traces left by all other words and in turn leaves its trace for all future uses of all other words. Meaning cannot be present to the user because meaning is a function of a never-ending play of differences between signs. It is a matter of '*différance*': of the play of differences and of the infinite deferring of one sign to the rest (see Derrida 1981: 26).

The weaknesses in Derrida's central argument have been well diagnosed by Ellis (Ellis 1989: 52ff.). In the first place it is based on a significant distortion of Saussure's original point. That was that meaning was a function of a word's place in a defined system of contrasts (such as the determinate qualities under the determinable 'colour'). What validity there is in that original point does not extend to the claim that the meaning of a single sign defers to the meaning of every other sign. In the second place the original point is destroyed by

Derrida's extension of it. The original point is that 'orange' gets its meaning from *some specific* contrasts (orange vs green, vs blue and so on). The point is taken away altogether if 'orange' is held to get its meaning from a contrast with *everything else*. Indeed the idea that 'orange' contrasts with everything else is nonsensical. It doesn't contrast with 'bovine' or 'molecular'. From this we can see, as Ellis notes, that Derrida's claims would destroy meaning altogether. They are not part of a theory of meaning but a way of saying there is no such thing as meaning. If there are no specific contrasts informing our understanding of 'orange', if it is not part of a *limited* series of contrasts (under the determinable 'colour'), it has no meaning for us. I understand you when you say the ball is orange rather than blue, green and so on. I would not understand you if you said the ball was orange rather than *anything else one might care to mention*. Take away the notion of specific, limited contrasts within which words are embedded and the notion of meaning goes altogether. One word is as good as another, because no word is closer in terms of likeness and difference to another. Suppose a friend and I are inspecting my malfunctioning car engine. She says: 'You need a new alternator belt.' That has meaning because of the limited range of things it could be contrasted with: new spark-plugs, a new engine block and so on. Linguistic meaning is a function, in part, of human beings' ability to make distinctions and therefore divide the world up in certain ways. Our languages contain items with meaning because they embody specific distinctions we draw.

The Derrida view is productive of the most grossly counter-intuitive consequences. It would entail, for example, that the meaning of every word in a language changes when any one new word is added to the language. It entails that two language users do not understand the same thing by a word if the vocabulary of one is more extensive than that of the other. One cannot but agree with Ellis that 'metaphysics of presence' (and its allied fallacy 'logencentrism') in Derrida is a straw man whose demolition in no way establishes Derrida's ideas about language (Ellis 1989: 35–7). Some past philosophers may have thought that meaning, truth and reference were guaranteed by the unmediated and therefore infallible grasp of concepts, thoughts and things. But it is sheer nonsense to claim that it characterises 'virtually the whole of western theology and philosophy since Plato' (Jantzen 1998: 187, glossing Derrida). The partial, limited, fallible and mediated character of our knowledge of the world, our selves and our language is the theme of many a Western philosopher and a commonplace in analytic theory of knowledge and philosophy of language.

The common-sense view that a great many words name things would be common folly if it assumes that words are like luggage labels and acquired meaning just by being hung onto objects. We saw in Chapter 2 that the meaning of a word cannot be identical with the thing it names. Something acquires the property of being a symbol because it is employed by human beings in a certain way. Meaning is a function of use. But that the 'words are simple labels' theory of language is false does not show that Cupitt is right in asserting that meaning is solely a matter of a sign's relation to other signs (1997: 21), as if we could leave the world out of the picture altogether. One employment of words is to refer to things. That employment can shape the meaning of a word. The evolution of a word's meaning may be explained by the history of human attempts to refer to something with it and thus by a history of human interaction with the world. Consider one of our stock examples: 'sedimentary rock'. The dictionary defines sedimentary rock as 'rock formed from sediment: the deposition of organic and inorganic materials on ocean floors, river beds and the like; sediments harden with pressure and like forces to form rocks such as shale'. The phrase gets its meaning from its place in the language, and, in particular, within theories of geology which make distinctions between processes of rock formation, but it would not have had that place if human beings had not discovered things about their world. The phrase and its origins show, *contra* some followers of Derrida, that it is not the case that signs are 'always already within the play of signification, not measurable against extralinguistic reality' (Jantzen 1998: 188). Geologists developed hypotheses about the causal processes which account for the structure of rocks. In so doing they confronted evidence which led to the tripartite division of rocks into sedimentary, metamorphic and igneous. We need to understand the development of those hypotheses in relation to geological discoveries to understand the origins of our phrase's meaning – not 'the play of signification'. And that understanding will show that the phrase is 'measurable against extralinguistic reality'. We can judge whether the system of hypotheses that produces the tripartite division is well-evidenced or not. It is conceivable that (though not perhaps *how*, given the well-entrenched character of relevant hypotheses) extralinguistic reality could show the tripartite division to be false. Thus 'sedimentary rock' could drop from usage or have its meaning changed. Note, *contra* both Saussure and Derrida, that someone could understand the dictionary definition of the phrase and make some use of it while being ignorant of the tripartite division of which it is a part. They may know nothing of 'metamorphic rock' and 'igneous rock'. Let us suppose that in their ignorance they think all rock is sedimentary rock and are unaware even of the names for other kinds of rock. That does not entail that they do not understand 'sedimentary rock', albeit their geological knowledge is woefully limited. They hold some false beliefs about sedimentary rock.

Back to Cupitt. How does Cupitt come to embrace the manifest absurdities of linguistic constructivism? He does so by systematic confusion of metaphysical questions, on the one hand, with semantic and epistemological questions on the other. He has committed a grave sin against Devitt's third maxim: settle the realism issue before any semantic or epistemic issue (Devitt 1997: 4). There is no clearer confirmation of this than Cupitt's commitment to that old chestnut that realism looks to the world finally to confirm one theory of reality true (1997: 32; realism is committed to a One Truth Universe according to Cupitt 1990: 114–15). But we have seen the poverty of this argument. The realist can happily accept the thought that a final theory of things may be in principle impossible (if there are aspects of reality which forever are beyond our descriptive resources) and the realist can easily embrace a fallibilist conception of human knowledge.

The caricature of realism which Cupitt parades in his books portrays the realist as an addict for certainty and stability in human enquiry. The rise and fall of theories in the various branches of human enquiry disturbs realists. They want meaning and theory to stay the same forever and always. However, why Cupitt thinks they should be upset by the ebb and flow of conjecture and theory is hard to follow. They know that human words are true only so far as they faithfully represent the one real world which exists apart from human theorising. They will see theory change as clear confirmation of the fact that it is one thing to say how things are but quite another for things to be as we say they are. It is because of this distinction that we cannot determine our theories to be true by fiat, but must keep on developing and weeding them. By contrast, if the world is all words, we should be able to make our words come true. We need not fear that the world will refute them.

Cupitt's texts preaching global anti-realism are full of reminders of the flux of human meaning and theorising. This is the burden of *The Sea of Faith*. He evidently believes that a realist outlook is decisively undermined by the realisation that meaning and thought changes, that no language or body of human theory stays the same forever. Realists must think that 'the great words of philosophy, religion, ethics and so forth' stand for unchanging essences (back to the 'metaphysics of presence'). It comes as a shock to their outlook to be told, in contrast, that linguists see languages as 'historically evolving and living systems' (Cupitt 1993: 46–7). Realists have a certain view about truth-bearers. Sentences, and the symbols which compose them, must have a fixed meaning. Once we see that meaning fluctuates, then we abandon realism. Of course, no realist will reason thus, unless very confused. Realism's founding postulate – that how we say things are is one thing, how things really are is another – rules out this endeavour to resist the fluctuation of meaning. Realism could only be disturbed by fluctuation in meaning if it was addicted to absolute certainty – a guarantee that words had meaning and reference giving a guarantee that theories were true. Realism according to Cupitt must be addicted to a form of linguistic and epistemic foundationalism which assures us that some words have meaning and reference because they hook onto given aspects of reality. That will then give us basic statements which can be judged true of reality upon inspection. Thus a fixed and certain theory of the world can be produced. But, of course, these classical foundationalist thoughts about meaning, truth and certainty run counter to realism's core postulate. Linguistic and epistemic atomism of this kind is precisely designed to close the gap between thought and things which realism says must be kept open. Realism must reject what Cupitt describes as a 'pre-established harmony between thought and being' (1987: 13–14).

Cupitt's core argument surely lies in the territory just described. It leads to the conclusion that realism must be false because the only world we can in principle know is a world constituted by our language. There is no possibility at all of comparing truth-bearers with truth-makers unless that which produces the truth-bearers (mind or language) forms, shapes or creates the truth-makers. Language can only be in contact with a world that is made by it. Realism therefore entails the most abject, despairing scepticism: 'There is no way we could ever detect the establishment of a "real" intelligible world-order out there independent of us, because we can none of us know anything prior to or apart from our initiation into the linguistic, world-ordering human community' (Cupitt 1986: 61).

Facts are 'sentence-shaped' because 'our minds impose our grammar onto the world'. We could not grasp any fact that was not 'sentence-shaped'. Therefore all facts have to be created by the power of our language (Cupitt 1990: 36). Herein lies Kant's discovery: 'The ordered world we see is the creation of our minds, and has to be so, for there is no other way we could know it' (Cupitt 1984: 138).

This is a familiar theme in idealism and in coherentist accounts of truth. The core claim is that the plausibility of realism in general, and of the particular view that true statements correspond to states of affairs in a mind-independent world, requires that we be able to compare our judgements with uninterpreted reality. In fact, we cannot do that. In order for us to check on whether any judgement is true, we must make another judgement. Then all we end up doing is comparing one judgement with another judgement (see Alston 1996: 87ff. for a detailed exposition of this argument). We could not compare our judgements with an uninterpreted reality, because we could make nothing of such a reality. We only have 'facts' about the world because we have concepts and judgements to apply to reality: 'nothing is *there* until the spectator has interpreted what she has seen in terms of a theory and has expressed herself in language' (Cupitt 1997: 19). That means that the notions of fact and objectivity only enter in once we have the means for conceptualising and making judgements about reality which come from possession of a language. So objectivity has to be given with and in language and cannot 'as realists suppose' be something external to language (1997: 19). Realism is thus defeated by the simple reflection that there is no uninterpreted, unconceptualised experience. It needs the notion of an uninterpreted, unconceptualised given to make use of its conception of truth as a matter of correspondence to the mind-independent. We could not make use of such a given, even if *per impossible* we were aware of it. We do not even need to posit an external reality to explain the fact that our experience is stable, coherent and shareable with others, because 'it is precisely the function of language to order experience in this way' (Cupitt 1986: 61).

Realism is not so easily defeated. Suppose my wife affirms that there is an ammonite fossil in a flint in the garden. I affirm that there is not. We go and look at the flint and, lo and behold, it contains an ammonite fossil. I have compared my judgement with the world and found it to be false. I have not compared it with another judgement but with the thing the judgement is about – the flint. It is true that I cannot register that I am wrong and my better half is right save through making a judgement, using concepts and employing part of English vocabulary. But there is all the difference in the world between surmising, opining and judging that there are ammonite fossils in the garden and finding that there are (here through seeing and touching them). Cupitt is guilty of a truly gross fallacy if he thinks we can move from 'You could not register the fact without using language' to 'Language creates the facts which you have registered'. It is equally absurd to contend that language accounts for the order in our experience. Language, in one respect, enables us to order our experience. We are able to put the things we experience into kinds because of the linguistically rooted concepts we have. But that I see fossils in flints when my attention is directed to a particular patch of Surrey is not down to the state of English in the United Kingdom at the start of the twenty-first century. (It would actually make sense to say of me that I had seen and noticed the fossils, even if I had no way of describing them as such, but leave that point aside.) English usage did not create ammonites, their fossils, or raise some of those fossils to the surface soil of this part of the British Isles. There is an obvious equivocation on 'experience is ordered by language' to which Cupitt is blind (compare our discussions of Runzo in Chapter 3).

But, it may be objected, the flint with which you compared your judgement was not something wholly independent of you and your linguistic community. It was reality as conceptualised by you, as you have been taught and socialised into conceptualising it. It was not reality as it is in itself. Language therefore enters into the construction of what you saw (thus argues Appelros 2002: 8 and *passim*). This defence of Cupitt will not wash. The flint with its fossil was conceptualised by me with the help of the resources of English. But that was not something I did to the flint analogous to what I might do to the liquid jelly when I pour it from the bowl into the sculpted jelly mould. The character of the flint was not changed. It did not acquire characteristics it did not have before. Above all: it did not become mind-dependent after I conceptualised it. All the application of my conceptual and linguistic resources did was enable me to recognise what there was to be recognised. If the piece of hard stuff really is flint and if it really contains a fossil ammonite, then this is true of the flint-in-itself. How the flint appeared to me is how the flint truly is – how the flint would have been if there never had been any human beings, speaking English and disagreeing (foolishly) with their spouses. Conceptualised flint is the same as unconceptualised flint.

Cupitt is just wrong to say that there is no way we could ever discover a real intelligible world-order independent of us, and further off the mark in alleging that our induction into a linguistic community provides a barrier to such a discovery. The truth is that we can detect facts about a real, intelligible world because, having been initiated in a human community and acquiring the epistemic resources it passes on to its members, we can distinguish between true and false judgements about it. We do so because we use the community's resources to investigate the world. Its resources were in fact shaped by human interaction with a real intelligible world-order out there independent of us, so they are apt for the purpose. The real, intelligible world can cause us to discard parts of our talk and theory (witness the disproof of phlogiston theory or the belief in cosmic ether) and cause us to acquire new talk (witness plate-tectonics and the viral theory of disease). The real, intelligible world is quite capable of telling us when we conceptualise fruitfully and correctly and when not, albeit that all human enquiries are beset by a measure of uncertainty. The world does not have to be a creation of our minds in order for us to know it. The harmony (only ever partial, given the fallibility of human thinking) between reality and the mind is established through the growth of the mind in contact with and influenced by the reality in which flesh-and-blood human life is set. Without that harmony, *homo sapiens* would have had a hard time evolving.

Politics and Reality

In the chapter which follows we shall have occasion to take brief look at the feminist critique of the concept of God. That critique is directed to a particular point: the traditional concept of the divine is implicated in attitudes which are anti-women. It comes as a surprise to find some feminist writers arguing that for the much more general conclusion that the very notion of there being universal truths is sexist or imperialistic. This conclusion bears upon realism, since it is tantamount to the denial that there is a way things are independent of how we think things are. It is part of an assertion that the way things are is somehow a function of our political interests. Since this form of global anti-realism has been offered in critique of realism in religion it is worth our notice.

The view to be discussed is set out in the following quotation from Julie Hopkins, worth reproducing at length because it gives us the full meat:

> Traditionally in the patriarchal West, truth has been considered an objective reality, to be deduced through reason and then tested empirically. Elite councils of men who wielded power in the church, or science or politics have claimed that their objectivity is God-given, corresponding with metaphysical laws. Welch argues that this understanding of knowledge, far from being value-free, is a strategy undertaken in order to dominate; for so-called objective reality is in fact laden with the presuppositions and prejudices of those who hold hegemonies of power and who project these onto a fictitious *tabula rasa*. Welch agrees with the French philosopher Michel Foucault that westerners should give up the pretension of speaking in universal and dogmatic categories and recognise that a just and peaceful future lies with a new epistemology, which she names the 'political economy of truth' in which every group, class, race, sex and religion has the right to name for themselves what is true and liberating. [Hopkins 1996: 68]

Many things are going on in this remarkable passage. It is drawing on the contentions of Sharon Welch in her *Communities of Resistance and Solidarity: A Feminist Theology of Liberation*. Hopkins' most striking claim is that different political and other groups should have the right to name for themselves what is true. This does not appear to be the claim that all groups should have the right to put forward their own opinions as to what is true. That would amount to a simple plea for liberty in thought and expression and for open debate in matters religious and political. Such a rehash of old-fashioned liberalism is not a new epistemology. No, Hopkins' view is not that our opinions are expressive of our political interests and strategies, but that knowledge is. She seems to be asserting that the very idea that there is objective truth and knowledge is politically oppressive.

Hopkins' mentor Welch affirms something similar. She states that the ideal of universal or absolute truth is intrinsically correlated with oppression (Welch 1985: 72). Feminist theologies of liberation must embrace some form of relativism about truth-claims (1985: 84). The suggestion we have before us then appears to be this: innocent realism is politically oppressive. The argument for this conclusion goes something like this:

1 Realism holds that truth is a function of correspondence with a human-independent world.

2   Point (1) suggests that knowledge claims should not be put forward
    on the basis of our political needs and ideals.
3   But inevitably all knowledge claims reflect political needs and ideals.
4   Realism will thus lead to the illusion that some knowledge claims do
    not reflect political needs and ideals.
5   Realism will therefore end up privileging some knowledge claims
    and some political needs and ideals under a false guise of
    correspondence to the real.

Solution: abandon the idea of objective knowledge and that which
supports it – realism.

Readers will be astonished that anyone could take up the position
outlined. There is a much less drastic diagnosis of the ills Hopkins
describes. Knowledge is of what is the case. What is the case is so
(leaving aside some facts in the human world), quite independent of our
political needs and ideas. In the past, oppression has taken the form of
the powerful claiming as knowledge things which merely reflect their
political needs and ideals. They have thus repressed the opinions and
experiences of those without power. The remedy for this ill is to be
found *within* a realist conception of how things are. That conception
invites us to distinguish those grounds for knowledge claims which are
trustworthy and those which are not. We do this by reference to the
distinction between, on the one hand, grounds which are genuine
indicators of the truth of what is claimed as part of knowledge and, on
the other, what passes for grounds, namely considerations (like political
ones) which are not genuinely truth-indicative. Thus we establish as the
only relevant criterion for someone's voice to be heard and given weight
in debate as to what is known in religion (or in anything else) that they
have something truth-indicative. Thus are the weak given epistemological parity with the powerful. Knowledge can never be oppressive
and the oppressors can never lay claim to ownership of knowledge.

Hopkins and Welch could be complaining about dogmatism in
religion. Dogmatism, as we have said over and over again in this study,
is not at home in innocent realism. Dogmatists offer some knowledge
claims as to be accepted without question and without due evidence
being given for them. Dogmatism is defeated by critical thinking.
Realism encourages critical thought.

I have just argued that realism is politically liberating – and
obviously so. But feminist philosophers and theologians do not see it
like that. Welch sees her realisation (as she would have it) that
traditional understandings of God and human nature merely reflected
'unnecessary relations of power and domination' not as evidence that
those understandings were not based on truth-indicative grounds, but
as demanding a new definition of truth (Welch 1985: 30). Welch is for
example suspicious 'about the intrinsic imperialism of Western

conceptions of truth' (1985: 21). She, along with many feminist thinkers, wants to worship at the shrine of Foucault. And Foucault has shown (though how is never quite clear) that all knowledge is power. This is not the jejune thesis that knowledge of the world gives us power to influence it but the startling claim that truth is the product of the forms of constraint which function in a society. Each society has a 'regime of truth'. It adopts certain types of discourse and makes them function as true. All the various techniques by which we distinguish the true from the false and acquire knowledge of the truth are a function of power in society (see Foucault 1980: 131, cited in Welch 1985: 10). On the surface this seems like a variant on the strong programme in the sociology of knowledge (of which more in Chapter 7) according to which social and institutional structures are sufficient for the production of what *passes for* truth and knowledge in a society. That programme may suggest a relativist understanding of truth, though it does not entail it. But Welch wants the relativism. She wants the truth of assertions (certainly of assertions about God) to be a function of political needs and ideals. What is true equals what is politically liberating (1985: 31) and she thinks that Foucault has given her the licence to make this equation. He can only have done that if he has shown that truth-makers bend to human political concerns. But that is magic again.

Not every feminist thinks that good, liberating politics produces a doctrine about truth-makers. Jantzen points to the problem for feminists in saying that truth, as opposed to what many count as truth, is determined by relations of power. She complains that in that case there would be no recourse against 'might is right' (Jantzen 1998: 224). What the powerful say could not then be the subject of external critique. Despite Jantzen's good sense on this point, it seems to be integral to postmodernist feminism to toy with the notion that truth-makers can be fashioned according to political and other relative concerns. Without at least a temptation to this denial of innocent realism, the scope of feminist theorising must be severely limited and its pretensions to produce a reform of the entirety of the academic life rejected. Consider in this regard the enterprise of producing a 'feminist science'. Much may be meant by the idea of a feminist science. Many of its proponents want it to refer to a science whose *content* will be different from the old, patriarchal brand. This means that *what is discovered* by feminist scientists will be different from what is discovered by patriarchal scientists. Advocates of feminist science want to say that the 'fingerprints' of the origins of knowledge are left over all knowledge. Knowledge is produced by flesh-and-blood human beings from within socially and politically charged circumstances. Thus what is discovered by those human beings remains forever imprinted with its social and political origins. 'All knowledge is socially situated' is the battle cry (see

Harding 1993: 57). Thus scientific thinking is always of an age and can never escape its historical locatedness (1993: 65). But surely the content of scientific claims is true of nature as it is independently of all human thinking? Not so for the proponents of feminist science. Harding tells us that nature itself does not correspond to our true claims, but only 'nature as an object of knowledge' (1993: 65). Then we are back with the familiar story: the denizens of the non-human world are no different from the items in the human world. Scientists' interactions with non-human objects culturally constitute them. Trees, rocks, planetary orbits, and electrons always appear to natural scientists only as they are already socially constituted in some of the ways in which the human world is constituted. Science can thus be integrated into 'democracy-advancing projects' (1993: 69). Science can be led by feminism to produce some results rather than others.

So, many feminist thinkers want to politicise science, knowledge and truth. They wish to make science serve political ends in the way in which Lysenko wanted biology to serve the aims of Soviet Socialism. Their aims are doomed to frustration because, as we have seen, it is not the case, because it could not be the case, that how human beings think, politically or otherwise, shapes the world that lies beyond human representations. It would be tedious to repeat the arguments for this conclusion yet again. This is more addiction to magic. There are in any event many full and incisive critiques of the feminist science project in the literature (see Curthoys 1997; Gross 1994; Gross and Levitt 1994; Sokal and Bricmont 1999).

Why cannot thinkers like Harding see the obvious? The obvious is as follows. Yes, knowledge is acquired by human beings in social, personal and historical contexts. But if what they acquire is genuine knowledge, it is of what is true. So what is known bears no imprint of those contexts or of the people who discovered it. If it is true that I know that there are nine planets in the solar system, then my knowledge is not relative to me or my social situation. When I enunciate this knowledge, I speak with a universal voice. The knowledge bears nobody's fingerprint because it is of what is so, independent of the beliefs, values or situations of any human beings. There are nine planets regardless of whether we are good democrats or regular contributors to the *Reactionary Times and Feudal Herald*. The knowledge is mine but in principle anyone's, regardless of their social situation or whether they agree with me in matters political. That is the obvious truth about genuine knowledge. We want to know why feminist theory cannot accept it. The answer is this. The obvious represents a denial of a holy feminist truth: that all knowledge reflects a standpoint. Why is that a holy truth? It is held to be entailed by a core feminist belief about the knowing subject, namely that he or she is not a pure spirit but a human being shaped by historical and social circumstances.

The holy truth is stated by Jantzen thus: 'we cannot escape our cultural and linguistic web to stand in some place from which objective knowledge can be obtained' (Jantzen 1998: 188). To deny this and affirm that we could ever have 'a view from nowhere' is to assume that human beings can function as 'disembodied and unsituated minds' who deny their foundation in 'natality', that is their birth via women into a life governed by material and discursive conditions (Jantzen 1998: 146). My claims about the status of the knowledge that there are nine planets are for Lorraine Code a denial of the truth that 'there are no dislocated truths' (Code 1993: 30). I can only make them because I suppose, falsely, that knowers can achieve the view from nowhere. But then I must have false beliefs about human subjects. I must think that human beings can 'through the autonomous exercise of their reason ... transcend particularity and contingency. The ideals presuppose a universal, homogenous, and essential "human nature" that allows knowers to be substitutable for one another' (Code 1993: 16).

So here we have it: innocent realists think that truth (at least, as it concerns the denizens of the non-human world) is 'dislocated' and politically neutral. They think, unless they are out-and-out sceptics, that human beings can attain to knowledge of such dislocated truth. But they can only do that if they think that human subjects are dislocated. They must hold ideas about the self which indebted to a misguided Cartesianism or Positivism. They think, falsely, that human ideas can somehow escape their location in history (Harding 1993: 73). They cannot because human subjects cannot. The last two steps of the feminist argument against realism are thus kicking in:

4 Realism will lead to the illusion that some knowledge claims do not reflect political needs and ideals.
5 Realism will therefore end up privileging some knowledge claims and some political needs and ideals under a false guise of correspondence to the real.

Oh what confusion reigns here! We have in the first place a most blatant incoherence – one that comes with the standard relativist package. Certain claims about the human subject are advanced in support of the conclusion that objective knowledge is not possible and that we cannot speak with a universal voice. Yet the claims are only cogent in argument if they themselves are spoken with a universal voice. If truth is but truth-from-a-standpoint, then it can after all be true from the standpoint of wicked, oppressive, patriarchal epistemologists that there is a universal human nature and thus that there are 'dislocated' subjects who can speak with a universal voice. So long as wicked, oppressive, patriarchal epistemologists are consistent, they cannot be refuted. There are no facts outside their system which can refute it. What is a fact depends on your outlook. Unless the feminist claims about human nature are spoken with a universal voice and can be seen to have authority as such, then we are back with the trap that Jantzen pointed up (but alas fell into herself): might becomes right. The attempt by feminist epistemologists to expose 'scientific' work which expresses a partial, biased – because masculinist – point of view can only be spoken in a universal voice. The accounts are authoritative if they are true diagnoses. If they are true, they are true for anyone, anytime. Why? Because if seen to be true, they are seen to rest on genuine truth-indicative grounds. But those grounds can't be truth-indicative only from some standpoint. As Thomas Nagel points out, the serious attempt to expose what is relative to some group or limited outlook in a way of thinking, can only end up confirming something that is universal and objective (Nagel 1997: 16) – that is, that such-and-such opinions do not represent the objective truth and cannot be sustained with a universal voice.

Above and beyond the incoherence of feminist thought on this matter, there is the plain fact that the notions of truth and of knowledge as being expressible with a universal voice do not depend on contentious views about the human subject as being somehow independent of others, devoid of values and capable of an impossible God-like vision of things. An example might help. How was the fact that there is a ninth planet discovered? In 1905 Percival Lowell noted disturbances in the orbits of Neptune and Uranus. He hypothesised that these were due to the gravitational force of some adjacent body. He predicted the location of this body, but had not located it by his death in 1916. In 1929 another astronomer at the Lowell observatory, Clyde W. Tombaugh, used Lowell's predictions and photographed the sky with a more powerful telescope. In 1930 he found Pluto's image (he named the new planet after the God of the Underworld) on three photographs. Neither Lowell nor Tombaugh were dislocated selves. They presumably had political views. But, *contra* Harding, their discovery that there was a ninth planet bears no fingerprint. The proposition is true for anyone regardless of social and political situation. It is based on grounds which are devoid of social and political fingerprints: evidence about the orbits of other planets, well-confirmed hypotheses from gravitational theory and images of the ninth planet itself. Lowell and Tombaugh were human selves living in relation to others. Unless they had been inducted into the intellectual traditions associated with astronomy, they could not have made their discovery. But these are intellectual traditions, not social or political ones. That does not mean that they are value-free, far from it. It does mean that they enable their participants to focus and reason about a subject matter and discern what is relevant and irrelevant to discovering facts about that subject matter. The occupants of such intellectual traditions do not need to be Cartesian egos (though poor Descartes is mightily caricatured in these debates). Flesh-and-blood human beings of both genders and of diverse ethnicities, political persuasions, sexual orientations and so on can share in intellectual traditions. They can (and is not this just *obvious*?) focus on what is relevant to a subject matter, reason, weigh up evidence, use instruments of observation and experiment and discover what is true.

None of the above implies that human enquirers have to escape their historical and social settings if that means they have to acquire God-like powers. Human beings can think and they can direct their thought to the *object*, to what lies beyond them. Of course, when they discover truths about their world, they are able to speak with a universal voice. If we like, we can say that they thereby escape their location in history (Harding), their cultural and linguistic web (Jantzen). They can, *contra* Code, exercise reason and transcend particularity and contingency. They do these things all the time. It is quite easy. It is simply a matter of discovering what is the case about a world which is cognitively and ontologically distinct from these flesh-and-blood human beings. (Of course it is often not easy. Human enquiry is riddled with bias. If we give in to personal or other forms of prejudice, we miss the truth by miles. There are countless ways of being stupid and some ways of acquiring insight take much learning and intellectual labour. Feminist epistemology is not telling us this jejune tale, because the tale is only intelligible if we contrast prejudiced judgement with the real possibility of judgement led by the object.)

When something about the mind-independent world is discovered, a fact is established which is good for anyone, anywhere. Thus the discovery of the ammonite in the garden establishes something which can be put in a universal voice and which bears the imprint of no particular person: at this location in space and time there is a fossil ammonite.

Feminists on realism and the impossibility of objectivity are mystery-mongers. They want to make what is an everyday occurrence into an impossibility. They do so by associating that occurrence with high-flown views about human selfhood. The everyday occurrence is rather explained by some commonsensical facts about human beings as enquirers. As only intellectuals can, feminists produce clouds of theory only to miss the obvious. At a deeper level, we have seen that the attack on innocent realism by some feminist theologians shows a commitment to the magical point of view implicit in linguistic constructivism.

Chapter 6

Contrastive Anti-realism

Contrastive Anti-realism

It is easy in general terms to state what contrastive, theistic anti-realism amounts to. It asserts that while the theories and discourses of other areas of human enquiry, such as science, can be taken to intend to refer to realities independent of human representations, theistic theories cannot. The problem is that most forms of contrastive, theistic anti-realism are comments on the success of theistic thought and not on its intent. These forms of theistic anti-realism simply amount to one or another version of atheism – the denial of the existence of a transcendent reality which ensures an underlying providential order in things and through which human beings can gain an ultimate good. It is quite impossible in a work of this scope to provide an adjudication of the question of whether a generic theistic vision of reality is plausible/implausible, let alone true/false.

We noted in Chapter 1 that many thinkers who judge theism to have failed in its intent to refer to sacred, transcendent reality go on to develop anti-realist interpretations of theism. They do so either by translating religious talk into talk about something else (reductionism) or by finding a non-cognitive use for such talk (instrumentalism). Feuerbach and Julian Huxley served as examples of such moves.

Reinterpretations of theistic symbols following the above pattern are capable of generating much heat in the philosophical and theological literature. Yet the project of reinterpreting religious language *if* one is convinced that it fails of its intended reference is harmless enough provided that it is seen as revision and not as description. If it is the former, there is no question of its adequacy as an accurate account of the intent and meaning of religious language. The theist should indeed welcome the possibility that others may see value in theistic symbols even after judging their referential intent to have failed. Revisionary attempts of Huxley's sort may bring out resonances in theistic symbols which are valuable for all parties.

In this chapter we shall be interested in those forms of theistic anti-realism which say that we cannot take seriously the intent of theistic symbols to refer to something transcendent. It matters who the 'we' is here. Below we shall note arguments from Don Cupitt and feminist writers to the effect that, given certain contemporary and political ideas (orthodoxies), we moderns (or: postmoderns) cannot use theistic language to refer to anything like the God of traditional theism. Moral advance and political evolution have made it impossible to use the symbols with their traditional intent. This is revisionary anti-realism with a difference. What is claimed is that the revision is mandatory for all with a contemporary conscience.

We could establish a true descriptive anti-realism if we had a well-established theory of meaning which told us that no language could refer to things transcendent. There is a path from verificationist theories of meaning to a descriptive, contrastive anti-realism. The problem with this particular form of anti-realism is of course that verificationist theories of meaning are very weak indeed (as noted in Chapter 4 above). Even if accepted as accounts of the nature of cognitive meaning, it is not evident that all forms of theism fall foul of verificationism (see Hick 1974 for an attempt to marry theism with a verificationist criterion of the meaningful). So we will not pursue this line of enquiry further.

More traditional descriptive anti-realism is to be found in the pages of Feuerbach. There is indeed an element in the argument of *The Essence of Christianity* which prefigures Positivism (presumably because it reflects the influence of Positivism's ancestor David Hume). Feuerbach tells us that we can make no sense of an existent that we cannot potentially perceive (Feuerbach 1957: 200). The limits of what we can think are set by the limits of what we can experience. But there are other arguments in Feuerbach for theistic anti-realism than this crude, proto-verificationism. They are based around the theme that belief in a transcendent ground of reality is obviously false. The 'obviously' is important in the last sentence. Merely considering a statement false cannot give us ground to question its apparent intent or meaning. But if someone were to say while pointing to your pet dog 'That elephant is looking a little ill', you would be entitled not to take the apparent attempt to refer to an elephant seriously. Something is seriously wrong with this piece of discourse. Feuerbach thinks that theism is obviously false in part because he thinks that materialism is obviously true. All our experience shows that spiritual realities, namely, ideas and values, only exist and have power because they are entertained and used by flesh-and-blood creatures. They only have effects in the real world because material human beings act in the light of them. Theism understood in its realist interpretation would have us believe that something non-material and ideal is the true reality on which all other things depends. This contradicts the only warranted generalisation we can make about the relation between the material and the spiritual. Making it, we must come to the conclusion that material human beings are the creators of the spiritual God, not the other way round (see Feuerbach 1957: 100–110).

The appropriate response to the materialist strand in Feuerbach's anti-realism is that at best it will take us to the view that transcendental theism is false, not that it is obviously false. Materialism may be seen by many as a world view which has been proved by the advance of natural science or as the merest common sense by others. But reflection will surely establish that to deny it is not like denying that grass is green or that the Sun rises in the east every day. It is a metaphysical outlook with many things in its favour but also many things against. World views which deny it are not thereby ripe for reinterpretation or worthy of being dismissed as obviously non-referential in force. This verdict on the status of materialism is plain common sense (but see D.Z. Phillips below).

Under the heading of showing that a discourse is obviously false comes the charge that it is obviously incoherent. What is wrong with embracing a self-contradiction is that at least one of a set of self-contradictory beliefs must be false. The presence of obvious self-contradictions in a theory is the presence of obvious falsehood. Obvious self-contradictions in what people say legitimately raise the question of how their words can be reinterpreted. It is important that we distinguish obvious from non-obvious incoherence in this connection. If someone tells me that they have drawn a perfect triangle with four sides, the incoherent character of the utterance is so blatant as to take logical falsehood into the realms of nonsense. What they say becomes the subject of diagnosis. But if someone tells me that they have drawn a perfect triangle whose internal angles add up to 200 degrees, I need assume only that they have strayed into falsehood because they cannot measure angles properly or have trouble with mental arithmetic. What they say is logically false and can be demonstrated to entail a contradiction, but it is not obviously contradictory. Part II of *The Essence of Christianity* contains chapter after chapter alleging contradictions in the theological, that is, realist, interpretation of religion. It follows from what has just been argued that, if these accusations were valid, they would not support the descriptive anti-realist project unless they showed that the theological interpretation was obviously incoherent. In itself a valid charge of incoherence suffices merely to show that the theory in question is necessarily false, not that its meaning cannot be taken at face value.

We now have two questions to ask about Feuerbach's assault on the coherence of theism. Does he establish theism's incoherence? Does he establish that this incoherence is obvious? Our answer to the first question begins by noting that in order for Feuerbach to derive contradictions from the key beliefs of theism he has to import philosophical principles of his own. Thus in arguing for a contradiction in the very idea that God exists, Feuerbach contends that for something to have existence independent of my mind it must be capable of involuntarily affecting me. He then concludes that God must exist in space and God must be capable of being perceived (Feuerbach 1957: 200). The principle employed here is to the effect that real things must be capable of affecting the senses and therefore be in space. The theist can certainly accept that real things must have causal power independent of the power of our thoughts about them. It does not follow that they are perceptible – if it did many unobservable entities in science would cease to be real. Feuerbach states that real existence is 'sensational existence' (1957: 200) and then accuses theism of incoherence in asserting that God exists while denying God of all the attributes of this real, sensational existence. But the incoherence is only there if there is a prior acceptance of Feuerbach's criteria for the real.

Similar inadequacies can be seen in Feuerbach's attempt to show that there are contradictions in theism's talk of the divine attributes. He notes that we give substance to talk of God possessing love, understanding and of God doing such things as creating by employing a human meaning to these characterisations. But then we are urged to purge our conceptions of divine attributes and actions of all human connotations. The result is contradiction (1957: 221). The contradiction is only there if we accept there is no *via media* between using human language univocally of God and not using it at all. That is a principle imported to generate the contradiction but one which few reflective theists will accept; without it there is no contradiction.

It should be admitted that in his discussion of the 'contradiction in the nature of God' Feuerbach has lit upon a genuine tension in the expression of many forms of theism. This could be said about many of the chapters in Part II of *The Essence of Christianity*. There are tensions and paradoxes in the many particular versions of theism, tensions arising from the generic concern to speak of something transcendent. Theists, however, will argue that a paradox is not yet a contradiction and they have spilled much ink suggesting ways in which their ideas can be understood. Our brief discussion moves to a verdict on the two questions arising from Feuerbach's treatment of the 'contradictions' in theism: he has not made good his case for saying that there are such contradictions and it therefore follows that generic theism is not obviously self-contradictory, albeit all will recognise tensions and paradoxes in theistic thought.

D.Z. Phillips

D.Z. Phillips is well-known for arguing over the best part of four decades that transcendental theism is not false but unintelligible and a hopeless construction placed upon talk of the divine by philosophers. The word 'God' does not denote a thing, an existent, an object (see

Phillips 1970b: 17, 85–6, 130–31). It can be characterised as a referring expression, but only if we abandon any attempt to treat is as analogous to what we commonly call referring expressions. If his case could be established, then a realist interpretation of theistic discourse would be out of the question. He has also emerged as a champion of Feuerbach's negative case in *The Essence of Christianity*. Phillips thinks with Feuerbach that realist interpreters of religion are faced with an impossible choice: either an unacceptable anthropomorphism or an account of the divine riddled with incoherence. I will briefly explore how Phillips takes up the cudgels on behalf of Feuerbach.

Phillips assumes that if we say that God is an existent then it will follow that God is one of a kind, a being amongst beings, something whose reality can be 'assessed by a common measure which also applies to things other than God' (Phillips 1993: 62). What he means by this complaint is perhaps indicated by his comments on how to interpret statements in theism about what God was like or up to before human beings emerged in history. Such statements, he tells us, do not mean that God existed before men in the same sense in which mountains, rainbows or rivers so existed:

> These are all empirical phenomena and my beliefs concerning their prior existence allow me to ask questions about what they looked like, how long they had existed, whether some of these empirical phenomena had ceased to exist, and so on. Nothing of this sort makes any sense where God's reality is concerned. [Phillips 1993: 104–5]

By this argument Phillips assumes that to say that God is an existent is to say that God exists as an object among other objects in a vicious sense: God must be like an empirical thing. The realist interpreter of theism will, of course, accept that we use a common measure of what is real outside of the human world, namely, what has causal power independent of our thoughts about it. But this is far from admitting that all things which are real by that measure enjoy the same mode of existence. Depending on the precise conception of the *theos* employed, theistic thinkers can agree with Phillips' contention that it makes no sense to ask what the eternal God looks like, how long it has existed (though some will have an answer: forever), or how it is changed since human beings came on the scene. Phillips makes the same assumption as Feuerbach: things which exist independent of the human world must be empirical things, objects in space and time. This is the force of the Phillips principle 'if God is an existent, he must be an object among objects'. Theists with a radical perspective on divine transcendence will, of course, assert that it is not sufficient merely to deny that God is not an empirical object. The divine mode of being is so different from empirical things that God in fact is absolutely simple, therefore without properties and consequently not in any genus. This markedly non-anthropomorphic conception of deity might even deny that God is an existent – since God is being itself. But the God of Aquinas and Maimonides is still something that is non-empirical and real by the common measure of reality employed in this study.

Phillips' endorsement of Feuerbach's contention that 'God' cannot refer to a metaphysical subject appears to be based firmly on the equation of real subjects with empirical subjects. Phillips affirms that there is an 'internal relation' between such properties of God as that God is the creator and that God is love. So no one could be said to have a knowledge of God if they did not have knowledge of God as creator, as love. Therefore Feuerbach was right to insist that God is not a metaphysical subject who possesses these properties (Phillips 2001: 94–5). We have to interpret such predicates as 'grammatical predicates of a grammatical object, not descriptions of an independent existing object of which they happen to be true' (2001: 95). The endorsement of Feuerbach in this argument only works if we assume that all subjects of predication are like empirical subjects: their properties are possessed accidentally. There seems to be nothing, outside of Feuerbachian dogma, to stop a theistic thinker affirming both that God is like empirical objects in being a subject of predication, but unlike them in possessing all its key attributes essentially. God could not continue to exist as the thing God is and yet lose such properties as being the creator and being loving.

Phillips thinks he has a knock-down argument against the conception of God as a metaphysical subject. That conception needs a notion of God transcending the world, as being in some significant sense apart from the world (see Chapter 1 above). It thereby falls into the following trap: it makes no sense to talk of 'the world'. Theism which has a metaphysical subject needs to think of the universe as a thing and of God as its source, ground or cause. But it makes no sense to speak of the universe as a thing. It cannot be spoken of as the class of all things, because we could not identify this class as being different from other classes. There are no criteria to identify what would belong to the class of 'everything'. The world does not have the unity of a thing or of a class of things (see 2001: 70).

What are we to make of the point that there is no thing (the universe) which we can say the *theos* transcends? The argument certainly points to a problem in how to make intelligible the context in which talk of a metaphysical subject makes sense. But surely the problem has a solution and it is along the following lines. What is meant by 'world' when it is said that God transcends the world is the cosmos. The cosmos is the collection of spatio-temporal objects thought of as forming an ordered physical whole. The things which God transcends are assumed to be all spatio-temporally related to one another and to be bound together by a fundamental set of physical stuffs, forces and laws. The notion that all spatio-temporal things form part of a cosmos in this sense is to be found at the origins of Greek natural theology and thus forms both the historical and logical basis for philosophical thought about a *theos*. It is difficult indeed to see what Phillips can have against it. With the notion of a cosmos we have a home for the cosmological argument, since we can ask whether the ordered system of physical things is self-contained or requires some cause or ground external to it. Phillips objects to the cosmological argument that we cannot ask who made the world or 'everything'. There could be no process or development leading to the world's existence and asking for the cause of everything is odd since we explain the cause of something by referring to something else (2001: 69). But of course purveyors of the cosmological argument will accept that there is no *physical* process that is the making of the world. And they will say that we must seek a cause or ground of all *finite* things or of all *things which come to be and pass away*. Phillips' dismissal of metaphysical questions is really quite weak. There is no striking new vindication of Feuerbach here.

One of the fundamental differences between Phillips' approach to the reality of God and the approach defended here is that he does not see the necessity of a metaphysical subject in order to tackle the problem of evil in human life. Indeed, on Phillips' oft-repeated view, any attempt to search for a transcendent source of moral order in things external to human beings and the moral lives they lead entails moral corruption. Since we have relied so much on an account of the relationship of theism to the perception of evil, a brief treatment of Phillips on evil is in order (for a fuller treatment see Byrne 1998: 136ff.).

Phillips defends what I have called a Socratic response to evil (Byrne 1998: 42) and reckons it to be at the essence of a religious perspective on life and the world. Socrates told us that the good man cannot be harmed. This means for Phillips that part of what is involved in the development of moral awareness is the acquisition of standards of good and harm such that the worldly way of measuring these things is abandoned. A true response to evil will enable evil to be overcome in the life of the individual to the extent that, like the Socrates of the *Apology* and the *Phaedo*, evil can be defeated through transcending the worldly standard of what is harmful. The ego will have been so transcended that no harm can come to the self from any external source. Phillips writes of the authentic religious response to evil arising out of acceptance of its very pointlessness. That means giving up the idea that it is part of a higher plan which will benefit those who suffer evil in the long run. Acceptance of evil's pointlessness means dying to the self; it means transcending self-centredness (Phillips 1977: 115–16). On his account, I would be correct in thinking that the language of theism arises out of an awareness of evil but wrong in thinking that such language introduces the thought of some higher, ultimate order which will lead to the defeat of evil in the end. That cosmic hope represents an outlook which has not accepted evil's pointlessness and has not died to the self. Religion represents a perspective on life and the world in which 'The beliefs assess the facts, not the facts the beliefs' (Phillips 1970b: 166). The believer has a new measure of good and evil articulated in the language of theism which entails that goodness is internal to the good person, who has so died to the self that evil is incapable of harming him or her.

My argument to the effect that forms of theism put evil and good in the context of a wider teleology backed by a metaphysical postulate is the precise reverse of an appropriate religious perspective for Phillips. Whereas I regard the authentic religious response to evil as involving the hope that good will triumph over evil in the objective order, he views that hope as corruptive. I regard the religious view of the good life as uniting the drive to moral worthiness and the expectation that such worthiness will bring right relationship to some transcendent goodness, which will in turn give us an invulnerable and imperishable good. He regards the good life as purposeless. It does not include or depend on a belief that good will triumph over evil in the objective order. The categorical demands of morality can be so embraced by the self that its notions of harm and evil are transformed, with the result that the self becomes invulnerable to evil no matter what happens in the world external to the self (Phillips 1970a: 33). Thus Phillips has a conception of goodness devoid of teleology.

Phillips' view of the human good is worth taking seriously. It is not, I would contend, that which has been customary in the concrete forms of theism found in the world's history. If I am right about that, his reading of religious language is revisionary. He would not accept that point and he has one major argument to show that morality and the good life must be divorced from any kind of metaphysical teleology. If it were sound, my defence of theistic realism would be broken-backed. Phillips' argument is based on the point that if the defeat of evil and the promotion of good in human life are linked to a teleology they will end up recommending morality as being to our long-term advantage. The hope will be that doing good and resisting evil will lead to the crowning of the moral struggle by an externally guaranteed happiness. This necessarily corrupts, for it serves to recommend morality as something which brings about some external good. That destroys the categorically binding character of morality. What becomes categorically binding and of supreme importance is the gaining of this external good, for example, blessed union with God in the life hereafter (see 1970a: 29–33).

Once more, Phillips moves much too swiftly in rejecting traditional understandings of theism. His critique of belief in morally grounded teleology assumes that those who believe in such a teleology will see good acts as merely instrumentally good. But this is not so. Theism in its various concrete forms tells us that the doing of good and avoidance of evil in one's own life are the constitutive means of attaining the perfected state. They are in and of themselves ways of entering into right relation with the *theos*. Acting well in part constitutes the end striven for. This is quite compatible with contending that the full good and the final defeat of evil can only come with other things, things which are external to the moral life, so that the full value (not *all* the value) of good action is realised only in the transformation of life promised in religion. Theodicies can recognise that there are things we can do in our own lives to defeat evil. Good conduct itself can be included in this list. But they will contend that unless good conduct is seen as an integral part of some larger, teleological whole some significant part of its value is lost.

The above reply to Phillips' knock-down argument thus accuses him of confusing two ways in which good conduct can be the means to a final end: it can be a *constitutive* means or an *instrumental* means. Only if it is the latter, is the kind of theodicy that goes with standard theism reductive. But on standard theism, good conduct will be a constitutive part of a final good, not a mere instrument to its realisation.

This is perhaps the point to deal with John Kekes' major objection to theodicy. Kekes offers an argument for the following conclusion: we know in the nature of the case that theodicy cannot work and thus that the theistic perspective as I have outlined it is false. It suffers from an obvious incoherence and thus was never a candidate for realist interpretation. The incoherence is simply seen. Theism tells us that the world as it appears to us is beset by evil. It promises us a transcendent mechanism which has the power to defeat evil and ensure our final good. Because this mechanism exists, the world is morally ordered underneath. According to Kekes, this passage of thought must be self-stultifying. The theistic perspective supplies the premise which shows that it cannot be rationally held: the world appears to be evil and disordered. How it appears is the best guide to how it truly is. Any reason we might give for believing that the world contains a deeper order must come from the world as we experience it. But we experience it as evil and disordered, therefore in the nature of the case it can provide no ground for believing in a *theos* (see Kekes 1990: 27–8).

We must admit that a major motive for belief in a transcendent God does provide evidence against that belief: the fact of evil in human life. The theist, however, will surely respond to Kekes that matters are not that simple. There is more to 'the world as we experience it' than he suggests. The general pattern of events as we experience it suggests no moral order to things. Yet there are specific facts revealed in our experience which can provide grounds for thinking that the general pattern of events does not provide a conclusive verdict. These specific facts will include the starting-points for the traditional arguments of natural theology. They will include what is disclosed in religious experience and revelation. There is a tension but no contradiction in the thought that 'how things appear' is complex. The world appears to lack a moral order, but a deeper look may give us grounds for thinking that our first sight of its appearance is deceptive.

Cupitt and the Autonomy of the Religious Requirement

In *Taking Leave of God*, Cupitt is convinced that we can no longer use religious language to refer to something that is transcendent. Instead it gives voice to something within us: the religious requirement (more of that anon). Given that he is a contrastive, revisionary anti-realist in *Taking Leave*, does he come out as a theological instrumentalist or theological reductionist? For the most part, he is the former. He states that the modern believer must use the old language expressively (1980: 93). He affirms that faith must now be expressed with a variety of 'as ifs', and thus speak *as if* there were a personal God, an unknowable transcendent (1980: 139). These points suggest that religious statements have no truth value and that symbols like 'God' have no referential force in a reformed theism. On the other hand, there is at least one place where Cupitt gives ways in which statements about God can be translated into statements about the religious requirement, thus giving them a truth value (1980: 103). That makes theistic symbols referential, but the reference is to an aspect of the self. The predominant view is undoubtedly the instrumentalist one.

Cupitt's revisionary realism is a clear example of the liberal thinking about theism described in Chapter 1 and illustrated there by reference to Julian Huxley. Like Huxley, Cupitt judges the theistic tradition of his culture to be false but nonetheless thinks that a worthwhile use can be made of its symbolism. Much of the religious life associated with that symbolism can survive the discovery that it is literally false. There need be nothing incoherent about this programme. And one might expect that folk who do believe in the contentions of some theistic tradition would welcome rather than condemn those unbelievers who can continue to make some positive use of the traditional symbolism. The question to be pursued with regard to Cupitt's revision is how persuasive it is, both in its negative verdict on the tradition and its positive account of how religious life can be salvaged from the wreckage. The problem with Cupitt's statement of modernist, religious liberalism in *Taking Leave of God* is its fatal combination of dogmatic, confident assertion that no sensible, moral person can embrace a realist understanding of theism with the poverty of argumentation in support of this contention.

Cupitt's negative case has two main strands in it: metaphysical-cum-epistemological and moral. The metaphysical-cum-epistemological strand includes the claim that theism is incoherent, as when he states that the idea of a God who is a disembodied person makes no sense (1980: 90–91). But Cupitt's argument on this score is undeveloped and, as noted in relation to Feuerbach, irrefutable proof of the incoherence of traditional theism is hard to find. Moreover, as pointed out in Chapter 1, a realistic interpretation of theism can be delivered by a wide variety of metaphysical systems, not all of which espouse the standard, Western conception of deity as a disembodied spirit. Cupitt takes us through the traditional proofs of God's existence and concludes that they do not work (1980: 21–33) and makes much of the point that the problem of evil makes difficulties for the argument from the design (1980: 28–9). While many will agree with him in these conclusions, his discussion does not advance the issues, not least because it is unable to take account of the revival of natural theology in the writings of Richard Swinburne and others (see Swinburne 1991).

Cupitt's central contention in support of his negative case is that 'a radical and permanent change in the human condition has taken place' such that theism, realistically interpreted is no longer credible (Cupitt 1980: 17). While this point mainly relates to Cupitt's moral case against theism, it connects with the metaphysical and epistemological claim that belief in an objective God is no longer possible once the West abandoned Aristotelian physics (1980: 99). This does raise an interesting issue. I have contended that, whatever metaphysical wrapping core theism comes in, it contains generically a commitment to a telic, providential world-order. There is a moral power sufficient to defeat evil which is over and above human and mundane powers. One might think that what modern science shows is that the world is devoid of purpose. This perception is frequently cited as a reason for abandoning theism (cf. Murdoch 1970: 79). But, whatever the merits of the claim that there is no providential order in things, it cannot be said to be established by the refutation of Aristotelian science or the absence of appeal to purpose in post-seventeenth-century science. Scientists no longer suppose that each natural thing acts for the sake of a final cause. They appeal to efficient causation alone. But that does not stop the postulation of a God who gives ends to the world and history. This point was made long ago – by early modern scientists such as Robert Boyle (see Boyle 1973). That there is no teleology in reality outside of human and animal agency is not a scientific thesis but a metaphysical thesis. It would be true if materialism were true, but that is a matter of philosophical suasion and not scientific proof.

By far the most important part of Cupitt's negative case is the moral argument that commitment to human autonomy rules out acknowledging a transcendent *theos*. Cupitt is not alone in this assertion. Other post-Christian thinkers make it. Hampson affirms that no self-respecting feminist can believe in a transcendent god because 'the relationship to such a God must ultimately be always heteronomous' (Hampson 1996: 9). This contention is founded on the notion that obedience and worship are due to a transcendent God, but worship and obedience are incompatible with autonomy. The argument is familiar to those with a knowledge of contemporary analytic philosophy of religion. A famous paper by James Rachels launched a debate around the 'proof' that as autonomous moral agents we cannot recognise any being as worthy of worship, since the role of being a worshipper is incompatible with being a morally autonomous agent (Rachels 1981). Let us note two initial oddities in this line of argument in Hampson. It is not, strictly speaking, belief in a transcendent, objective *theos* that demands attitudes of worship and obedience from us. It is rather, belief in a transcendent deity who is personal. We have argued, to take just one example, that the impersonal divine Unity of forms of pantheism is a candidate for a transcendent deity conceived realistically, but the appropriate attitude due to it may be contemplation rather than worship and obedience. A further problem with the Hampson argument also infects Cupitt's negative moral argument. How can any premises about what are appropriate or praiseworthy human attitudes convince us that something is the case (that there is no transcendent God)? Supposing we set great store by autonomy and are fully convinced by Hampson, Rachels and Cupitt that we cannot be autonomous if we acknowledge the existence of a traditional deity. That may just tell us that we cannot be what we want to be. Why should the world be such as to satisfy our moral ideals? It is more consonant with innocent realism to be sceptical than welcoming of such arguments from our ideals to what is the case.

If this point is urged against theism's critics, it will have to be urged in equal measure against those religious apologists who argue from our moral needs to the conclusion that we must believe in a God. The many variants on the theme that we need transcendent help to defeat evil if morality is not to be pointless will become suspect for the same reasons urged against our anti-realists. (This difficulty in moral arguments for theism is explored in Byrne 1998; see p. 40 for an initial airing.)

Cupitt's use of the autonomy theme is much more extensive than Hampson's. If modernity has killed the positive case in natural theology for belief in God, it has also transformed human beings into creatures with a craving for autonomy in moral and religious life. We are told 'theological realism can only be *true* for a heteronomous consciousness such as no normal person ought now to have' (Cupitt 1980: 12; note that as an argument for God's non-existence this contains just the problem highlighted above). The moral development of human beings into creatures who must have autonomy is aided by the intellectual change which has seen science 'show' that there are no values in the world and that all values are human creations (1980: 3). Cupitt has found one piece of firm ground here: theism taken realistically rules out the fact–value distinction in its classic form. That is to say, if there is a transcendent *theos*, then we cannot say that all values are projected on to the world and that reality contains no objective value. Generically, theism is committed to thinking that there is a transcendent reality or ground which is the embodiment of supreme value. It is not valuable because human attitudes, feelings or decisions of principle make it such. Generic theism demands a metaphysic of objective values.

We have yet to explore why Cupitt thinks autonomy demands the falsehood of any objectivist metaphysic of value. We observe a problem in the link he makes between these two notions. Cupitt runs an argument claiming that certain specific moral values are incompatible with believing in a God. He contends that disinterestedness as a value is out if there is a God dispensing rewards and punishments after death (1980: 68–9). But if values are not objective, so that the value of disinterestedness reflects human choice, then it is hard to see how such an argument can be probative. I can, presumably, choose not to have disinterestedness in my value-set if a projective theory of value is true. Then the force of Cupitt's argument on this score collapses. At best his argument becomes: if you want to be disinterested, you won't believe in God.

If values are not 'out there', then it is not objectively true that autonomy itself is a good. Is not Cupitt's entire argument then in danger of unravelling? Supposing someone said to themselves: 'The last thing I want to be is fashionable. I choose to be a heteronomous agent. I will positively relish selecting an authority to whom I will give absolute obedience.' Cupitt may contend that autonomy is the one value that we cannot eschew. The decision not to be autonomous is one that the individual has to make for him- or herself. True, but autonomy is something which can be given up. The state of living in autonomy can be ended. Cupitt is here faced with a major dilemma. He has a moral critique of belief in traditional theism. Certain moral values (disinterestedness, autonomy) are threatened by theism's truth. It is contrary to conscience to embrace theism. No normal person ought now to have a religious consciousness based on traditional theism. But he says that there is no objectivity to value. What then is the force of the 'ought' in his argument? There is a kind of modern atheism based on a moral critique of religion (usually Christianity). We can trace it in numerous nineteenth-century thinkers. But a necessary condition for its coherence is that the conscience which protests against the evils of religion is reliably formed. Without an objectivist account of value, we will be hard-pressed to give sense to the notion of a reliable formation to conscience. It will not be a conscience that is aware of what is truly valuable. Yet if Cupitt were to embrace an objectivist metaphysic of value, his metaphysical critique of theism would begin to wobble. He could not run the line that the world outside of human consciousness is just as natural science describes it and no more.

What does Cupitt see in autonomy that makes it so morally and spiritually important? This is hard to answer. He links autonomy to 'internalisation' – that process whereby 'meanings and values are withdrawn from external reality and sucked into the individual subject' (1980: 3). It is certainly important for moral and spiritual progress that people live by values which they make their own, that is, values which they are fully committed to and which are authentically theirs. Yet it is hard to see how this is connected with the notion that values should be the product of our autonomy and not found in external reality. It may be important that people act on beliefs of which they are fully persuaded, fully committed to. But that is not incompatible with regarding the beliefs as corresponding to what is true of the world around them – rather the opposite. Why cannot I, by the same token, internalise values which I take to be discovered rather than invented by me? Cupitt will have none of this. He sings a paean to autonomy, declaring that moderns have come to realise that they can make spiritual progress only if they live their own life, one arising out of their own freedom (see 1980: 4). He urges:

> What matters is spirituality; and a modern spirituality must be a spirituality for a fully-unified autonomous human consciousness, for that is the kind of consciousness that modern people have. That in turn means that the principles of spirituality cannot be imposed on us from without and cannot depend at all upon any external circumstances. On the contrary, the principles of spirituality must be fully internalised *a priori* principles, freely adopted and self-imposed. [1980: 9]

In the light of the above it is claimed that it is spiritual vulgarity and immaturity to demand an extra-religious reality for God or to attempt validate religion by any external facts (1980: 10). It is especially wrong to think that we are to obey a divine commander. God becomes a symbol for the religious requirement. Cupitt writes that the religious requirement ('the central principle of spirituality') commands us to achieve the highest degree of autonomous self-knowledge combined with self-transcendence (1980: 9). Self-transcendence is the disinterestedness we have met before.

Once more we face the problem that Cupitt's thought appears to lack even the most minimal coherence. The religious requirement, spirituality, makes demands of us. It is even spoken of as directing us (1980: 9). But what then becomes of autonomy? Waiving the paradox that the value placed on autonomy ought to allow some people to give it up, how can we set such store by autonomy and yet find it directing us to give up reliance on self and, Buddhist-like, strive for a complete disinterestedness? If freedom is the great spiritual value, I can surely be allowed to be free to be self-centred. It is hard to see how we can be autonomous and yet be subject to a religious requirement which directs me to realise a specific value in my life. It is hard to see how my freedom is any less hampered by a requirement/demand located in the human self than one located externally. Cupitt's autonomy in the end is circumscribed by some universal, essential traits in the human self. In order to flourish we have to be disinterested. Here we confront a dilemma already hinted at: he cannot say the equivalent of 'whatever you do, do what you authentically and autonomously want' while at the same time urging the necessity of self-transcendence. Well, he can, but at the cost of a big assertion about the human essence: liberation can only come if we are disinterested. However, we would not then be free to stay sunk in selfishness. An objective value would have reared its ugly head.

Cupitt must give an objective value to freedom and disinterestedness in order to run his argument, even while he denies that there is any such thing as objective value. If that were not a big enough hole in his argument, we have noted above that it seems implausible to argue that our autonomy would be hampered if moral values are objective. That something is a fact does not make us believe it. Even if there is a proof of the fact, proofs do not coerce assent – people are perfectly free to think irrationally and incoherently. Beliefs can be sincerely and devoutly held and yet correspond to facts. A way of coming to 'internalise' beliefs is to come to accept them at the end of a process of examining grounds for them. That is a way of making the beliefs my own. All this could be true, *mutatis mutandis*, of coming to embrace objective moral values autonomously.

We have seen that Cupitt is in trouble because he wants us to exercise our moral and spiritual freedom in ways which he regards as good, worthwhile and liberating. He is right in this desire. Suppose that I was free not merely to espouse the ideals I judged to be good, worthwhile and liberating, but also to determine, by fiat, what ideals really were good, worthwhile and liberating. Freedom of this latter would be worthless, since if I had this freedom what values I chose could not matter to me. Exercise of freedom in moral (and factual) judgement matters precisely because there is a difference between correct and incorrect judgement. One of the bad (*the* bad?) things about not having freedom of thought and enquiry is that in those circumstances I am forced to give up truth in favour of what someone tells me is the truth.

It may be objected that so far I have omitted what is the most important element in Cupitt's (and Hampson's) argument. Subscribing to an objective God means signing up to the belief that spiritual growth and human flourishing come about through obedience to commands.

Here is a real sense in which objective theists are forced to abandon their role as autonomous and conscientious agents: they must be prepared to accept divine decrees for life and conduct as valid just because they are divine decrees. But, as James Rachels famously pointed out, 'to deliver oneself over to a moral authority for directions about what to do is simply incompatible with being a moral agent' (Rachels 1981: 44). If this is the unconfused core to Cupitt's argument, it is open to the range of replies to Rachels' attempt to show that being a morally autonomous agent is incompatible with recognising a God who demands obedience and issues commands to his worshippers. There is a vast array of replies to Rachels (expertly surveyed in Sagi and Statman 1995, Chapter 7). I shall merely pick out a few strands of argument to show that Cupitt has not discovered a strong argument against belief in an objective, personal God.

An obvious reply to Rachels is that if doing what is right consists in obedience to divine decrees, then there is still room for believers to exercise autonomous judgement. They have to determine what is and is not a divine decree and they have to determine what genuine divine decrees mean. This they could not do if they lacked intellectual autonomy. Perhaps it may be said that this is not true (that is, moral) autonomy, since believers in a personal God would not be working out for themselves what is right and wrong and then acting on that knowledge. But in a way they are: identifying and interpreting divine commands is an absolutely sure way of working out what is right and wrong, given that God is omniscient and omnibenevolent. What better way could there be if some form of personal theism is true? Such a policy is guaranteed to lead to action which is morally correct. The response to this would no doubt be: thinking and acting thus is not being morally autonomous because it is not acting out of a directly acquired conviction of right and wrong. The faithful act on the basis of an indirect pointer to value, not out of awareness of value itself.

At this point in the debate opponents of the Rachels-Cupitt line on autonomy will have to confront the question of what is wrong in acting on the authority of another. They have to deny that there is an overriding value in always acting on one's own direct convictions as to what is right and wrong. Sometimes it is right to put oneself under the direction of a central authority and act on its dictates. Autonomy, as defined by the critic of personal theism, is simply not a value which trumps all other values in all circumstances. The case for this conclusion can start with the fact that reasonable people will accept obedience to human law as proper in appropriate circumstances. It is necessary for the wise conduct of human affairs that we be subject to the authority of law and government. Law that is directed to the securing of the common good has a proper authority over our own personal preferences and values. 'Authority' is the key word here: where law has legitimacy, submission to law is not submission to mere might or power. Though I may act contrary to my own wishes at one level in obeying lawful authority, I can reason at a higher level that it is necessary that there be such authority and right that its particular commands are obeyed. I do this because I want the goods that come from living in an ordered community and judge that the law and government I face is genuinely directed to producing that community. I sacrifice some specific goods I want in favour of the general good I need to participate in.

A central reason why reasonable individuals are not addicted to the autonomy Cupitt apparently values is that they realise that their good is relational. Their overall good can only be sought in community with others. Pursuit of individual good in community requires restraint on one's autonomy and the acceptance of direction from those who have power over the community. One can only make Cupitt-style autonomy the acme of value at the cost of placing a commensurate, supporting value on individualism. But such individualism (the denial that the human condition and good are profoundly relational) will simply appear false to many. It will certainly be judged false by the theistic traditions Cupitt is trying to reject. From within them the human good will appear precisely to be relational in character and thus from within them Cupitt-style autonomy will not appear to be of supreme value. Cupitt's argument thus faces the following difficulty: there are problems in conducting a moral critique of types of theism by reference to the value of autonomy, conceived in a certain way. The value of autonomy thus conceived will not be persuasive, since it is only upon stepping outside those traditions that Cupitt-style autonomy will be seen to be of supreme value. The moral critique lacks a neutral vantage point and subsides into the assertion that some of us want to live a style of life incompatible with traditional forms of theism.

It is evident that the generic theism identified in this study sees the good for human beings as relational. A diagnosis is offered of the human condition which shows it to be beset by evil. Our condition is fundamentally flawed. A cure is offered which consists in living in right relation with a trans-mundane source of power and value. Alignment with this transcendent, sacred principle constitutes escape from evil. Liberation and salvation precisely cannot come about through a process consisting in an individualistic transformation of consciousness. It comes about through right relation to an other. The particular kind of theism Cupitt attacks sees that relation as consisting in loving union with a personal deity. Heeding the instructions for right living of such a deity cannot be fairly represented as being swayed by 'external guarantees and sanctions' (Cupitt 1980: 68). The good that would come from loving union with this reality, if it exists, can only be acquired if pursued for its own sake. In the same way, I cannot listen to Beethoven's late quartets for the sake of the pleasure they will give me as opposed to listening to them for their own sakes. I won't get the pleasure unless I regard the activity as intrinsically worthwhile. I will not get the rewards of the Christian's heaven unless I become the kind of person who loves God and the good for their own sakes.

Like so much in *Taking Leave of God*, Cupitt's autonomy critique only moves forward on the basis of crude caricature of the views he is attacking. Such caricature comes out in the way he portrays the God of traditional theism as 'an infinite, almighty and commanding being quite distinct from the believer, who requires absolute obedience' (1980: xii) and as 'an alien almighty and commanding will' (1980: 85). The traditional believer's God is in truth the source of his or her nature and of the order of reality in which that nature is set. Following God's decrees can only be a way of realising one's happiness, of pursuing flourishing as a human being and realising one's good. God cannot be an external authority set over and against the self. It is only in so far as a human being has lost his or her true self that God and God's decrees can be thus represented. Acting rightly toward God is the way in which one's true self can be found – if the theistic story is correct.

I thus conclude that Cupitt's contrastive theistic anti-realism is an utter failure. It makes the mistake of assuming that anti-realism is the only alternative to personal theism of the kind found in Christianity. Its intellectual and moral critique of personal theism lacks any kind of probative force. The anti-realist humanism espoused is barely coherent.

The Feminist Critique

We have seen in the previous chapter that feminist thinkers are inclined to embrace a political conception of truth and knowledge. We discovered that such a conception is hard to understand. There is another strand in feminist thinking in religion which is superficially much more comprehensible. It centres on the claim that the traditional conception of God is a valorisation of the male desire for power and domination. The traditional concept of God is an idealisation of the *male* subject writ large. The feminist point about the concept of God gives rise to an argument against a realist construal of theistic language: such language cannot be taken as having a serious intent to refer to a being beyond human representations, since it is so obviously a projection of human (that is, male) desires onto reality. As one feminist critic of theism puts it: 'the further monarchical monotheism rationalises the object of its experiences, the more *obviously* susceptible it becomes to deconstruction as an anthropomorphic projection which divinises male political power' (Raphael 1994: 523; italics mine). The 'obviously' in this verdict is crucial. A denial of the realist intent of theistic discourse is supported to the extent to which it is obvious that the dominant motive in the employment of such discourse is something analogous to wish-fulfilment.

The feminist critique has its roots in Feuerbach's contentions in *The Essence of Christianity* to the effect that religious beliefs are the means whereby deep-seated human needs are objectified. He states that the dogmas of religion are the 'realised wishes of the heart' (Feuerbach 1957: 140). Feminist theologians and philosophers of religion find a strong positive correlation between, on the one hand, the wishes of the male heart for the possession of power and the exercise of dominion over others and, on the other, the belief that there is an omnipotent deity:

> This cold deity is the legitimating construct of the patriarchal desire to dominate and control the world. He is the eternal King, the Chairman of the board, the President of the institution, the Guru of the youth, the General of the army, the Judge of the court, the Master of the universe, the Father of the church. [Heywood 1982: 156]

It may be thought that there is in Chapter 1 of this book an easy reply to this Feuerbachian critique. There it was argued that theistic realism was not tied to the intent to refer to the God of standard, Western theism. The core meaning of *theos* we stipulated as necessary for realism was that of a transcendent source of moral order in the world. This need not entail that realism only comes with an attempt to refer to an omnipotent creator. Process theists deny that there is a creator who possesses the classically understood attribute of omnipotence and the God of Process thought is one that feels and suffers with creation, rather than being a 'cold deity'. But Process theism is hardly a version of theistic anti-realism. It claims to be closer to living religion than traditional philosophical accounts of God.

The point about the many varieties of theism can be added to. It is relatively easy to show that even so-called 'classical theism' does not in intent valorise the alleged male desire for power. If we attend to the way in which traditional philosophical theology has characterised the attribute of omnipotence in relation to the rest of the divine nature, we see it contains influential currents of thought which present divine power as precisely *not* human power raised to its maximum limit. This is done most notably by the deep-seated contention that the nature of any one divine attribute is affected by its relation to the others. In respect of omnipotence, this means the prevalence of the thought that God has no power to do evil (and thus no power to use might for unjust ends). God cannot exercise power as human beings exercise it: to dominate and deny others the opportunity to flourish. Divine power is fundamentally different from human power (see for example Swinburne 1977: 158–61). It follows that to think justly about the divine power is to see that we cannot use human power as its model. On the contrary, in the light of a conception of divine power we have to judge human power as something imperfect in its fundamental nature, not just in degree. In true thoughts about the divine, the transcendent is not modelled on the human, as Feuerbach has it. Thought about the transcendent is the attempt to gain a perspective for thinking critically about the human. Traditional theists can thus be as stern critics of the male lust for domination as can feminists. Human power is paltry; it is false coin. (For more on this see Byrne 1995a.)

Has the feminist critique thus been turned? Well, not quite. We should note that some feminists consider that it is not the specific attribute of omnipotence that displays the patent masculinist character of thought about a transcendent deity. There is a more general critique. It can be found in Grace Jantzen's *Becoming Divine*. Part of the critique is based on the thought that traditional theisms all value rational consciousness. God is the acme of rationality. This disembodied rational consciousness is presented as the perfection of personhood. Our good consists in becoming like this thing. After death, we can become disembodied consciousnesses, leaving behind the feelings and ties that came with having a body. It is not important for our identities as persons to be embodied and gendered subjects. We will flourish when we become like the ungendered, disembodied rational mind who is God (see Jantzen 1998: 28–31). But all this is masculinist. It is a fact, affirms Jantzen, that philosophers and theologians in Western traditions have taken their cue from Plato. Rationality is characteristic of the male. Female life is in contrast rooted in the bodily and the passional. Females are therefore bound to be further away from the divine than males (1998: 31–2). Thus is the traditional God revealed to be a masculinist construct and therefore oppressive.

Jantzen goes further. Tied to the ideal of the rational subject, human and divine is 'an implicit investment in the symbolic of death' (1998: 29), since the human self cannot reach its true end – likeness to and consequent union with God – save through death. Embodied life must be left behind. True fulfilment only comes with death. Theism is part and parcel of the 'necrophilia of western philosophical and religious thought' (1998: 8). This notion – that we can only flourish and become God-like after death – has dire consequences for the social and political order (1998: 155). Jantzen goes further still. She, along with many feminist critics of traditional notions of God, thinks it is sufficient to raise doubts about the cogency of that notion to point out that it has been used for oppressive ends: '... the assumption of the centrality of this concept of God is disrupted by the consideration that, even on a most generous reading, it has been used to legitimate the most appalling sexism, racism, colonialism, and technological exploitation of the earth ...' (1998: 66).

The political critique of traditional theism has got deeper, but it is not yet forceful enough to disturb a realist interpretation of its discourse. Feuerbach's arguments, if sound, have the power to show that on a second look religious folk have not intended to refer to a transcendent *theos*. But that is only because he aims his arguments at the right target. He endeavours to show that a necessary condition of using theistic language is that one be moved by the desire to project human desires and needs (or, put another away, that using theistic language is a sufficient condition for expressing the relevant desires and needs that one use theistic language). He can affirm this because, as noted above, he takes theism when interpreted as if it had a transcendent reference to be obviously and necessarily false. If we try to adopt the false, theological reading of talk about God seriously we generate blatant incoherence. Because of this we can set aside the possibility that anyone was ever motivated to embrace theistic assertions through the genuine awareness of reasons. Hence, we must search out the motives behind the show of reasons offered in support of theism. But then we have seen that there is little reason to accept Feuerbach's case for the patent incoherence of talk about a transcendent God. Freed from Feuerbach's materialist and empiricist dogmas, we can quite easily accept that many people embrace some form or other of theism because they are persuaded by due consideration of relevant grounds. We may think that one and all these versions of theism are false. The grounds need not persuade us. But the mere fact that we think other folk's beliefs are false is not a reason for giving a suspicious interpretation of their meaning or seeking an account of the motives that lie behind them. They just think differently from us. Welch roundly asserts that theologians cannot refute Feuerbach's theory of religion as a projection (Welch 1985: 5). But they can. They can do so by pointing to the possibility of having genuine reasons for believing in the God theology describes. If there are such reasons, then not all belief in God is projective.

Jantzen provides no grounds whatsoever for the contention that people who think differently from her have no genuine reasons for believing in a conscious mind which controls the universe or for believing that human blessedness comes only with a life after death. As we noted in the previous chapter, she does toy with the idea that all knowledge claims are but the expression of political interest. But if they were, then so would her claims be and it would be sufficient to reply to her feminist philosophy of religion: 'it doesn't suit my interests'. There would be no intellectual challenge in it. Traditional theisms such as Christianity, Judaism and Islam embody world views different from that adhered to by Jantzen. If they can be embraced rationally, then they can be embraced without reliance on the desire to denigrate women. They need not be motivated by a love of death and hatred of life. They need not be embraced by those who wish for a license for oppression.

Consider Jantzen's charge that a traditional God feeds on an image of human personhood which overvalues rationality and detachment but devalues embodiment and the things which go with it. We can note straightaway that such a conception need have nothing to do with the denigration of women. It could only do so on condition that it is associated with the thought that women are less rational and autonomous and more tied to things bodily than men. No doubt a great many Western thinkers have had that view, but it seems monumentally confused. There is surely no proper sense in which male human beings are less tied to their bodies than female human beings. An easy diagnosis offers itself. Many past Western intellectuals have been misogynists. They have let their misogyny colour their theology and their anthropology. But the view that there is a disembodied creator is not of itself misogynist. There is no way in which, in the absence of other highly tendentious beliefs, it implies or entails a view that women are lesser persons than men.

How about the charge that thinking of God as disembodied in itself leads to a devaluation of embodied life? Well, of course we can find many thinkers who make that link. But the link is in no way necessary. It can equally go the other way. That this world is the creation of a perfect and good God implies that it is shot through with goodness and glory. Hence, earthly creation is to be esteemed. There are many specific forms of theism which set great store by the health and integrity of the body and by the importance of the good and just community of embodied human beings. Judaism will do as an example. If the West's culture has for centuries been founded on forms of theism, does this mean that it has been characterised by hatred for things bodily and physical? To pose the question is to see how feeble is the attempt to link belief in the traditional God with a denigration of the human body or the physical world. A brief list of characteristic features of Western civilisation confirms the verdict: naturalistic forms of art (directed as well at the human form), the development of natural science, the pursuit of earthly justice and the amelioration of the human condition in ethical and political thought and life.

The above will also make us refuse to accept without demur talk of the necrophilia embedded in 'the Western male imaginary'. The living forms of theism in the Western tradition are characteristically world- and life-affirming rather than the opposite. It is true that it is highly characteristic of systems affirming some determination of generic theism to hold that the defeat of evil and finitude in human life depends on a life to come. In so far as Jantzen disagrees with this generic affirmation she simply has an intellectual disagreement with many religions and philosophies. She must respect that some people think differently from her. Anyone viewing the issues in that spirit will also recognise that there is a logic to the typical movement of thought within theism to see human flourishing as completed by the conquest of death. There are no grounds for suspicious interpretations so far. Alas, Jantzen does not see matters thus. She contends that any world view interested in salvation/ liberation as a state beyond the grave is thereby committed to a morally blind acceptance of injustice this side of eternity. She opposes talk of human flourishing to talk of salvation. The former is focused on life in the here and now, the latter on the life hereafter. If we focus on flourishing, we see the importance of material well-being in this life and hence of justice on earth. If we focus on salvation, we embrace a privatised religion removed from political and social involvement (see Jantzen 1998: 169–70). This argument is of a similar quality to Cupitt's on autonomy. It is based on hopeless caricature.

It is true that we can read some traditional theists as dismissing the earthly concern for social justice and material well-being altogether. Augustine's account in *The City of God* of the Christian as a pilgrim in the earthly city is suggestive of this reading (see Augustine 1972: 381, 620). But we should not allow any general opposition between the concepts of human flourishing and salvation. It is quite alien to many mainstream forms of theism. Consider here just one example: Aquinas' moral theology affirms that blessedness consists in the vision of God in a life to come. Yet it is integral to his view that a life lived according to the virtues is the precondition of such blessedness. To be the kind of person who is fit to enjoy a relation to God it is necessary to have developed a certain kind of character. The living of a life manifesting the virtues is not on this account to be opposed to a desire to be saved for the next one. Virtuous conduct is in any event a way of participating in right relation to God, since it is a manifestation of God's eternal law within us. Aquinas, and the virtues tradition generally, has taught that the virtues can only be fully manifested in the individual against the background of the just community. Aristotle, Aquinas' mentor in moral philosophy, is crystal clear in Book I of the *Nicomachean Ethics* that the master art in human affairs is political science because the human good is not self-contained in the sense of being private to the individual. It is social (see Aristotle 1941: 930/I, 2). If we started to investigate determinate forms of theism in detail, we would see even more clearly that Jantzen's argument is based on a false 'either-or'.

Jantzen is equally wide of the mark in her claim that the concept of God becomes suspicious merely because some people have used it to justify evil. It is very easy to see how the justification is possible even while the concept of God is innocent. The notion of deity is in part the notion of a supreme source or locus of value. Wicked people need to hide their wickedness from others and from themselves. They will thus represent evil as good. If they believe in God, they will represent their evil as God's will, since all that is good is in accordance with divine will. The movement of thought involved is exactly the same as when evil people claim that justice is on their side. Reflect on how many evil human projects have been presented as in the service of justice. There is nothing in the very concept of justice (the giving to each of their due) that will prevent evil people from presenting evil as good by appealing to justice to mask their wickedness. How could the notion of justice and its core definition prevent that? Concepts cannot stop human beings becoming evil in thought and deed. Concepts cannot stop people misusing them. By the same token, there is nothing in the concept of a providential source of goodness which prevents evil people from saying that their acts are in accordance with divine dictates. How could the concept prevent people from misusing it? Furthermore, it is by reference to the core of the concept of the divine, as it is by reference to the core concept of justice, that we can detect its misuse. If we find people claiming divine sanction for appalling behaviour, we know just in knowing the behaviour to be appalling that they misuse the concept. Nothing in the human world we truly judge to be evil can in fact be sanctioned by God. That is a tautology. The tautology cannot prevent people passing off evil as divinely sanctioned, because it cannot prevent people being evil or mistaking evil for what is good. What Jantzen wants, it would appear, are concepts which would be immune to human misuse, error and evil. She is not going to find them. To blame words and concepts for evil deeds and thoughts is another example of the magico-childish view of language documented and criticised in this study.

We embarked on the discussion of Cupitt and feminist thinkers because of the distinctive character of their critiques of traditional conceptions of God. They are not simply arguing for atheism, agnosticism or some kind of religious naturalism (cf. Huxley). It is their contention that, given certain contemporary and political ideas, ideas which amount to holy orthodoxies, we cannot use theistic language to refer to anything like the God of traditional theism. Realism has passed its sell-by date owing to an ethical and political transformation found in contemporary thought. Our probing of this notion has not revealed much substance to it. No doubt if one affirms Cupitt's belief in autonomy, or if one affirms that political liberation from gender and social injustice is the be-all and end-all of the human good, one will not avow any form of traditional theism. Many contemporary ideas of the ultimate good are not compatible with the ideas of the good found in traditional forms of theism. But that is simply to register an area of intellectual disagreement. What is gratuitous is the air of exposé which accompanies such disagreement. This is always liable to evince the tiresome expression of intellectual arrogance if it is not justified by a thorough and judicious analysis of its object. The stance of a hermeneutics of suspicion is a standing temptation to bad (that is, arrogant, unfair and dismissive) ways of thinking, since it allows its proponents not to treat the objects of their critiques as equal partners in an intellectual debate. It should accordingly be used sparingly.

Scepticism?

We have affirmed time and again in this study that realism invites scepticism. It affirms a gap between world and human subject. Most of our beliefs are true or false of a world which does not in any way depend on them. Realism's founding motto is that 'thinking cannot make it so'. Realism with respect to theism has the natural implication that the doctrines of any particular version of theism cannot be guaranteed to be true. All are fallible.

From the above we can generate a very simple argument against theistic realism:

1 Religious faith involves wholehearted commitment to the truth of doctrine.
2 If theistic realism is true, wholehearted commitment to doctrine is impossible (because all religious claims would have a measure of uncertainty).
3 Therefore theistic realism cannot be true.

The argument speaks of wholehearted commitment to doctrine. It might be more accurate to state that living faith involves wholehearted commitment *to God*. But for realism any particular affirmation of God's reality would be tinged with uncertainty and subject to reasonable doubt. Thus realism in fact rules out the possibility of appropriate relation to God. The believer can no longer dwell in the presence of God. Phillips makes this point in an amusing caricature of Psalm 139. The Psalmist affirms the believer's state as a person who dwells in God's presence:

> If I ascend up into heaven, thou art there;
> If I make my bed in hell, behold thou art there.

But if the realist philosopher of religion were right, then the Psalmist would have had to say:

> If I ascend into heaven, thou art probably there;
> If I make my bed in hell, it is cumulatively likely that thou art there. [Phillips 1988: 9–10]

One of Feuerbach's reasons for rejecting the thought that 'God' refers to a reality independent of us is that religion needs absolute certainty as to the existence and nature of God, but cannot have it in those circumstances:

> Religion gives up its own existence when it gives up the nature of God; it is no longer a truth when it renounces the possession of the true God. Scepticism is the arch-enemy of religion; but the distinction between object and conception – between God as he is in himself, and God as he is for me – is a sceptical distinction, and therefore an irreligious one. [Feuerbach 1957: 17]

Matters are worse for the realist than thus far suggested. It is not merely that realism applied to theism has a general tendency to promote a fallibililist, agnostic view of religious belief. Lived theism only comes in one concrete form or another. And concrete forms of theism disagree over the precise nature of the divine and its relations to human beings. Such conflict generates further agnosticism. Religious diversity encourages scepticism. It has been plausibly argued (in McKim 2001) that diversity among and conflict between different accounts of the divine entails that religious faith must be governed by 'the Critical Stance'. This stance has two component principles. The 'E-principle' obliges religious folk to examine their beliefs in the light of diversity. The 'T-principle' obliges them to hold their beliefs tentatively (see McKim 2001: 140–41). We might avoid the Critical Stance if we argued, as Runzo does (see Chapter 3), that diverse religions do not intend to give conflicting accounts of the one, human-independent divine reality.

The best response to this charge that realism destroys authentic faith is to tough it out.

Toughing it out in this context amounts to embracing the fact that realism entails uncertainty as inevitable and indeed welcome. Realism forces an epistemic gap between theistic claims and their truth. This gap is an inevitable consequence of the fact that particular, concrete forms of religion have an intellectual content. That intellectual content has to be judged to be true (to some degree or other) by the adherent of faith and no amount of passionate commitment to the putative object and content of faith can make the content come true. Basil Mitchell puts this point simply and well: 'The serious [religious and ethical] options that actually confront us are deeply involved with subtle and complex visions of the world' (Mitchell 1995: 68). If all concrete forms of faith have an intellectual content, embody a subtle and complex vision of the world, then it cannot but be that thinking them true is one thing, their being true is another. It cannot but be that the gap between the thought of their truth and their actual truth needs to be bridged by truth-indicators (reasons or grounds of some sort). In which event, in the (very likely) absence of conclusive reasons for one form of faith and against the others, epistemic certainty in religion is a matter of more or less, and is subject to severe restrictions.

Thus epistemic uncertainty is the inescapable consequence of the fact that each religion has an intellectual content. The premise behind the reply can be questioned. The Wittgensteinian interpretation of religion in Phillips effectively denies that religion (in Phillips a reworked Christianity) has an intellectual content. We have seen above that he takes religion to be an affirmation of a moral perspective on the world, one bound up with dying to the self and seeing the pointlessness of good. This notion of an authentic religious outlook has a place in the writings of Tolstoy and Wittgenstein as well (see Vaughan Thomas 1997). I have argued against its ethical and religious adequacy in *The Moral Interpretation of Religion* (see Byrne 1998, especially Chapter 6). My main contention now must be that Mitchell is descriptively correct. Actual, living forms of religion do have an intellectual content, do embody concretely different visions of the world. There is a generic vision/intellectual content to all theisms: an affirmation of a moral teleology to the world and human life. With intellectual content comes the possibility of falsehood and error, and thus epistemic uncertainty.

Note that not even making 'God' refer to the human essence in the manner of Feuerbach will remove intellectual content and the possibility of error from religion. There can be, and notoriously are, different views about our species-being. If talk of God really refers to important human attributes, there can and will be debate about what those attributes are. There is still a gap between making a claim and it being true. What is needed to avoid the gap is either the view that there are no beliefs in religion (see Phillips *et al.*) or the view that the divine reality is constituted by our beliefs. Neither of these views is acceptable.

Chapter 7

A Realist Interpretation of Theology?

Realist Disciplines

Thus far we have pursued the question of whether the governing intent of theistic discourse is to refer to a transcendent God, an extra-mundane source of a providential order in the world. A positive argument for answering the question in the affirmative was given in Chapter 1. That argument turned round the point that typical theisms were responses to evil in human life. They promise that evil can be overcome and defeated through relationship with a transcendent reality and by virtue of its guarantee of a teleological, moral order to reality. Chapters 2 to 6 have supported this line of thought by defeating the arguments, both global and specific, which would make it impossible to see the governing intent of theistic discourse as coherent. We have made it plain that the realism expounded and defended thus far does not amount to the assertion that some version of theism is true. Many people will judge that all and every specific version of theism is false. They can do that without inspecting each and every one if they reject the underlying assertion of a moral providence in all of them (as does John Kekes in *Facing Evil*). They are then at liberty to make use of theistic symbols for other ends than to refer to a transcendent *theos*.

We noted in Chapter 1 that questions about the intent of generic theism and the success of that intent do not exhaust the questions about religion that we can pursue under the banner of realism. We can ask whether theology can be interpreted as a realistic enterprise. This question can be understood by analogy with the corresponding question about science. Theology we understand as the discursive elaboration and exploration of claims about the divine. Correspondingly, we understand natural science as the discursive elaboration and exploration of claims about the material world. There is no such thing as theology *simpliciter*. For the sake of convenience, we shall take Christian theology as our example of such a discursive elaboration and exploration. We shall pursue the question of whether it can be interpreted realistically by taking natural science as our point of comparison.

There are many ways of understanding the question 'Can science be interpreted realistically?' It could be a question about the intent of scientific theories and hypotheses. It is so understood when we consider the debate between 'theoretical realism' and 'instrumentalism' as defined by Haack. Theoretical realism affirms that 'scientific theories are genuine, true or false, statements'. Instrumentalism affirms that 'scientific theories are not genuine, true or false statements, but instruments for making observational predictions' (Haack 1987: 276). In order to move beyond questions about the intent of scientific statements we have to consider other realist theses about science. Haak lists a further three:

1 Cumulative realism – later scientific theories are limit cases of earlier ones in the same domain.
2 Progressive realism – as science proceeds, it gets progressively nearer the truth.
3 Optimistic realism – current scientific theories are (mostly) (approximately) true. [1987: 276]

The details of these three theses do not concern me. Overall they hint at the following picture: science is a cumulative enterprise. As the history of science unfolds, science exhibits an increasing knowledge of what is the case. That in turn suggests a thesis about how scientific belief is to be interpreted. It is in significant measure the outcome of genuine real-world influences. So that, if we are giving an account of how scientific ideas come and go, we will have to make reference to the fact that scientific thought and practice are shaped by cognitive contact with natural reality. The story of science is a human story, but one which is comprehensible only if we assume that human theory and practice are being in part, at least, shaped by what the world is really like. If there is a progressive, cumulative structure to the development of science, this strongly suggests real-world cognitive contact and influence; otherwise the accumulation of reliable belief would be the merest accident.

Realism versus non-realism in the interpretation of science thus relates to broad hermeneutical questions concerning the character of scientific thought, discourse, practice and institutions. The different parties to the debate can admit that science is a human product, that it is to be interpreted as such and that it has a human explanation. But realists will hold, correctly, that there is an asymmetry between how we explain thought and activity directed at the discovery of the truth and thought and activity not so directed. They will further hold that this asymmetry is vitally important in the interpretation of science, since science shows through its cumulative character that it is successfully directed at the discovery of truth.

It follows that there are two ways in which a non-realist hermeneutic of science can be argued for. One way is to deny the asymmetry thesis outlined. Regardless of whether it 'tracks reality', science should be explained by the same array of human causes as explains any other complex of belief and practice. The explanation of science is not different in kind from the explanation of astrology. The other way of arguing for a non-realist hermeneutic of science is to deny that science exhibits clear marks of accumulation of truth and discoveries. In the rest of this chapter I shall contend that the asymmetry thesis holds. I shall highlight the fact that theology does not show any accumulation of truth and discovery in the manner of science and then draw the obvious moral that it deserves a non-realist hermeneutic.

Realism and the Explanation of Science

Proponents of the 'strong programme' in the sociology of knowledge deny the asymmetry between explaining belief which tracks reality and belief which does not. David Bloor holds that a true sociology of knowledge will exhibit the following features (amongst others):

1   It will be causal, that is, concerned with the conditions which bring about belief or states of knowledge.
2   It will be impartial with respect to distinctions such as those between truth and falsity, rationality and irrationality, success and failure. Both sides of these dichotomies will require explanation.
3   Its styles of explanation will be symmetrical. The same type of factor will explain true and false beliefs, rational and irrational beliefs, and so on. (see Bloor 1976: 4–5)

It is the third of these features in Bloor's portrait of an ideal sociology of scientific knowledge which does the work. No one will deny that mundane factors can be cited to explain how belief and knowledge arise. Belief and knowledge do not arise in human subjects out of thin air and this point must hold for true, rational and successful beliefs as much as for false, irrational unsuccessful beliefs. With the premise that true, rational and successful beliefs are explained in the same way as their opposites, Bloor gives himself license to conclude that sociological explanations are as much in order for scientific thought and practice as they are for anything else. Thus, for example, we can appeal to the structure of scientific institutions for sufficient explanations of scientific developments. Social influences, social causes, explain all.

  The symmetry thesis looks plausible if we take the truth and falsity of a belief in isolation from its rationality. To say that a belief is true is not to comment on how it is acquired. It is to say that its content matches what is the case. I might come to hold a belief that is true by the merest wishful thinking. By contrast, to say that a belief (in the sense of someone's believing something) is rational is precisely to comment on how it is acquired (and maintained). It is a belief acquired through awareness of evidence, reasons and the like, and/or after due reflection. Consider Alisdair MacIntyre's model explanation of the acceptance of Galileo's claims that Jupiter had moons in the early seventeenth century. The explanation will deal in observations and evidence that Galileo had made available. It will also refer to the canons of argument and enquiry which enabled astronomers to see that the evidence was cogent. Those canons are in turn made intelligible by reference to an account of the intellectual tradition of which they are a part (MacIntyre 1971: 245–6). To say that these astronomical beliefs were arrived at rationally is to say that awareness of grounds (against the appropriate background) was a necessary condition of their occurrence. This entails that societal factors *which do not include awareness of these grounds* could not have been sufficient to explain these beliefs. So, *contra* Bloor, the processes of reason do make people independent to a degree of sociological and psychological factors which are capable of generating belief (as MacIntyre notes, 1971: 246).

MacIntyre has a contrasting case of an irrationally acquired and maintained belief: the beliefs central to the witchcraft craze in early modern Europe. Here the explanation goes something like this. The belief that there were witches whose activities threatened the social good was the product of prevailing social tensions. These tensions generated certain emotions. The emotions sought an object, a rationale. The object and rationale were found in the witch, who thus became the scapegoat or the safety valve for powerful social frustrations. The explanation works by moving from social circumstances to the generation of emotions to production of a mechanism for the channelling of the emotions (1971: 245). Here no mention need be made of the awareness of grounds and the setting of such awareness in an intellectual tradition.

The early modern belief in witches could have been true for all that it was generated and maintained irrationally. The early modern belief that Jupiter had moons could have been false for all that it was the outcome of the work of reason. But nonetheless these two beliefs are not related to truth in the same way. If the witch belief had turned out to be true, it would have been the merest coincidence. The belief-producing mechanism was not open to the truth. Its character was such that its overwhelming tendency was to hide reality from participants in the witchcraft craze. The opposite holds for the astronomers. There is an inbuilt tendency for rational beliefs to be true, for they are the product of processes which open the human mind up to the influence of grounds and reasons – things which are *prima facie* indicators of truth. It is through the influence of truth-indicators that the mind is open to real-world influences on what it thinks.

Now we can see why a hermeneutics of science – such as that embodied in the strong programme in the sociology of knowledge – which ignores the success and truth of scientific hypothesising will not do. Interpretations of science have to take account of the possibility that it accumulates truths and discoveries on pain of wilfully ignoring striking evidence of the global operation of reason in science. Where a system of thought and action offers evidence of accumulation of this kind, then it looks as if it is characterised by procedures which open the mind to truth. And those are the procedures of reason. Beliefs which are the product of rational procedures are to be explained differently from those which are not. If a system of thought shows no evidence that it has been open to the truth, that is a strong indication that is not the product of genuinely rational procedures. That such a system of thought has been closed to the truth, and with it real-world influences via truth-indicators, is in turn indicated by the absence of accumulation of insight and discovery in it.

We have reached the conclusion that to interpret a discipline of thought realistically is to see its evolving conclusions as the outcome of real-world influences. Explanations of those conclusions which do not mention processes which are open to real-world influences cannot be sufficient. Accumulation of insight and discovery is the mark of real-world influences. We have very strong reason to interpret the disciplines of natural science realistically because science does show the clear presence of the accumulation of insight and discovery. It can be said without fear of reasonable contradiction that, thanks to the development of natural science, human beings know much more about their world than they did 200 or 300 years ago. Accumulation of insight and discovery into the things, stuffs and structures that make up the world via science is a clear refutation of the postmodernist opinions about knowledge and subjectivity outlined in previous chapters. The accumulation claim with respect to science can be made 'without fear of reasonable contradiction'. We have seen in previous chapters that fashionable constructivist ideas about truth and reality are unreasonable. They cannot therefore defeat the accumulation claim. Nor is the accumulation claim the equivalent of other claims that we ought to be sceptical of, such as the claim that science will progress to a final, complete or absolute theory of things. In fact, we know that the history of science is the history of the construction and abandonment of theories. Past theories have risen only to fall and induction therefore suggests the process will continue with present and future theories.

An obvious objection to the accumulation claim now arises: if the history of science shows a continued process of the rise and fall of theories, in what does the alleged accumulation of insight and discovery in science consist? The answer to the objection is that there are continuities of reliable belief preserved across theory change in science. In the first place, we can note that much existential knowledge is preserved across theory change. Harré asserts:

> ... it is in existential statements that most of the permanent advances of science are preserved, against a background of shifting hypotheses. Knowledge of the existence of chemical atoms, bacteria, genes, subatomic particles, and so on constitutes the hard core of scientific knowledge, while our ideas as to the constitutions and capabilities of these entities develop and grow and change. [Harré 1972: 52]

One way of marking the striking accumulation of discovery that science has produced is by saying that we have much greater knowledge of the things, stuffs and structures that make up the world than we did previously. Not all existential claims survive theory change. We no longer believe that there is such a thing as phlogiston or the ether. But science exhibits the ability to test and reliably confirm or disconfirm existential statements about the world. Hence, reliable beliefs as to what things, stuffs and structures there are accumulate. Biological theories may change with time, but it is now a reliable and permanent belief of the scientific community that there are viruses. Time and time again, science exhibits the pattern illustrated in our example of the discovery of Pluto in Chapter 5. Existential hypotheses are formulated on the basis of indirect evidence, the means of confirming them directly are found and then they are decisively confirmed. Thus existential knowledge grows and the presence of real-world influences on scientific thought is established.

The permanent, accumulating part of science is not wholly confined to reliable existential belief. There is, in truth, no absolute contrast between existential and theoretical belief in science. This contrast cannot be absolute because when scientists posit hitherto unknown entities or stuffs (such as a ninth planet or a sub-microscopic agency of disease – viruses) they are postulating things with certain causal properties. The ninth planet had to be something with mass and the consequent capability to affect the orbits of other planets. Because entities are postulated with causal properties, they come with theories attached. Beliefs about the causal properties of entities can change as theories change, but there must be some continuities across such change otherwise belief in entities' existence will not survive (see Psillos 1999: 256–8). Biological theory may evolve new accounts of the properties of viruses, but unless there is continuity across such evolution the reliable belief that there are viruses will not survive evolution in theory.

The fact that much existential belief established in earlier science remains valid for later science shows that the coming and going of theory in science is not total. Reliable belief in what things, stuffs and structures make up the world accumulates because causal hypotheses established earlier stick. So there is theoretical continuity amidst much change and evolution. It can be independently argued that analysis of theory change in science (such as that from Newtonian mechanics to contemporary mechanics) reveals continuity amidst change (see Psillos 1990: 108–11). If the prior theory was successful (for example, was capable of uniting diverse bodies of data and fruitful in predictions), some of its theoretical mechanisms and laws will be preserved, even if their validity is now limited to a restricted domain. This is the case with Newton's laws. Theory change is sometimes total. Renaissance theories of medicine have gone. But sometimes it is not. Some past theories can be seen to generate 'stable and invariant elements in our evolving scientific image' (Psillos 1990: 109).

We have a given a *prima facie* case for regarding natural science as productive of accumulating insight and discovery into the world. Its ability to track truth and be open to real-world influences is in part a reflection of what Rom Harré describes as its 'moral order' (Harré 1986: 12). The idea of science as a moral order is linked to MacIntyre's emphasis on the provenance of some beliefs in intellectual traditions, traditions where canons of argument and evidence can be established. One of the reasons why science tends to produce reliable beliefs about the world rests upon the fact that the scientific community is bound by norms of proof and evidence. For example, as everyone knows, experimental results in science are not valid unless they come with the means to enable other experimenters to repeat the experiments and reproduce the results. There are agreed standards of good work and good reasoning in science and those standards are productive of beliefs which everyone, in or outside the community of scientists, can rely on. They enable scientists to be open to real-world influences. This is not to say that all work and reasoning done by those who are counted, whether by themselves or others, as members of the scientific community is good. There are noted past and present examples of fraud and bias in science. (This is something that the feminist critique of science can occasionally throw up: see Code 1993: 27–30 for an example.) But it is by reference to the moral order/intellectual traditions established in the sciences that such bad reasoning and practice can be exposed.

The Case of Theology

The scene is set for asking the question of whether theology (in the person of Christian theology) can be interpreted via a realist hermeneutic. A short and decisive deductive argument is now available to the sceptic of theology:

1   All disciplines of thought that can be interpreted realistically show
    the accumulation of reliable belief.
2   Theology does not show the accumulation of reliable belief.
3   Therefore theology cannot be interpreted realistically.

Premise (1) has been established through consideration of the example
of science. Premise (2) is obvious, it will be claimed. Consider this
question: do we know anything more about God than we did at the
dawn of Christian theology nearly 2,000 years ago? Answer: No. During
that period many theological theories have come and gone in Christian
thought, but there has been no accumulation of insight and discovery
whatsoever. The stock of reliable beliefs about the Christian God, about
its attributes and plans, has not increased one iota. Whereas the
undergraduate physicist in a contemporary university has vastly more
reliable beliefs about physical reality than Aristotle, Galileo and
Newton, the undergraduate theologian has no more reliable beliefs
about divine reality than Augustine, Aquinas and Calvin. By virtue of
its intellectual traditions and modes of discovery physical science has
been open to influences from physical reality and its practitioners have
been put in cognitive contact with that reality. Theology has not
possessed intellectual traditions and modes of discovery of an analogous
kind to enable its practitioners to be open to influences from divine
reality and its practitioners have not been put in cognitive contact with
divine reality. The academic discipline of theology is simply not
productive of reliable beliefs about God – or about anything else for
that matter. It cannot be understood realistically. QED.

   The simple deductive argument for the non-realistic hermeneutic can
be reinforced by reflection on the absence of a morality of knowledge
and enquiry in Christian theology. If we consider the way in which some
disputes in Christian theology have been settled, we find that it is
frequently through non-argumentative, non-rational means. A defender
of theology may be impressed by the manner in which mainstream
Christian theology settled on the conclusion that the first and second
persons of the Trinity were of equal status. Arianism was defeated.
However, if the manner of that defeat is explored even superficially it
soon becomes apparent that it was power which defeated Arius and his
followers. Wiles remarks on the crucial character of the actions of the
Emperor Theodosius I, who acceded to the throne of the Eastern
Empire in 379. The death of the Emperor Valens spelled the end of
Arianism. Laws and edicts in 381 forbade Arians from using churches
or assembling in groups (Wiles 1996: 32). To read an account of the
Council of Nicea and the way the Emperor Constantine ensured a
victory for the anti-Arian party, leading to an Imperial banishment for
all those bishops who would not sign the new profession of faith, is to
realise the extent to which the outcome in favour of what we now style

orthodoxy was not the result of canons of argument meeting objectively established evidence. It was the outcome of power, both ecclesiastical and political (see Nigg 1962: 126–7). This is a conclusion which applies to many 'resolutions' of theological debates in history. We can see why this should be so. A noted feature of Christianity, and of all religions, is its ability to split into sects once doctrinal issues surface. Safe in their own sects, theologians are free from the danger of having their opinions refuted by evidence and argument. Each sect will tend to have its own way of weighing up theological evidence and its own approved methods of argument. There is no shared rule of faith across sectarian divisions. Thus what was thrown up by the greatest schism in Western Christianity was not merely differences on specific theological claims but also a rule of faith controversy. There can be no assured answer from within the methods of theological enquiry as to whether, for example, Luther added to the stock of reliable theological beliefs when he affirmed the priesthood of all believers or the necessity of justification by faith alone. There is nothing in this alleged discipline of thought analogous to the morality of scientific knowledge.

The above reflections on the prevalence of sectarianism in religion and on the absence of agreed rules of faith make it implausible to suggest that the problem with theology is that it has yet to find its Galileo or its Newton. It is not just that theology has not had sufficient time to develop the intellectual traditions and methods which will enable it to start accumulating reliable beliefs about the divine. There is rather something structural and endemic about its non-cumulative character. (Reflections below on the hiddenness of God will further support this point.)

Note what this simple non-realist argument is not saying. It is not saying 'here is a proof for the non-existence of God'. It is not even offering a proof for the unknowability of God. There may be a God and some beliefs about God may be established as reliable. But such beliefs seem to be few in number. As between, and even within, religions we can find no assured means for establishing any significant body of reliable belief about the deity's attributes and plans. We can understand why this may be so. Theistic systems will agree that the divine is transcendent and as such does not manifest itself to human faculties in a ready way. By contrast natural realities are immanent and do manifest themselves to human faculties. Moreover, many forms of theism hold that the divine is personal. They thus hold that God-manifestations depend on the free choice of God. This means that there can be no expectation that if I can perceive God in some given circumstances, then you will be able to perceive God in those same circumstances. God is thus not an object of shared investigation in the way physical objects are. In the light of these points we might then accept, at least for the sake of argument, that we know enough to know that divine reality cannot be the object of

inter-subjective investigation in the same way natural reality is. Fair
enough: but that should entail that we do not invest in theological
enquiry for the purpose of acquiring a body of reliable belief about
God. We know enough to know that we must be theological agnostics,
theological sceptics.

Does this mean that theology is an area where unreason and
unreasonable belief reign? Not necessarily. In contrasting the processes
which led to the spread of witchcraft beliefs in early modern Europe
with the spread of the belief that Jupiter had moons, Alasdair
MacIntyre thinks of the former as controlled by rationalisations, not
reasons. The mask of reason is used to hide from agents the non-
rational forces that really govern their thought and action. The
complex of belief and behaviour that was the witchcraft craze cries out
to be interpreted suspiciously. We cannot take its participants' thoughts
and words at face value. But that theology cannot be interpreted as a
realist discipline does not entail that it must be interpreted suspiciously
or that the arguments of its practitioners are but rationalisations and
masks.

Consider an example. Luther's treatise 'On Christian Liberty'
contains two of the most famous tenets of his theology: the priesthood
of all believers and the primacy of faith, not works, as the means to
justification. There is a rational structure to Luther's exposition and
defence of these tenets. They are interrelated. Given the primacy of faith
in justification, the person of true faith has a special dignity that comes
from being rightly related to God. Nothing else is needed. The primacy
of faith is linked to the sufficiency of hearing God's word in salvation.
No other channel of divine grace than this is required. Hence, there is no
need for a separate class of priests to be that channel. Both tenets are
supported by arguments which appeal to Scripture. Luther tells us that
Scripture contains no distinction between ecclesiastics and lay people
(Luther 1961: 65). Numerous passages are cited to support the absolute
primacy of faith over works in justification (see 1961: 56). Arguments of
a philosophical kind also support the primacy of faith doctrine. Thus we
are told that human beings have a twofold nature: spiritual and bodily.
Salvation is of and by the acts of the spiritual element, not the bodily.
And what the soul needs is to hear the Word of God and accept it in
faith (1961: 53–4).

So there is an argument in this classic piece of theology. From a
mixture of philosophical and scriptural premises the primacy of faith
tenet is established. The priesthood of all believers is shown to be
implied by the first tenet and then is independently supported by
Scripture. There is no reason to consider that these arguments are a
mere show or a mask for non-rational causes of belief. Thus we can say
that theological thought illustrated by this instance is minimally
rational. Its conclusions can be backed by arguments and reasons.

However, our sample piece of theology also shows why this discipline is of its nature incapable of advancing to a stock of reliable beliefs about an independent reality. There are no agreed canons for interpreting the 'data' of this discipline or, in general, for deciding which premises it draws upon are indicators of truth and which not. Luther cites Romans 10:10 'For man believes with his heart and so is justified' as a proof text for his primacy of faith doctrine. But whether that is the right interpretation cannot be established to the satisfaction of all those who consider themselves adepts at the discipline of theological reflection. His distinction between the spiritual and bodily elements of the human partakes of all the tendentious and inconclusive character of philosophical reflection. And the connection between it and the primacy of faith doctrine depends on further links of soul to faith and of body to works which are equally tendentious.

Luther is illustrating the following feature of theological thought for us. It can be and is moved by reason and argument. Data can be cited in support of its conclusions. But there are no agreed canons for interpreting the data and no agreed canons for determining good and bad inferences from data. Very crudely put, there are no inductive standards of a public kind which enable the citing of evidence in arguments to be viewed as settling what is true and false. By contrast, astronomy slowly built up such standards. That enabled it to establish some truths with certainty and build on them in order to establish further ones and so on.

Theology displays reason and argument. But it lacks the means for establishing which arguments are cogent and which are not. It is perpetually doomed therefore to interminable discussions of the same issues. It is thus constitutionally incapable of yielding any reliable beliefs about its putative subject matter.

Theology: a Divine Source?

At the opening of his *Church Dogmatics* Karl Barth claims, not without some equivocation, that theology *qua* dogmatics is a science (Barth 1975: 10–11). But dogmatics is not possible as a science except as an act of faith. Without faith it would be irrelevant and meaningless, 'idle speculation without any content of knowledge' (1975: 17). But faith is not the product of human action. It is the gift of God (1975: 18). This means that it is down to God's grace whether theology is true: 'the decision as to what is true or is not true in dogmatics is always a matter of divine election of grace' (1975: 21). Here Barth gives us a good example of a widespread theme in the interpretation of the status of theology as a critical discipline. It is guided to its end – truth about God – by its object, God.

We can take from Barth's words the suggestion that the divine itself can establish the truth of theological claims. Theology, if it is true and genuine knowledge, is the expression of faith. Faith is given by God. This thought finds its echo in many attempts to indicate that true theological thinking is conducted under the guidance of the Godhead (in Christian terms, the Holy Spirit is frequently cited as the source of guidance). In contemporary philosophy of religion, the echo can be caught in Alvin Plantinga's argument that belief in God and in 'the great things of the Gospel' may be directly produced in the believer by divine action on a *sensus divinitatis* and by the internal instigation of the Holy Spirit (see Plantinga 2000: 172–6 and 249–52). Plantinga's thought is that human nature could be so designed that, via possession of the *sensus divinitatis* and the action of God upon it, warranted true belief in God can be generated in a non-inferential fashion. Belief in the further things particular to Christian theology is the product of the interaction of the data for these further beliefs in revelation (Scripture) and the action of the Holy Spirit upon the believer who hears/reads Scripture. The result is faith and the accompanying belief in the doctrines of Christianity.

What we have in the above line of thought is the prospect of getting the divine cavalry to ride to the rescue of Christian theology. It does have standards for interpreting its data and checking its inferences from those data. The standards come from divine action itself. The standards will be seen to be in place if we accept a Christian account of human nature and the sources of knowledge open to it. People who are not convinced of Christian truth will be blind to the existence of these standards and so theology will be seen as a groundless exercise to them. Plantinga's aim is to show that there can be no neutral assessment of the question of whether Christian belief is warranted. Those who think it is true will see it as warranted, because they will have the relevant beliefs about human nature and God enabling them to see how Christian beliefs can be generated. Non-Christians will lack these beliefs and will thus see Christian beliefs as unwarranted. The *de jure* question of whether Christian belief is warranted cannot be separated from the *de facto* question of whether it is true (Plantinga 2000: 169).

Plantinga's contentions and the general line of thought traced from Barth might be seen as a challenge to the argument of this chapter. For I have argued that we can demonstrate the appropriateness of a non-realist interpretation of theology in its Christian version without determining the question of whether God is real. Regardless of whether the Christian God exists, we can see that the discipline of Christian theology is not building up reliable beliefs about that God. But perhaps if we view theology from the non-neutral standpoint of Christian faith itself, we will reach a different conclusion.

My reply to this Barth/Plantinga-based critique is: No – bringing in this machinery will not help. The core of the reply comes to this: even those who think that the Godhead does implant theological beliefs into people will have to concede that the process has not worked to establish an increasing stock of reliable beliefs about this God. What do Christians know more about God now than they did 800 years ago? The core of the problem besetting such attempts to see deity itself as supplying warrant for beliefs about it is that the alleged processes are undetectable. Plantinga has no means of deciding which religious beliefs are the product of the *sensus divinitatis* and the internal instigation of the Holy Spirit other than by judging their truth (that is, their agreement with what he takes to be Christian authority). These 'faculties', sources of warranted belief, are undetectable in their operation. In general terms, to say that the true theology is that which is an expression of faith will not help us to detect which it is because different theologies will equally claim this mantle and there is no external criterion for determining which systems claim it rightly and which do not. Compare Plantinga on the *sensus divinitatis*. He states that those who do not have a belief in God have their *sensus divinitatis* disordered by sin (Plantinga 2000: 213ff.). But he is unable to support the suggestion that this sinfulness shows itself elsewhere in these people's lives. It does not destroy their knowledge of other things that do not depend on their knowing a God. It does not mean that their conduct is more sinful than the conduct of those people whom Plantinga claims have a functioning *sensus divinitatis*.

Here is an obvious fact about the Christian religion (and others): it displays an inveterate tendency to sectarianism. Groups and sects split off, motivated by differences over doctrine and/or practice. Some survive; some do not. Each one claims that it genuinely has the witness of God and true faith. Yet there is no established means for eliminating some sects on intellectual grounds. The ones that do not survive, like Arianism, are often as not defeated by processes which are not truth-directed. We can contrast this inveterate sectarianism with what happens in science. Great divergences may exist in the scientific community between different groups of researchers. Not all questions get resolved. Yet there are processes (back to 'the morality of scientific knowledge') that weed out the cranks, the fanatics, and that establish in very many cases which ideas have run their course and which others can be added to the permanent and growing stock of reliable belief. The root problem in appealing to divine aid in the guidance and direction of true theology is that God has been notably lax in establishing some cast-iron, external signs for distinguishing between the fruitful, authentic lines of theological enquiry from those which are not. God could make the truth about the divine more manifest, but God chooses not to. That is an aspect of divine hiddenness. God chooses not to make the truth about

God obvious, when presumably, God could. McKim cites a number of reasons for thinking that God is hidden from the generality of the human race (McKim 2001: 10–12). They include the following. It seems believers can readily lose their faith, indicating that the reality of God cannot be overwhelmingly obvious. Countless numbers of people, otherwise sane and normal, claim to have no awareness of God. Believers often claim that they have no clear and strong sense of the divine presence. The long-term and extensive preoccupation with finding proofs of God's existence suggests that God's existence is not obvious. Whether people find it hard or easy to believe in God depends very much on their background culture. If the possibility of belief in God can be so easily effaced by culture, then the reality of God cannot be obvious.

What the Barth/Plantinga line of thought does is connect an apparatus to the promotion and rejection of conclusions about God's being and nature. The apparatus can include newfound faculties and cognitive states such as faith produced by the deity itself. The core problem is that the cogs in the apparatus do not connect with anything. At least they do not connect with anything which would help even those who style themselves Christians and theologians to recognise who has the truth about God and who has not. The apparatus is therefore of no use in providing the missing morality of knowledge that would enable Christian theology to function as a realist discipline.

Theology in Pragmatic, Liberating Mode

Given the argument thus far, we cannot take seriously Torrance's affirmation that theology is the science of the living God (Torrance 1985: 67) confronting 'the objectively given fact of God's self-communication' (Torrance 1969: 347). Academic theology is not controlled by real-world influences. As noted above, theology can be and is moved by reason and argument. Data can be cited in support of its conclusions. But there are no agreed canons for interpreting the data and no agreed canons for determining good and bad inferences from data. Theology begins from human understandings (even if they are thought to be understandings of divine words) and proceeds by human understandings (Pailin 1990: 5). The canons of theological evidence and interpretation are not such as to assure us that theological discourse tracks the truth. Some of it may, but which, if any, portion of the discourse tracks the truth is not something that can be established by public argument. This is where the contrast with natural science lies. Hence, David Pailin's verdict on theologians is correct: 'Their judgements ... are to be seen as only tentative insights perceived from relative stances' (1990: 30). This judgement applies to scientists too, but it is not the final verdict on their surmises, since some of those, indeed many, can be credited as reliable beliefs about a world existing independently of human representations.

The above verdicts about the severe limitations upon the validity of theological conclusions are hardly new. They are commonplaces among many contemporary theologians. Sallie McFague, for example, contends that a radical theological agnosticism is now in order given the epistemology established by the conditions of postmodernity (McFague 1987: x–xi). We cannot lay down theological truths any more but must advance metaphors and models in a 'highly sceptical, heuristic enterprise' (1987: xii). In much the same spirit, Gordon Kaufman contends that the putative object of theological discourse – God – is not in fact a reality over and against us but a construct of the human imagination (Kaufman 1995: 32–3). This contention is a recognition of the fact that theology cannot demonstrate itself to be a discipline which tracks the character of a reality independent of human representations. Thus, our verdict on the realist pretensions of academic theology is accepted by a large swathe of liberal theological opinion. Theology's detractors may be tempted to build on this verdict: if theology does not add to the sum of human knowledge, perhaps it should be pursued no further. We find, however, that non-realist scepticism about theological discourse is paired with a new justification for producing more and more of it. This justification is pragmatic. Far from scepticism about theological propositions leading to doubts about the viability of the enterprise, it leads in many minds to a renewed license for speculation. Since theological speculation cannot be constrained by real-world influences, we have that much more room for new theologies devised to suit our practical interests. Theology can take flight again and be doled out by the yard in consequence.

Kaufman tells us that we can construct an idea of God (1995: 38). We are to do so under the guidance of our practical purposes: 'The purpose of theological construction is to produce concepts (and world-pictures and stories) which make possible adequate orientation in life and the world' (1995: 39). Prosecution of the purpose is justified on the ground that human action and life is dependent on having 'some conception or picture of the overall context, the fundamental order, within which human life falls' (1995: 38). McFague moves in the same direction: from scepticism about the possibility of assured truth in theology to a pragmatic justification for continuing with theological construction. If we set aside the question of which theological theory is true, we are allowed to take up the question of which 'heuristic, metaphoric' theology is a better portrait of Christian faith for our day (McFague 1987: xiii). That question is pragmatic: we are to produce and develop such theological models as are 'most helpful in the praxis of bringing about fulfilment for living human beings' (McFague 1987:

187 n.13). Theology can fly precisely because it is not reality-constrained. It flies as liberation theology. Each interest group, each socio-political faction, can generate a theology – understood as a constructive working-out of theological symbols in the light of that group's political, ethical and social concerns. Hence, we have Sharon Welch's effort, referred to earlier in this study, to construct a 'Feminist Theology of Liberation'.

We have now documented a movement of theological thought which accepts a sceptical verdict on theology as a realist enterprise but insists that it does not amount to strong reason for foreclosing on the prosecution of theology. Readers who have followed me thus far will not expect me to accept this attempt to save theology's bacon. This is too easy a way of dealing with the fact that academic theology does not produce reliable belief.

We need to take issue with Gordon Kaufman's claims for its continuance in the context of contemporary scepticism about its grounds and results. Kaufman's scepticism about a science of God shown in *An Essay on Theological Method* is reinforced in *In Face of Mystery* in a number of ways. One way is by means of the assertion that a creator God as traditionally conceived is inconceivable in the light of suffering in the world (Kaufman 1993: 3). Another reinforcement comes through the claim that the large-scale questions about human life and the cosmos to which the traditional belief was an answer are mysteries, inscrutable to the human understanding (1993: 240). There can be no laying down a doctrine of divine things with any certainty in the light of these points. There can only be theology understood as an open, democratic conversation (1993: 67). Kaufman confronts the question I would ask at this juncture: what is the point of engaging in the conversation if we can be assured that no reliable beliefs about the mysteries of life will result from it? Why should we not suspend judgement on them (1993: 240)? His answer to his own question is simple: we have to act and therefore to make choices on matters metaphysical and therefore we had best do this in the open (1993: 241). But on this point we can disagree. First, we can make a distinction between a basic choice we might make for, on the one hand, the Kantian-style conclusion that there is some power or other on the side of goodness and against evil and for, on the other, a detailed theological account of God. The former choice might be justified on the grounds of a Jamesian 'will to believe' argument. But that is not at all to say that further choices between one developed theology and another are licensed. The basic choice is expressive of the commitment that evil can be defeated somehow and that thus the human good is attainable somehow. Second, we can point out that if we have to choose how to live, then we had best do it with the best knowledge available of what the world is like. Now if the best knowledge available tells us that we can reach no reliable beliefs about a God, then we have to choose accordingly and not put our own constructions in the place which we should leave open for ignorance and mystery. It is our reliable beliefs which we need to act on. Relying on those will lessen the chance that our actions will misfire.

Kaufman affirms that there are two vital questions humanity confronts. How is human flourishing to be conceived? How is God as the focus and/or source of the search for flourishing to be conceived? But if we know enough to know that there is little certainty and thus authority in detailed conceptions of God, then we know enough to know that we should pursue the first question while setting aside detailed answers to the second. We have to get on with the job of considering the nature of human flourishing while knowing that, if there is a God, God is hidden. Kaufman thinks that the human imagination constructs pictures of God (1993: 56). But we are not going to get a sure foundation for answering the question about human flourishing by relying on our imaginative constructions. The point, then, against Kaufman's theological constructive method in the face of admitted mystery is this: it will lead us to fudge important questions about how we should act and orient ourselves in the world by allowing us to give ourselves answers to pertinent questions about reality to which we are not in fact entitled. I see an example of this danger in two of Kaufman's definitions of God. A prominent definition of God in *In Face of Mystery* is 'that to which we can give ourselves and our lives without reservation, the proper object of our unqualified devotion, that in terms of which human life in the world can most properly be oriented' (1993: 237). So: God is the whatever it is we identify after seeking the focus and sum of our values. There are no inherent problems with this definition, so long as we understand its character. But it fits in ill with the following definition Kaufman also supplies, for the reason that the use of both definitions together begs an important question. Kaufman's other definition of God reads: 'that reality ... orientation on which evokes our human moral and creative powers ..., encouraging their development and enhancement by promising significant human fulfil-ment (salvation) in the future' (1993: 79). Here 'God' no longer appears to be merely the name for the focus and sum of our values but rather an agency, a source of power, which can promote human salvation. A religious sceptic will want to insist that we must separate the search for the focus of our values from the search for a reality orientation on which evokes our powers and makes for our fulfilment. It is precisely the point of many religious sceptics that there is nothing external to ourselves that can make for fulfilment and flourishing, or at least nothing other than us is known to be pursuing this end. Human agency is the only morally oriented agency there is, or that we know about. Thus questions are begged.

Mikael Stenmark has carefully documented an important, and disturbing, consequence of the heady combination of theological scepticism and theological pragmatism. This is the proliferation of theological arguments from the desirability of certain theological notions to their validity (see Stenmark 2000). This move can be seen in McFague's *Models of God* from which we have quoted above, but Stenmark cites numerous authors who conduct essentially the same manoeuvre. It is typical of the genus 'liberation theology'. Indeed it is hard to see how the genus can flourish if it is forbidden to argue from the ethical, political and social ideals of some group identified as oppressed to the validity of one conception of God over another. In McFague, the manoeuvre is shown in her argument that theology is about the construction of models and models are recommended on the basis of the attitudes and actions they encourage. We need to adopt the models of God as parent, lover and friend and abandon those of God as monarch and ruler in order to meet the needs of an 'ecological, nuclear age'. Thus we can recommend the model of the world as God's body because it 'encourages attitudes of responsibility for and care of the vulnerable and the oppressed' (McFague 1987: 78). Stenmark puts his finger on the danger of this approach to theology via pragmatic construction: we normally do not think that our political and other ideals are sure guides to the nature of reality (Stenmark 2000: 141–2). We know that we ought to be open to the very genuine possibility that what we would like to be true, morally and politically, may not be true. It is an open question whether the world is such as to gratify our moral and political desires. If we ignore the question, we risk living in a fantasy world.

Theology as pragmatic construction looks as though it is going to fall into a gigantic trap. It will be no more than a grand exercise in wishful thinking. It will turn what some 'we' would like to be true into what it is in fact true. We can remind ourselves, yet again, that it is fundamentally against the spirit of innocent realism to think that human desires in and of themselves are a guide to the character of truth-makers. Theological pragmatism appears to be a denial of the independence of the world demanded by realism. It should be stressed that such a denial is unpragmatic. To approach the world in the spirit of expecting it to be shaped as human ideals would like it to be shaped is to embark on a practical stance fraught with dangers – the dangers inherent in unheeding optimism and wishful thinking.

The formal gap between our ideals and the 'models' produced by constructive theological pragmatism could be closed with either of two moves. The first move consists in adopting the view of truth and reality found in Welch and the second consists in claiming that we merely have to act *as if* our theological models are true, and thus can cancel any doxastic commitments that would otherwise arise from them.

We have already discussed and dismissed the first move in Chapter 5. It would remove the scandal of wishful thinking from theological discourse only by recreating it on a vaster scale and indulging in the magical view of words and reality typical of linguistic constructivism. However, credit must be given to Welch for seeing that constructive theological pragmatism is inherently unstable (because open to the charge of rank wishful thinking) unless it adopts a new concept of truth, a new 'episteme' (see Welch 1985: 11 and 30). But we saw in the previous chapters that this alternative 'episteme' has nothing to recommend it. If theological pragmatism depends on it, then it is doomed.

The second move is hinted at in McFague's account of 'metaphorical theology'. It is based on the assumption that all language about God is human construction and as such 'misses the mark' (McFague 1987: 23). She states that theology has an 'as-if' quality (1987: 37). Let us run with this hint. We can construct images, metaphors and accounts of God to meet our perceived social, moral and political ends without indulging in the vice of letting what we wish to be true determine what is true for us because we merely think and act *as if* God were thus and so. This will obviously solve the formal problems indicated in Stenmark's criticisms of theological construction. 'Acting as if *p*' does not entail 'believing that *p*'. Considerations such as our needs and desires can bear upon acting as if, while they do not bear on upon the formation of belief. But if the formal problems in theological construction are removed, deeper ones remain. If theological construction in the service of liberal, left-wing social and political thought is mere 'as if', it would appear to be dangerous daydreaming. It is daydreaming because instead of putting forward socio-political programmes on the basis of such facts about ourselves and the world as we can determine, it sets off in the direction of fantasy. Serious thought on these matters is surely going to be based on enquiries into what is the case with us and with the world in which we live. If we cannot have any reliable beliefs about divine beings, then we need to set aside thoughts about them in working out our socio-political policies. The daydreaming becomes positively dangerous to healthy practical debate in so far as theological constructivists create an association between their own political programmes (invariably left-leaning programmes) and thoughts about the divine. Even if the theological images constructed and employed are not meant to be true in any standard sense, the impression is created that to be a Christian, or whatever, involves signing up to the political policies promoted. But there is no reason why it should. To read McFague, Welch and Kaufman is to be clear that they are left-wing thinkers in favour of nuclear disarmament, 'green' economic policies and the like. The standard raft of 'pink', internationalist, vaguely pacifist and anti-capitalist political views of a certain type of Western academic may be impressive or not. Whether it is so is to be determined by political reflection and argument. But why should attachment to the central images and narratives of the Christian (or any other) faith be associated with this standard raft? Theological constructionism is always bound to attach a spurious religious authority to what passes as political commonplaces in certain quarters. There is absolutely no reason why they should have that authority, especially as constructivists contend that there is nothing to be discovered here about what the Almighty favours in the way of political programmes.

The above worries can be given greater focus by turning to Mary Daly's announcement of a pragmatic criterion for theological truth. In *Beyond God the Father* she lays down that we are to ask of any theological statement or image: does it help or hinder the creation of a new society in which sex-role socialisation can be defeated and human becoming established? (Daly 1985: 20–21). There is an obvious political assumption here (present throughout the book), namely that radical feminism's analysis of the nature of human flourishing and what hinders it is correct. Many people, including the present author, would disagree profoundly with that. Some would like to argue with Daly about her analysis of personal and social flourishing and contend against her assaults on the 'sex-gender system'. They can therefore properly object that this specific piece of socio-political analysis should not get mixed up with the authority of the sacred. If we cannot produce truth-indicative reasons in favour of any detailed account of the divine, we should not let our political concerns fill in the detailed account for us. What we should do is acknowledge the force of theological agnosticism and the consequent difficulty of providing a divine warrant for any political programme. We just cannot know enough about the divine for it to be yoked to our political analyses and aims. Healthy political debate will be hampered if we associate political action with the aura provided by the sacred – more especially when, on the premise that the divine is substantially hidden, we cannot have independent arguments for or against its political leanings. This association of politics and the aura of the sacred is precisely what Daly offers us. She states that the divine is somehow manifested in women's creative political struggle: 'the emergence of the communal self-awareness of women is a creative political ontophany. It is a manifestation of the sacred . . .' (1985: 34). I find it impossible to take such a statement seriously. If one reads critical accounts of the way in which radical feminists behave collectively and individually, especially in the academic sphere, one will be inclined to describe the manifestation of communal self-awareness of such women as the opposite of sacred (see Hoff Sommers 1994, *passim* for ample support for this judgement).

There is another issue which Daly's stance hides. This is the issue of the identification in liberal theological constructionism of human flourishing with social and political liberation. Daly's criterion of theological truth evinces the common thought that the constructive theologian takes earthly, social justice (construed in a certain fashion) to be identical with human liberation/salvation. But this assumption should be seen to be controversial precisely in the context of discussions of the nature of the divine. It is integral to the notion of the divine that the final human good should be seen as consisting in right relation to it. The multifarious conceptions of the divine will relate that final good to the good achievable in personal and social living on Earth in different ways. But to think that there is a divine reality of some kind must entail being alive to the question of how far human flourishing in this life is the sum and substance of the human good. All too often, as with Daly, liberal theological constructivists give the clear impression of having worked out a conception of the human good in secular terms (that is, in terms minus any possible relation to a transcendent source of moral order) and then trying to yoke the categories of the divine to it. This move is implicit in McFague's insistence that we must work out theological symbols 'for our day' (McFague 1987: xiii).

What is fundamentally problematic in a pragmatic criterion of theological truth? What is pragmatic, what works for us, depends on what is true. Whether destruction of 'sex-role socialisation' will produce human flourishing for men and women depends in large measure on what is the case in a world which exists independently of our representations.

Philosophy – a *Tu Quoque*?

I have tried to establish in this chapter that theology cannot be considered to be a realist discipline. It gives no sign of being controlled by real-world influences. It is not productive of reliable beliefs about God. We should be theological agnostics. These strictures are open to an obvious response: how can a philosopher make such play of the non-realist character of theological discourse, when philosophy is in exactly the same boat? Philosophy is not a realist discipline. It does not add to our stock of reliable beliefs about the world. Consider a striking illustration of this fact. Aristotle's strictly philosophical writings, such as the *Nicomachean Ethics*, are still important parts of the philosophy syllabus in the Western academy. But his scientific writings are of purely antiquarian interest. Aristotelian physics is dead; Aristotle's philosophy lives. Conclusion: physics has advanced in its understanding of the world since the fourth century BCE; philosophy has not.

Some will object to this characterisation of philosophy. Philosophy has advanced. We can contrast the undergraduate philosopher at the

end of his or her first year with Aristotle. The former knows a good deal
more, for example, in logic (about the nature and range of valid
inferences), than Aristotle. Philosophers argue for theses and some of
these theses get established. Has not this book brilliantly established
theses about matters connected with realism?

Let us ignore this riposte on behalf of philosophy. I will concede the
point that philosophy is not a realist discipline for the sake of argument.
So I will accept that that does not add to the stock of our reliable beliefs
about the world in order to get a debate going. This concession need not
deliver the conclusion that philosophy is worthless as a discipline of
intelligence. Here is one response. It can be argued that philosophy is
productive of practical knowledge, even if not of reliable beliefs. It
creates and depends on knowing-how, not knowing-that. It does not
yield increases in the stock of facts stored our intellectual locker. But it
is productive of understanding. It is perpetually necessary because the
human intellect is constitutionally liable to get itself into knots. It is the
job of philosophy to provide the means of sorting out these knots. It is a
second-order activity. Its aim is to clarify and keep sharp the conceptual
tools that first-order activities, such as physics, employ. The practical
knowledge it produces consists in a set of skills in analysis and argument
which are helpful, indeed vital, if the human tendency to fall into
conceptual confusion is to be resisted. Philosophy is not productive of
the kind of knowledge that adds to the stock of things we know to be
the case or that increases our theoretical knowledge. If it deals in facts,
the facts are obvious ones, assembled as reminders for those who are
conceptually confused. Consider the main argument of this book.
Variations on the theme of linguistic constructivism have been rebutted
by reminding ourselves of the fact that talking, thinking and believing
cannot of themselves determine the nature of reality. No one really
denies this when they are not doing philosophy. But a whole raft of
theorists need reminding of it on pain of falling into the most profound
confusions.

We can continue with this defence of philosophy. The understanding
we may hope is made possible and kept alive by the knowing-how in
philosophy is not merely an antidote to conceptual confusion. It enables
intelligent discussion of important issues about the human self which
discovers the facts accumulated in natural science. These issues include
those about matters to do with value. What values should we live by?
What values are needed to keep science and other disciplines in being?
Are some areas of scientific research more valuable for human
flourishing than others? Such questions could be multiplied. Raising
them and discussing them in the intellectually rigorous way made
possible by the skills in argument and conceptual distinction provided
by philosophy enables the results of science to be digested by an
informed human understanding.

Philosophy's character as a discipline which does not (on the concession made in this section) accumulate new facts but does keep alive forms of human understanding is shared by other parts of the humanities. The theologian's *tu quoque* may be extended to include the humanities as a whole. Do not the humanities, like theology, exhibit a clear failure to accumulate reliable beliefs about the world? Again, we may be reluctant to accept the premise that the humanities yield no new facts (cf. the study of history), but again we can accept the point for the sake of argument. Some examples may seem to illustrate the thought that humanities disciplines do not accumulate reliable beliefs about the world. The study of literature in the various departments of an arts faculty may throw up some new facts – about the biography and literary productions of a great author. But, in the main, the study of literature, let us concede, does not do this. Yet it is the means of keeping alive, through dialogical engagement with texts, a living sense of the meaning and value of great works of literature. Great literary critics, such as F.R. Leavis, are not necessarily possessed of more facts about the works they write about, but are expert in bringing out and making available the meaning and value of the objects they study. Only through the kind of critical engagement with texts (which they exemplify in its highest form) can the meaning of literary texts be kept before us. Critical engagement with literature in a disciplined context is based on forms of knowing-how and it is vital if certain important forms of human understanding are to be kept alive.

We are here gesturing toward the familiar distinction between natural and hermeneutical sciences, with the hermeneutical ones having as their province the realm of human meaning displayed in culture. The latter are not productive of knowledge about what is the case in the manner or to the extent of the former. The hermeneutical sciences are productive of understanding. This understanding is vital to the living of an examined life. It is the product of a self which can engage in reflective examination of its aims, values and modes of thought. Even if we concede that the hermeneutical sciences do not accumulate facts, they are still sciences in the sense that they conduct their business through argument and other forms of critically guided thought. And they are important and inescapable. It is in truth impossible to contend or argue that they are otherwise. If someone were to contend that only cumulative disciplines, only the natural sciences, were worthwhile intellectual pursuits, were capable of producing true knowledge, then he or she would have made a claim that belonged to the search for human understanding. Such a contention would be one which is part of the hermeneutical sciences. It could be made good only by engaging in arguments which belonged to the arts faculty and not the science faculty.

The above points could be greatly expanded upon, but enough has been said to indicate how we may justify the contention that if something is not a realist discipline, then this does not mean it is not a worthwhile discipline at all. So this is where the *tu quoque* from the theologian has got us: yes, philosophy is not a realist discipline; but, no, this does not mean that philosophy is a worthless waste of time which has no place in the academy. That very response shows that our argument on the status of theology in this chapter cannot amount to a proof that theology is not a proper part of the academy. The self-image some theologians have (to the effect that their enquiries generate reliable beliefs about God's characteristics and intentions) is false. But there is plenty of room left to argue for the necessity of disciplined reflection on the divine in an academic context. A space for such argument is there in the brief remarks above about the hermeneutical sciences, human understanding and the examined life. One important question of value which the human understanding is faced with is this: are all values human-centred or not? Are there any values which are, in some sense, transcendent? We have seen in this study that such questions are vital in reflection on the nature and significance of evil in human life. The examined life is not possible unless it confronts them because it is not possible unless it confronts the fact of evil. Such questions are the kind of questions which theology can address.

It is not for me to determine what the nature and status of theological reflection should be in the academy. What this chapter has done is lay down a challenge for the theologian, rather than provide a proof that theology is worthless as a discipline of thought. Theology cannot be sensibly conceived to be a realist discipline. Its reflections give no sign of being controlled by an object external to itself. It does not give us ever-more reliable beliefs about the divine. It is a not a science of God in that sense. Criticisms have been offered of one response to this realisation: liberal, theological pragmatism. Plenty of room is left for alternative accounts of the nature and basis of theological reasoning.

Bibliography

Alston, W.P. (1995), 'Realism and the Christian Faith', *International Journal for the Philosophy of Religion*, vol. 38, pp. 37–60.

Alston, W.P. (1996), *A Realist Conception of Truth*, Cornell University Press, Ithaca and London.

Appelros, E. (2002), *God in the Act of Reference*, Ashgate, Aldershot.

Appiah, A. (1986), *For Truth in Semantics*, Blackwell, Oxford.

Aquinas, St T. (1964), *Summa Theologiae*, vol. 3, McCabe, H. tr., Eyre and Spottiswood, London.

Aquinas, St T. (1975), *Summa contra Gentiles*, Anderson, J.F., O'Neil, C.J. and Pegis, A.C. trs, University of Notre Dame Press, Notre Dame.

Aristotle (1941), *The Nichomachean Ethics*, in McKeon, R. ed., *The Basic Works of Aristotle*, Random House, New York, pp. 927–1112.

Augustine, St (1972), *The City of God*, Knowles, D. tr., Penguin, Harmondsworth.

Ayer, A.J. (1971), *Language, Truth and Logic*, 2nd edn, Penguin, Harmondsworth.

Baker, G. and Hacker P. (1984), *Language, Sense and Nonsense*, Blackwell, Oxford.

Barth, K. (1975), *Church Dogmatics*, vol. 1, part 1, Bromiley, G.W. and Torrance, T.F. trs, T. and T. Clark, Edinburgh.

Berger. P. and Luckmann T. (1967), *The Social Construction of Reality*, Penguin, Harmondsworth.

Bloor, D. (1976), *Knowledge and Social Imagery*, Routledge and Kegan Paul, London.

Boyle, R. (1973), 'A Disquisition About the Final Causes of Things', in Goodman, D.C. ed., *Science and Religious Belief*, John Wright and Sons/Open University, Dorchester, pp. 103–18.

Braithwaite, R.B. (1971), 'An Empiricist's Account of the Nature of Religious Belief', in Ramsey, I.T. ed., *Christian Ethics and Contemporary Philosophy*, SCM Press, London, pp. 53–73.

Brown, S. (1976), 'What is the Verifiability Criterion a Criterion of?', in Vesey, G. ed., *Impressions of Empiricism*, Macmillan, London, pp. 137–53.

Butler, J. (1961), *The Analogy of Religion*, Ungar, New York.

Byrne, P.A. (1995a), 'Omnipotence, Feminism and God', *International Journal for Philosophy of Religion*, vol. 37, pp. 145–65.

Byrne, P.A. (1995b), *Prolegomena to Religious Pluralism*, Macmillan, London and Basingstoke.

Byrne, P.A. (1998), *The Moral Interpretation of Religion*, Edinburgh University Press, Edinburgh.

Carnap, R. (1952), 'Empiricism, Semantics and Ontology', in Linsky, L. ed., *Semantics and the Philosophy of Language*, University of Illinois Press, Urbana, pp. 208–26.

Cicero (1997), *The Nature of the Gods*, Walsh, P.J. tr., Clarendon Press, Oxford.

Code, L. (1993), 'Taking Subjectivity into Account', in Alcoff, L. and Potter, E. eds, *Feminist Epistemologies*, Routledge, London, pp. 15–48.

Cupitt, D. (1980), *Taking Leave of God*, SCM Press, London
Cupitt, D. (1984), *The Sea of Faith*, British Broadcasting Corporation, London.
Cupitt, D. (1986), *Lifelines*, SCM Press, London.
Cupitt, D. (1987), *The Long-Legged Fly*, SCM Press, London.
Cupitt, D. (1990), *Creation out of Nothing*, SCM Press, London.
Cupitt, D. (1993), 'Anti-Realist Faith', in Runzo, J. ed., *Is God Real?*, Macmillan, Basingstoke and London, pp. 45–55.
Cupitt, D, (1997), 'Free Christianity', in Crowder, C. ed., *God and Reality*, Mowbray, London, pp. 14–25.
Curthoys, J. (1997), *Feminist Amnesia*, Routledge, London.
Daly, M. (1985), *Beyond God the Father*, Beacon Press, Boston.
Derrida, J. (1976), *Grammatology*, Chakrovorty, G. tr., John Hopkins University Press, Baltimore and London.
Derrida, J. (1978), *Writing and Difference*, Bass, A. tr., Routledge, London.
Derrida, J. (1981), *Positions*, Bass, A. tr., Athlone Press, London.
Descartes, R. (1984), *Meditations*, in Cottingham, J., Stoothoff, R. and Murdoch, D, trs, *The Philosophical Writings of Descartes*, vol. II, Cambridge University Press, Cambridge, pp. 1–62.
Devitt, M. (1997), *Realism and Truth*, 2nd edn, Princeton University Press, Princeton.
Devitt, M. and Sterelny, K. (1987), *Language and Reality*, Blackwell, Oxford.
Dummett, M. (1973), *Frege: Philosophy of Language*, Duckworth, London.
Dummett, M. (1975), 'What is a Theory of Meaning? II', in Guttenplan, S., ed., *Mind and Language*, Oxford University Press, Oxford, pp. 97–138.
Dummett, M. (1978), *Truth and Other Enigmas*, Duckworth, London.
Dummet, M. (1991), *The Logical Basis of Metaphysics*, Harvard University Press, Cambridge MA.
Dummett, M. (1993), *The Seas of Language*, Clarendon Press, Oxford.
Ellis, J.M. (1989), *Against Deconstruction*, Princeton University Press, Princeton.
Feuerbach, L. (1957), *The Essence of Christianity*, Evans, M.A. tr., Harper and Row, New York.
Foucault, M. (1980), *Power/Knowledge*, Gordon, C. ed., Harvester Wheatsheaf, London.
Gerson, L.P. (1990), *God and Greek Philosophy*, Routledge, London.
Glymour, C. (1982), 'On Conceptual Scheming', *Synthese*, vol. 51, pp. 169–80.
Goodman, N. (1980), 'On Starmaking', *Synthese*, vol. 50, pp. 211–15.
Gross, B. (1994), 'What Could a Feminist Science Be?', *The Monist*, vol. 77, pp. 434–44.
Gross, P.R. and Levitt, N. (1994), *The Higher Superstition*, John Hopkins University Press, Baltimore and London.
Haack, S. (1987), 'Realism', *Synthese*, vol. 73, pp. 275–99.
Haack, S. (1996), 'Reflections on Relativism', in Tomberlin, J. ed., *Philosophical Perspectives 10. Metaphysics*, Blackwell, Oxford, pp. 297–315.
Hampson, D. (1996), 'On Autonomy and Heteronomy', in Hampson, D. ed., *Swallowing a Fishbone*, SPCK, London, pp. 1–16.
Harding, S. (1993), 'Rethinking Standpoint Epistemology', in Alcoff, L. and Potter, E. eds, *Feminist Epistemologies*, Routledge, London, pp. 49–82.
Harré, R. (1972), *The Philosophies of Science*, Oxford University Press, Oxford.
Harré, R. (1986), *Varieties of Realism*, Blackwell, Oxford.
Heal, J. (1989), *Fact and Meaning*, Blackwell, Oxford.
Heimbeck, P. (1969), *Theology and Meaning*, Stanford University Press, Stanford.

Hempel, C.G. (1952), 'Problems and Changes in the Empiricist Criterion of Meaning', in Linsky, L. ed., *Semantics and the Philosophy of Language*, University of Illinois Press, Urbana, pp. 163–85.

Heywood, C. (1982), *The Redemption of God*, University Press of America, Washington DC.

Hick, J. (1974), *Faith and Knowledge*, Collins/Fontana, Glasgow.

Hick, J. (1989), *An Interpretation of Religion*, Macmillan, London and Basingstoke.

Hoff Somers, C. (1994), *Who Stole Feminism?*, Simon and Schuster, New York.

Hopkins, J. (1996), 'Radical Passion', in Hampson, D. ed., *Swallowing a Fishbone*, SPCK, London, pp. 66–81.

Horwich, P. (1996), 'Realism and Truth', in Tomberlin, J. ed., *Philosophical Perspectives 10. Metaphysics*, Blackwell, Oxford, 187–97.

Horwich, P. (1998a), *Meaning*, Clarendon Press, Oxford.

Horwich, P. (1998b), *Truth*, 2nd edn, Clarendon Press, Oxford.

Hume, D. (1990), *Dialogues concerning Natural Religion*, Bell, M. ed., Penguin, Harmondsworth.

Huxley, J.S. (1957), *Religion without Revelation*, Parrish, London.

Jantzen, G.M. (1998), *Becoming Divine*, Manchester University Press, Manchester.

Kant, I. (1997), *The Critique of Pure Reason*, Guyer, P. and Wood, A.W. eds and trs, Cambridge University Press, Cambridge.

Kaufman, G. (1993), *In Face of Mystery*, Harvard University Press, Cambridge MA.

Kaufman, G. (1995), *An Essay on Theological Method*, Scholars Press, Atlanta.

Kearney, R (1984), *Dialogues with Contemporary Critical Thinkers*, Manchester University Press, Manchester.

Kekes, J. (1990), *Facing Evil*, Princeton University Press, Princeton.

Kirk, R. (1999), *Relativism and Reality*, Routledge, London.

Kretzmann, N. (1997), *The Metaphysics of Theism*, Clarendon Press, Oxford.

Kuhn, T. (1962), *The Structure of Scientific Revolutions*, Chicago University Press, Chicago.

Laudan, L. (1996), *Beyond Positivism and Relativism*, Westview Press, Boulder.

Le Poidevin, R. (1995), 'Internal and External Questions about God', *Religious Studies*, vol. 31, pp. 485–500.

Le Poidevin, R. (1996), *Arguing for Atheism*, Routledge, London.

Levine, M. (1994), *Pantheism*, Routledge, London.

Luntley, M. (1988), *Language, Logic and Experience*, Duckworth, London.

Luntley, M. (1995), *Reason, Truth and the Self*, Routledge, London.

Luther, M. (1961), 'On Christian Liberty', in Dillenberger, J. ed., *Martin Luther: Selections from His Writings*, Doubleday, Garden City, pp. 52–85.

Lyotard, J.-F. (1984), *The Postmodern Condition*, Bennington, G. and Massumi, B. trs, Manchester University Press, Manchester.

McFague, S. (1987), *Models of God*, SCM Press, London.

MacIntyre, A. (1971), 'Rationality and the Explanation of Action', in MacIntyre, A., *Against the Self-Images of the Age*, Duckworth, London, pp. 244–59.

McKim, R. (2001), *Religious Ambiguity and Religious Diversity*, Oxford University Press, New York.

Mitchell, B.G. (1973), *The Justification of Religious Belief*, Macmillan, London.

Mitchell, B.G. (1995), *Faith and Criticism*, Clarendon Press, Oxford.

Moore, A.W. (1997), *Points of View*, Clarendon Press, Oxford.

Murdoch, I. (1970), *The Sovereignty of Good*, Routledge, London.

Nagel, T. (1997), *The Last Word*, Oxford University Press, New York.

Nigg, W.N. (1962), *The Heretics*, Winston, C. and Winston, R. trs, Dorset Press, New York.

Pailin, D. (1990), *The Anthropological Character of Theology*, Cambridge University Press, Cambridge.

Patterson, S. (1999), *Realist Christian Theology in a Postmodern Age*, Cambridge University Press, Cambridge.

Phillips, D.Z. (1970a), *Death and Immortality*, Macmillan, London.

Phillips, D.Z. (1970b), *Faith and Philosophical Enquiry*, Routledge, London.

Phillips, D.Z. (1977), 'The Problem of Evil', in Brown, S.C. ed., *Reason and Religion*, Cornell University Press, Ithaca and London, pp. 103–21.

Phillips, D.Z. (1988), *Faith after Foundationalism*, Routledge, London.

Phillips, D.Z. (1993), 'On Really Believing', in Runzo, J. ed., *Is God Real?*, Macmillan, Basingstoke and London, pp. 85–108.

Phillips, D.Z. (2001), *Religion and the Hermeneutics of Contemplation*, Cambridge University Press, Cambridge.

Plantinga, A. (1969), *God and other Minds*, Cornell University Press, Ithaca and London.

Plantinga, A. (1982), 'How to be an Anti-Realist', *Proceedings and Addresses of the American Philosophical Association*, vol. 56, pp. 47–70.

Plantinga, A. (2000), *Warranted Christian Belief*, Oxford University Press, New York.

Plato (1963a), *Apology*, in Hamilton, E. and Cairns, H. eds, *The Complete Dialogues*, Princeton University Press, Princeton, pp. 3–26.

Plato (1963b), *Phaedo*, in Hamilton, E. and Cairns, H. eds, *The Complete Dialogues*, Princeton University Press, Princeton, pp. 40–98.

Psillos, S. (1999), *Scientific Realism*, Routledge, London.

Putnam, H. (1981), *Reason, Truth and History*, Cambridge University Press, Cambridge.

Putnam, H. (1989), *Representation and Reality*, MIT Press, Cambridge MA.

Putnam, H. (1990), *Realism with a Human Face*, Harvard University Press, Cambridge MA.

Putnam, H. (1992), *Renewing Philosophy*, Harvard University Press, Cambridge MA.

Putnam, H. (1994), *Words and Life*, Harvard University Press, Cambridge MA.

Quinton, A. (1966), 'The Foundations of Knowledge', in Williams, B. and Montefiore, A. eds, *British Analytic Philosophy*, Routledge, London, pp. 55–86.

Rachels, J. (1981), 'God and Human Attitudes', in Helm, P. ed., *Divine Commands and and Moral Requirements*, Oxford University Press, Oxford, pp. 34–48.

Raphael, M. (1994), 'Feminism, Constructivism and Numinous Experience', *Religious Studies*, vol. 30, pp. 511–26.

Runzo, J. (1986), *Reason, Relativism and God*, Macmillan, Basingstoke and London.

Runzo, J. (1993), *World Views and Perceiving God*, Macmillan, Basingstoke and London.

Russell, B. (1962), *An Inquiry into Meaning and Truth*, Penguin, Harmondsworth.

Sagi, A. and Statman, D. (1995), *Religion and Morality*, Rodopi, Amsterdam and Atlanta.

Saussure, F. de (1976), *Course in General Linguistics*, Baskin, W. tr., Fontana, London.

Schrader, G. (1968), 'The Thing in Itself in Kantian Philosophy', in Wolff, R.P. ed., *Kant*, Macmillan, London, pp. 172–83.

Scott, M. (2000), 'Framing the Realist Question', *Religious Studies*, vol. 36, pp. 455–71.

Searle, J. (1995), *The Construction of Social Reality*, Allen Lane, London.

Smart, R.N.S. (1966), 'Myth and Transcendence', *The Monist*, vol. 50, pp. 475–87.

Sokal, A. and Bricmont, A. (1999), *Impostures*, Profile, London.

Stenmark, M. (2000), 'How Should One Do Religious Epistemology?', in Lehtononen, T. and Koistinen, T. eds, *Perspectives in Contemporary Philosophy of Religion*, Schriften der Luther Agricola-Gesellschaft, vol. 46, Luther-Agricola-Society, Helsinki, pp. 136–51.

Swinburne, R.G. (1977), *The Coherence of Theism*, Clarendon Press, Oxford.

Swinburne, R.G. (1991), *The Existence of God*, rev. edn, Clarendon Press, Oxford.

Torrance, T.F. (1969), *Theological Science*, Oxford, Oxford University Press.

Torrance, T.F. (1985), *Reality and Scientific Rationality*, Scottish Academic Press, Edinburgh.

Vaughan Thomas, E. (1997), 'Wittgenstein and Tolstoy: the Authentic Orientation', *Religious Studies*, vol. 33, pp. 363–77.

Ward, G. (1996), *Theology and Contemporary Critical Theory*, Macmillan, Basingstoke and London.

Ward, G. (1997), *The Postmodern God*, Oxford, Blackwell.

Welch, S.D. (1985), *Communities of Resistance and Solidarity*, Orbis, Maryknoll.

White, A.R. (1970), *Truth*, Macmillan, London.

Wiles, M. (1996), *Archetypal Heresy*, Clarendon Press, Oxford.

Wisdom, J. (1953), *Philosophy and Psychoanalysis*, Blackwell, Oxford.

Wisdom, J. (1963), *Paradox and Discovery*, Blackwell, Oxford.

Wittgenstein, L. (1961), *Tracatus Logico-Philosophicus*, Pears, D.F. and McGuinness, B.F. trs, Routledge, London.

Wittgenstein, L. (1963), *Philosophical Investigations*, Anscombe, G.E.M. tr., Blackwell, Oxford.

Wittgenstein L. (1978), *Remarks on the Foundations of Mathematics*, Anscombe, G.E.M tr., Blackwell, Oxford.

Wittgenstein, L. (1981), *Zettel*, Anscombe, G.E.M and von Wright, G.H. trs, Blackwell, Oxford.

Index